MW01088798

The Globalization
of Chinese Food

ANTHROPOLOGY OF ASIA SERIES

Series Editor: Grant Evans, *University of Hong Kong*

Asia today is one of the most dynamic regions of the world. The previously predominant image of 'timeless peasants' has given way to the image of fast-paced business people, mass consumerism and high-rise urban conglomerations. Yet much discourse remains entrenched in the polarities of 'East vs. West', 'Tradition vs. Change'. This series hopes to provide a forum for anthropological studies which break with such polarities. It will publish titles dealing with cosmopolitanism, cultural identity, representations, arts and performance. The complexities of urban Asia, its elites, its political rituals, and its families will also be explored.

The Globalization of Chinese Food

Edited by

David Y. H. Wu and
Sidney C. H. Cheung

UNIVERSITY OF HAWAI'I PRESS
HONOLULU

Editorial Matter © 2002 David Y. H. Wu and Sidney C. H. Cheung

Published in North America by
University of Hawai'i Press
2840 Kolowalu Street
Honolulu, Hawai'i 96822

First published in the United Kingdom by
Curzon Press
Richmond, Surrey
England

Printed in Great Britain

Library of Congress Cataloguing-in-Publication Data

The globalization of Chinese food / edited by David Y. H. Wu and Sidney
C. H. Cheung.
    p. cm. – (Anthropology of Asia series)
    Includes bibliographical references and index.
    ISBN 0-8248-2582-9 (alk. paper)
    1. Food habits–China. 2. Cookery, Chinese–Social aspects. 3. Chinese–Ethnic
identity. 4. Chinese–Foreign countries. I. Wu, David Y. H. II. Cheung,
Sidney C. H. III. Series.

GT2853.C6 G56 2002
394.1′0951–dc21   2001053967

Contents

List of Contributions

Dr. Louis Augustin-Jean, Honorary Research Associate, Department of Anthropology, The Chinese University of Hong Kong, Hong Kong.

Professor Sidney C. H. Cheung, Associate Professor, Department of Anthropology, The Chinese University of Hong Kong, Hong Kong.

Professor Dai Yifeng, Professor, Department of History, Xiamen University, People's Republic of China.

Professor Doreen G. Fernandez, Professor, Department of Communication, Ateneo de Manila University, Philippines.

Professor Mohamed Yusoff Ismail, Professor, Department of Anthropology, University of Malaya, Malaysia.

Professor Sidney Mintz, Emeritus Professor, Department of Anthropology, Johns Hopkins University, Baltimore, U.S.A.

Professor Siumi Maria Tam, Associate Professor, Department of Anthropology, The Chinese University of Hong Kong, Hong Kong.

Professor Mely G. Tan, Professor, Social Research Department, Atma Jaya Catholic University, Indonesia.

Professor David Y. H. Wu, Professor, Department of Anthropology, The Chinese University of Hong Kong, Hong Kong.

Professor Zhuang Kongshao, Professor, Department of Anthropology, Central University of Nationalities, Peking, People's Republic of China.

List of Figures

List of Tables

Acknowledgements

This book began to take shape at the 5th Symposium on Chinese Dietary Culture in 1997 under the theme of 'Chinese Foodways in the 21st Century: Prospects of Globalization of Chinese Food and Cuisine', which was held at the Chinese University of Hong Kong and co-sponsored by the Foundation of Chinese Dietary Culture and the Department of Anthropology, CUHK. Several papers presented at the Symposium are now included in the book (Chapters 3, 8, 9, and 10). The book took much of its present form, however with the additional inclusion of papers presented at a workshop on 'Food and Ethnography', held in the summer of 1998 also at CUHK.

We would like to thank the Foundation of Chinese Dietary Culture (Taipei) for funding the Symposium of 1997, from which we were able to select several papers for inclusion in our book. For organizing the symposium we would also like to thank Ms. Chang Yu-hsin and other staff members of the Foundation, the Former Chairman of the Foundation, Mr. George Chau-shi Wong, and many attendants and discussants from the Chinese University of Hong Kong and other institutions around the world. We also would like to extend our gratitude to the Hong Kong Universities Grants Council for sponsoring the research project under which the Food and Ethnography workshop was funded. The project was entitled 'Cooking Up Hong Kong Identity: A Study of Food Culture, Changing Tastes and Identity in Popular Discourse (CUHK 314/95H)', and David Y. H. Wu, Maria S. M. Tam, Sidney C. H. Cheung, and Grant Evans were the investigators.

Finally, this book would not have been possible without the support and constructive comments of the following people: Grant Evans of the University of Hong Kong for enthusiastic encouragement of putting the selected English papers of the conference and workshop into a book; Maria S. M. Tam and Tan Chee Beng for spending considerable time and energy in organizing the conference and workshop; Chen Sea-ling and Tong Ho Yan for their research assistance, Mary Day for excellent and patient copy editing, Doris Lee for spending time on the final version, and Lam Hiu-yin and Joyce Chan for their secretarial assistance.

D. Y. H. Wu and S. C. H. Cheung

Foreword: Food for Thought[1]

Sidney W. Mintz

Students of food – social scientists, nutritionists and humanists alike – face a serious challenge in their work. The anthropologists among us need to gather data among living, active persons, observing and recording how people engage in all of the concrete tasks that lead up to, and that follow, the consumption of food: the gathering and hunting of wild plants and of animal foods; the planting and harvesting of vegetable foods; the care, breeding and raising of domestic animals for food; the processing by dehydration, canning and otherwise of those substances that become foods, such as bean curd, pickled vegetables, salted fish, and the distilled or fermented sauces and liquors that accompany them (Thompson and Cowan 1995); and – once the meal is consumed and the social relationships that mark it have been strengthened, and renewed – the cleaning up, the disposal of waste, the laundering of linens, and the washing of cooking instruments, plates and chopsticks.[2]

We engage in the hard work of careful observation and recording because we want to understand, in a concrete and particular manner, how food is produced, distributed and consumed, in all of its many forms. The history of eating is precisely that, a history – tied to environment, ecology, technical achievement and evolving cultural forms. All other life feeds; the human species eats; the foods of all other species are part of natural history; the foods of the human species have both a natural history and a history. The comparative history of human foods, like the comparative history of any other cultural achievement, thus forms an essential chapter in pan-human experience.

Accordingly, we aspire to understand what – other than as nourishment – food and its consumption mean for the life of humankind. That requires us to rise above the carefully-gathered materials we possess in order to analyse, on a much wider canvas, where our specific case fits, within the great range of variability that characterizes human eating behaviour. We recognize that cultural variety is typical of our species: variety in what we eat, in how we eat, in what meanings we bestow on our foods, or derive from them.

There follow in this volume contributions on the trepang or bêche de mer and birds' nests, on the ethnography of food behaviour, on street foods and coffee shops – the down-to-earth food substances, material culture and locational detail that allow us to come close to real people, satisfying real hungers. We know as we do our work that one man's food is another man's poison – that attitudes about food and the ways in which it should be eaten not only vary enormously, but also as often prove emotionally strong. Precisely because we do not feed like animals but eat like humans, our rules for eating may be enormously complicated. Among us human beings biological drives are always being mediated through cultural systems. Human behaviour without cultural intervention is difficult even to imagine; this is as true of our eating as it is of everything else that is physical and biological about us. Accordingly, it is no surprise to discover that, somewhere on the earth's surface, someone is eating practically everything that won't kill us, as well as a number of things that will.

What is more, we know that cultural materials have influenced or shaped eating behaviour for much of our history as a species. The most powerful evidence of this is the mastery of fire, which led among other things to the establishment of a whole treasure of foods, especially the cereals, tubers and legumes, that had been substantially inedible for us before control of fire. This is what leads us to be defined as 'the animal that cooks'. Among many peoples – as Claude Lévi-Strauss pointed out long ago – it is our cooking that distinguishes us most clearly from other animals. Many millennia after the mastery of fire, the domestication of plants and animals, which was surely the single biggest energy-capturing invention in history, eventually transformed human food behaviour almost entirely. Events of these sorts, which marked the development of our cultural variety over time and were due to active human interventions in nature, are eloquent evidence that we are historical animals. As social groups we vary behaviourally, not because of our biology, but because of our history, and these are histories that we ourselves have made.

Hence any study of human eating is simultaneously of our behaviour as members of a single species on the one hand and of our culturally specific, historically-derived, group-patterned behaviour on the other. Given cultural variation from society to society, the norms of any social group take on additional intensity when contrasted to the norms of a different group; the nature of Japanese food behaviour becomes even more clearly seen when it is contrasted with French food behaviour, say, or with Chinese food behaviour. The same will be true as between differently-privileged classes within the same society, though intrasocietal differences may not be so extreme or surprising as those which distinguish one society from another. Our humanity is divided by, and dramatized by, our cultural variety. What makes our species one – our capacity for culture – also divides us, because our cultures have distinctive histories, distinctive outlooks. The challenge we face, then, is to make the most possible sense of the food behaviour of any specific organized human group – but meanwhile never forgetting that that behaviour is particular and specific, and can be evaluated and analyzed eventually in relation to the whole vast range of human variety.

When such a view of human diversity is put together with the anthropological study of food over time, several features of the history of the field of food studies stand out clearly, even starkly. First and most importantly, the history of the study of food in the West has always been profoundly affected by the history of Western faith, particularly as embodied in three major monotheistic religions: Judaism, Christianity and Islam. It would be difficult to overemphasize the significance of faith in contrasting Western and other food patterns. Those three faiths all employed food and food practices zealously, in defining their beliefs. They used food and food practices in defining the nature of belief itself; in specifying the relationship of the believer to his god; in clarifying the relationships of believers to each other; and perhaps most of all, in marking off the relationship of believers to non-believers.

Nor was it simply that such peoples liked food and eating, or only that they cared aesthetically, or medically, about food in relation to themselves. Instead – or in addition – they endowed food with enormous power of a moral kind, as evidenced by the way food and faith were intertwined. Conspicuous among the food-related practices of these religions are food prohibitions and taboos. For example, there is the taboo against consuming animal blood among the Jews and the ritual emphasis on the consumption of certain foods, such as the flesh of the lamb, in Judaism; the use of the fast as a path to sanctity, as in the case of Ramadan and the Jewish holiday of Yom Kippur; the history of sacrifice of the edible and inedible, as in the story of Abraham and Isaac; the restriction of some consumption to specific periods and/or social categories, as in the Lenten festival of Christianity, and the special significance of Friday foods; and of course, in the codification of food practices, which began early in the histories of these religions. All such beliefs have served as effective means for bringing together the faithful, on the one hand, and in dividing the faithful from outsiders – 'pagans', 'heathen', unbelievers – on the other. Though the Old Testament in particular gives dramatic evidence of the role of food in Western belief, the holy books of all of these religions attest to the importance of food in the religious thought of the West. Though by no means limited to those societies, such beliefs are characteristic of them.

Scholars of food-related behaviour have been keenly aware of this noteworthy relationship between believing and eating, and between eating and belonging. William Robertson Smith, surely the first great scholar of food and religion in the West, deals with it at length in his most famous work, *Lectures on the Religion of the Semites*. It was Smith who first used the term 'commensality' to describe how humans ate with their god, because by their religious acts they were able to bring him to their table. In the history of Christianity, the relationship between eating behaviour, sacrifice, the holiness of food and the presence of the God is particularly poignant and visible. In the New Testament it is high drama, in the case of the Last Supper.

But the Old Testament too is rich in stories of food and its enormous symbolic power over those who believe, from the story of Adam and Eve and the apple, through the divided economic activities of Cain and Abel, and then Esau and Jacob, and in fullest display in the so-called 'abominations' of Leviticus and again in Deuteronomy, where the food code of the ancient Hebrews is first documented. The Old Testament provides perhaps the oldest written evidence of the intimate linkage between food and belief; both the New Testament and the Koran perpetuate that symbolic connection. And it is probably not surprising that the story of the Fall – the ejection of Adam and Eve from Eden for having 'sinned' – is accompanied by a terrifying passage in which Jehovah, the Hebrew god, tells Adam that thereupon he will make all living things 'meat' (food) for the sinners.

The historic importance of food in Western religious dogma has given rise to a rich anthropological literature as in the work of Claude Lévi-Strauss, Edmund Leach, Mary Douglas, and Gillian Feeley-Harnik, among many others. Mary Douglas attempts to explain the origins of the food code of the ancient Hebrews. To do so, she capitalizes on the work of Claude Lévi-Strauss. In Douglas's view, the categories of nature characteristic of Hebrew thought eventuated in the devaluation of those living things that did not fit into the categories. A student of Hebrew food taboos soon discovers that animals with cloven hooves who do not chew a cud, like creatures of the sea that lack scales and fins, are seen as abominations, freaks, monsters – dirty and unfit to be eaten. The categories are what become real; nature is bent to the categories, rather than the other way round. Though Douglas's analysis does not seem complete to some colleagues, and wrong to others (Harris 1986), its stress upon how things fail to fit into categories is provocative and persuasive.

Feeley-Harnik's *The Lord's Table* (1981) is concerned with other matters. She seeks to bring together the history of the Passover ritual of the Jews, the ceremony which celebrates the escape of the Jews from Egypt, with the Eucharist or communion. This is the sacrament which indelibly marks Christianity as that religion in which the body and blood of Jesus are shared symbolically by the communicants in the celebration of their faith. From the ceremony of the Jewish Passover, celebrating emancipation,

Feeley-Harnik hypothesizes the birth of a new faith, building on elements of the old. In both, food is of central importance.

These anthropologists deal, in one manner or another, with the intimate relationship between food and faith, as revealed in the Old and New Testaments. They are keenly aware of the place of food in Western religious thought, as well as of its connections to wider frames of social organization, including systems of kinship, patterns of marriage and much else. As students of food, it behoves us to think hard about the linkages, the connections, between food and its consumption and the institutional arrangements of any society that we study.

The anthropological phenomena to which these scholars refer are by no means limited to the West, of course. The study of taboo and prohibition, of rituals of purification, and of food-related behaviour that is also religious in character was first undertaken by anthropologists outside the West, and many such behavioural forms were first studied in so-called 'primitive' or preliterate societies. In Western societies, as in these other cases, such forms are also related to an overarching system for the provision of moral and ethical order and guidance. Yet in the case of the West, I think that these particular associations between monotheistic religion and food-related behaviour have a distinctive stamp or character.

There does not seem to be a comparably powerful association between food and any particular social or moral institution in the case of Asian food systems – in China, to take the largest case. On the one hand, it must be more than just chance that, in the West, so much distinguished scholarship should have been focused upon food behaviour in terms of its links to belief or faith. On the other, it is difficult to find a comparable link in Asia. One might perhaps think of the food taboos typical of the West in comparison with the treatment of the cow, say, in Indian belief. But beyond the sacredness of the cow and the role of *ahimsa*, or the sacredness of life, and except for Islam, food prohibitions on the Indian subcontinent appear to be linked primarily to caste and to hierarchy. Their connection to religious belief seems to be constructed more through the contrary themes of purity and pollution, than through specific religious codes, and differs substantially from that of the West. Why what appears to be such an enormous difference should set Eastern and Western belief apart is not at all clear – to this writer, at least.

The Far East, in particular, poses quite different questions for the student of food. When compared to Western belief, to a non-Asia specialist Han Chinese food-related behaviour seems relatively innocent of taboos and prohibitions. Though there exists an elaborate system of food guidance tied firmly to conceptions of health and sickness – to the 'balance' of the individual with nature, so to speak – particular foods do not take on the tremendous symbolic weight they have for so long possessed in Western religious thought. Dairy products, for example, once not much used,[3] seem to be viewed not so much with horror as with disdain or possibly contempt. Other animal foods, and products made from animals, whether much liked or not, seem to lack the heavy symbolic charge they often carry in the West. Disgust is not experienced at the thought of so many particular foods. What is meant here is not dislike or disinterest; what is meant here is disgust.

Indeed, it is possible that many Westerners distrust Han Chinese cuisine precisely because it is so open, and so unfettered by particular taboos. That dog, cat, snake or monkey, jellyfish or goose foot webs or chicken feet, may turn up in a meal is cause enough for worry among most Westerners. Compared, for example, to the Jewish rules of kashruth, which make some foods prescriptively edible, and others real abominations; or to the rules for Lent in Catholic belief; or to the fasting rules for Ramadan within Islam, Han cuisine seems marked principally by the relative absence of taboos, or of any heavy food-connected emotionalism. To be sure, feeding both the gods and the ancestors is part of Chinese religious ritual;[4] and considerations of health figure importantly in the Chinese food system. Moreover, it is seriously misleading to deemphasize the importance of food in Han culture. But the concern here is rather with the specific and emotionally powerful linkage of food to religious belief that is so typical of the West. Several scholars, remarking on the absence of strong food taboos in China, have suggested that recurrent famine may explain the absence of most such taboos.[5] That may be an adequate explanation, though one wonders whether there may not be more to it. Any reasons we advance for the absence of taboos we arrive at only by inference; the question of their absence persists.

Hence the contention here is that the development of an anthropological literature concerned with food and faith in the West does not yet have its match in the food anthropology of Asia, mainly because food has never played that particular role in Asian culture. This obvious difference can quite easily be changed into one of two questions: why has food in Asia not played such a role; or, contrariwise, why has food in the West been such a powerful ideological vehicle?

Students of Asian food systems have certainly provided us with considerable information and some useful analytical devices, such as the stress upon health and balance – the yin/yang, fan/ts'ai, hot/cold, wet/dry and clean/poisonous polarities.[6] But what seems most to be emphasized in studies of the Han Chinese food system, for example, is the central importance of food in the culture – a stress with which no one would wish to quarrel. To be sure, it does not take us very far interpretively, for it serves more as a statement of fact than as an explanation of anything else.

This writer is convinced that our fundamental strength as a discipline rests upon ethnography. The most important source of our contributions to theory come from ethnography. But we need to look as closely at functional interconnections between food systems and other subsystems of the society. In what spheres might we find structurally important resemblance to the links between food and faith that typify the West? If one reads Malinowski, or studies the potlatches of the Northwest Coast of America, one sees how political power can be hinged to food and its distribution. In the case of Asia, parallels may be linked to the structure of families; to the organization of ancestor worship; or to the veneration of local or craft deities. But the writer is an ignorant outsider. It is important that ethnographers of Asia undertake the detailed fieldwork that can build out from the particulars to the institutional links.

One can also suggest that we try to develop larger scale and more ambitious comparisons of Asian and Western food systems – comparisons to enable us to develop a better theoretical grasp of the subject matter. We cannot assume that the absence of studies of Eastern food practices comparable to those made by Douglas or Leach for the West, for example, is only the result of differences in cultural orientation. Large-scale comparisons, both historical and functional, between Eastern and Western food systems, might eventually enable us to discern similarities as well as differences. By limiting ourselves to one or the other sphere, we may be missing a chance to deepen our insights usefully. Even in regard to some contemporary aspects of food practice, this may be true. For example, the spread of Western fast food in Asia, neatly exemplified in Watson's *Golden Arches East: McDonald's in East Asia* (1997), deserves to be contrasted to the astonishing success of Asian cuisines in the West during the same decades, even though the forms of these two diffusions were radically different. In the case of McDonald's and similar enterprises, careful corporate planning has meant a focused approach to specific categories of consumers, even though it has turned out that consumers often have motives for buying quite different from those envisioned by the sellers. In the case of consumers of Asian foods in the West, the increasing success of Thai, Vietnamese, Japanese, Chinese and other Asian cuisines appears to have taken two quite different forms. The more important has been the unplanned but cumulative consequence of growing affluence, a rising interest in novelty, and more sophistication and daring among consumers. They cook less; they eat out more; and they are willing to try more new things. The second, less important yet still significant form, intersecting to some extent with the first, has been the growth of healthy eating outlooks, epitomized by the health food stores and now, by the organic food interest, which is beginning to cross class lines. Because these trends represent more random diffusion of ideas and cuisines, without corporate blessings, they appear to differ sharply from the corporate spread of American fast foods in urban Asia. So far, however, no serious attempt has been made even to compare or contrast these evidences of a vast exchange of food-related behaviours. Understanding the similarities and differences could tell us something about both these systems.

What this suggests is that anthropologists of food ought not to continue to look at Western and Eastern food practices as if they were on different planets, when we are given more evidence every day that they are not. As anthropologists who find the study of everybody equally important for what we seek to establish, we can benefit from bringing the unlike as well as the like together comparatively, thereby enriching our understanding of both civilizational spheres.

Notes

1 The author delivered this paper at the workshop on *Food and Ethnography*, held at the Department of Anthropology, The Chinese University of Hong Kong, in June 1998.
2 Jack Goody (1982:37) has outlined the steps involved as follows:

... the study of the process of providing and transforming food covers four main areas, that of growing, allocating, cooking and eating, which represent the phases of production, distribution, preparation and consumption:

Processes	Phases	Locus
Growing	Production	Farm
Allocating/storing	Distribution	Granary/market
Cooking	Preparation	Kitchen
Eating	Consumption	Table

To which should be added a fifth phase, often forgotten:

Clearing up	Disposal	Scullery

3 Needham (1999 VI [41]:5) points out that, during the period of the Northern Dynasties and the early Tang, milk and dairy products enjoyed a great vogue, as the leaders of the nomadic conquerors, drinkers of milk and *kumiss,* intermarried with members of the upper classes at the imperial court.
4 McCreery (1990) provides an illuminating account of – as he puts it – real food and fake money in describing Taiwanese offerings to the ancestors.
5 Anderson and Anderson (1977:393), for example, make this point.
6 Simoons (1991:23–25) provides a brief description of these contrasts.

References

Anderson, N. Eugene and Marja L. Anderson (1977) 'Modern China: the South', in Chang, K. C., (ed.) *Food in Chinese Culture: Anthropological and Historical Perspectives*, pp. 337–381. New Haven: Yale University Press.
Douglas, Mary (1966) *Purity and Danger: An Analysis of the Concepts of Pollution and Taboo.* London and New York: ARK.
Feeley-Harnik, Gillian (1981) *The Lord's Table: The Eucharist and Passover in Early Christianity,* Philadelphia: University of Pennsylvania Press.
Goody, Jack (1982) *Cooking, Cuisine and Class.* Cambridge: Cambridge University Press.

Harris, Marvin (1986) *Good to Eat: Riddles of Food and Culture*. London: Allen & Unwin.

McCreery, L. John (1990) 'Why don't we see some real money here? Offerings in Chinese Religion', in *Journal of Chinese Religions* 18, pp. 1–24.

Needham, Joseph (1999) *Science and Civilisation in China. Volume 6: Biology and Biological Technology* (compiled and edited by Francesca Bray). Cambridge: Cambridge University Press.

Simoons, Frederick (1991) *Food in China: A Cultural and Historical Inquiry*. Boca Raton: CRC Press.

Smith, William Robertson (1956 [1889]) *Lectures on the Religion of the Semite*. New York: Meridian Books, World Publishing.

Thompson, S., and J. T. Cowan (1995) 'Durable food production and consumption in the world Economy', in Philip McMichael (ed.) *Food and Agrarian Orders in the World Economy*, pp. 35–52. Westport: Praeger.

Watson, L. James (ed.) (1997) *Golden Arches East: McDonald's in East Asia*. Stanford: Stanford University Press.

The Globalization of Chinese Food and Cuisine

Markers and Breakers of Cultural Barriers

David Y. H. Wu and Sidney C. H. Cheung

The study of food practices in different cultures and societies has been an important part of anthropological inquiries. In recent years, anthropological literature on food has generated new theoretical findings on this important aspect of human behaviour that help to explain cultural adaptation and social grouping in a more general way. Among many new works on food, however, few studies address the Chinese foodways, despite their enormous and continual influence on local food habits around the world. Even classic works on Chinese food provide us with only basic information about China itself, or interpret Chinese foodways in the restricted local food scene and within Chinese history (Chang 1977; Anderson 1988; Simoons 1991).

We present Chinese food/cuisine and culture from a fresh angle and in the broad context of global existence. In this volume, authors make use of ethnographic examples collected within and beyond the boundaries of China to demonstrate the theoretical relevance of Chinese-inspired foodways, tastes, and consumption, in a manner echoing current anthropological discourse on the fluidity of identity formation (or the identification of Chineseness), and on the changing meanings of Chinese as deterritorialized, transnational, and translocal 'communities'.

Thematically divided into three parts, this volume engages in the discussion of Chinese food as a powerful, global force dated hundreds of years before the present time. The first section under the theme of 'Sources of the Globe (Chapters 1–3)', the globalization of Chinese food appears in the overseas Chinese trading network and migration. The second section, 'Chinese Food and Food for Chinese (Chapters 4–7)', focuses on the negotiation of ethnic, cultural, and national identities, when the idea of being Chinese as well as Chineseness is presented and represented in the local, regional, national, and international cuisines. The third section, 'Globalization: Cuisine, Lifeways and Social Tastes (Chapters 8–11)',

1

addresses modern consumerism and social stratification in connection with the Chinese cosmopolitan life outside of China.[1]

Recent Theoretical Concerns in the Anthropology of Food

Anthropologists have gone through stages in theoretical development and have in recent decades provided various thoughts about the power of food in psychic representation, ceremonial symbolism, social function, biological necessity, economic organization, and political identity. Major arguments can be found in an abridged form in a collection of essays *Food and Culture* (Counihan and Van Esterik 1997). Cases presented in this volume, which follow more recent anthropological interests in the 1990s, perceive culture and identity existing in the intercultural, inter-spatial, and transnational interaction as argued by Abu-Lughod (1997), Appadurai (1990, 1996), Friedman (1990, 1994b), Hannerz (1988, 1989a, 1989b, 1990, 1996), Clifford (1997), and Wilk (1999). In the present volume, however, the field materials presented reflect Chinese foodways as multi-cultural in nature, being in constant contact with non-Chinese sources that come from both inside and outside of China. To explore the cultural meanings of Chinese food or cuisine, the authors have employed not only basic participant observations and in-depth interviews, but also multi-sited field investigations, across time and space, in their attempts to better understand the fluidity and diversity of Chinese food in contemporary Asian societies (also see Foster 1991; Friedman 1990, 1994a; Hannerz 1988, 1989a, 1989b; Marcus 1995).

This volume's central theme of globalization reflects a new strand of interest and new efforts in the anthropology of food, and our investigations shed new lights on several theoretical fronts that have been proposed, discussed and debated among colleagues who have studied food cultures in other parts of the world. Our first concern is the question of what is the meaning of globalization of food? For instance, Sidney Mintz's *Sweetness and Power* (1985) documents the global scale of historical transition of one food item – sugar, tracing the changes in the consumption patterns and productivity in Europe and America, and telling the changing roles of sugar in social life. We want to explore Chinese food and political economy by using a similarly macro approach in time and space though on a much smaller scale. In several chapters here the authors are able to trace the changing socio-economic meanings of Chinese cooking ingredients or the emergence of regional cuisines; such as abalone, trepang, birds nest, shark fin, Cantonese cuisine, chop suey, Macanese cuisine, Taiwanese cuisine, and *yum cha* and *dim sum* that developed across national and geographic boundaries on several continents and during several decades or even centuries.

Globalization in the Old Chinese World of Food

Food has often been cited as a good example of globalization that makes connections among cultures, peoples and places (Hannerz 1996; Wilk 1999). We believe that 'Chinese food' makes a particularly strong subject of study to increase our understanding of the globalization process in human food distribution, cuisine variation and consumption. Our approach, global in scale and historical in orientation, joins a new line of inquiry into the cultural meanings of cultural commodities, consumption and modernization. We have been inspired by earlier work such as Appadurai's conception of treating cultural items as having a social life to be studied and documented (Appadurai 1986). A good example is his classic work on how cookbooks helped to construct and re-invent an Indian national cuisine (Appadurai 1988). Another more recent illustration of globalization of 'Western' fast food in Asia is seen in the investigation of McDonald's hamburgers by a group of anthropologists in major East Asian cities (Watson 1997). This type of work answers to Hannerz's calls in his earlier work on 'the world in creolisation' (1988) for the investigation of the Third World (Africa, Asia, Oceania, and South America) as modern, urban, post-industrial, capitalist self; not as remote, primitive, and exotic 'Other'. Hannerz (1990, 1996) and Appadurai (1996) both suggest from cultural materialist's point of view that the post-modern, post-colonial world must be understood within the context of consumption and the global political economy. While we agree with them, we also find their framework being tied to the post-industrial, Western world and deserving of reconsideration. Here, on the basis of research on 'Chinese' food and cuisine, we realize that Chinese food's global implications happened much earlier. The importation from Southeast Asia of trepang and bird nests to China, for instance, entered local official records in China since the seventeenth century (see Chapters 1 and 2). We see a different picture of the 'Chinese world', in which Chinese have already made global connections with 'local others' through 'international' trade network, travel, and migration.

As early as the fifth century Indonesian spices had been found in dishes on the tables of rich Chinese (Chang 1977; Goody 1982:108). Tan points out in Chapter 9 of this volume that Chinese settlements were established before the funding of Jayakarta (1527), which later was colonized by the Dutch and renamed the city of Batavia (in 1618). Chinese food ingredients and cooking methods should have already reached other parts of today's Indonesia even earlier, when the Ming emperor's envoy, Zheng He (whose Muslim name is Mahaci), visited the island chains to enforce political alliance and trading relationship. Today Chinese cooking cannot be separated from Indonesian foodways, as reported in Chapter 9. Chinese trade wares, including cooking utensils, of the Song Dynasty were unearthed in large quantities in Luzon and Borneo. Yusoff in Chapter 2 of this volume cited historical studies in Sabah to note that Zheng He visited the Sulu Seas in around 1405 AD to initiate bird nests trade. The old Manila under Spanish control had a sizable population of Chinese sojourners and traders in the seventeenth century. Thousands of Chinese regularly went back and forth between Manila and hometowns along the Fujian coast during the past four hundred years, making Southern Fujian cuisine an integral part of today's Filipino foodways (see Chapter 11). Wu's study in Papua New Guinea indicates that since the late nineteenth century, the indigenous people had already seen how Chinese cook their food (see Chapter 3) and adopted in their diet imported Chinese vegetables and one variety of taro (Wu 1977).

In this sense, China as a global force, and food practices in particular, may be examined in a historical depth of perhaps a millennium rather than just within the modern era. Certainly, as Dai points out in Chapter 1, Chinese trading for luxury food items precedes Western colonial, mercantile contacts of the eighteenth and nineteenth centuries and the trading monopoly in luxury seafood had never fallen outside Chinese hands. Dai's explanation makes clear how internal ethnic divisions paralleled occupational and commercial activities among the Chinese overseas.

Chinese cuisine has for centuries absorbed ingredients and methods that came from far corners of the globe (discussed in Chapters 1, 2, 3, 4, 9, and 11), and it continues to incorporate foreign and exotic elements to the familiar, local Chinese cuisines (Chapters 5, 6, and 7). Information about Chinese national and ethnic dishes (in Chapter 4) implies that in major cities of China, for centuries, or even millenniums, they have exhibited multicultural, multi-ethnic, and transnational characteristics.

Then, what is Chinese cuisine? Historically speaking, there was never one 'national cuisine' but many regional Chinese cuisines, due to geographical differentiation and social stratification (Chang 1977; Goody 1982; Anderson 1988; Simoons 1991). In Kaifeng, the capital of Northern Song (960–1127 AD) for instance, 'restaurants served a variety of regional cooking, catering for refugees as well as for the grand families who had come there from distant parts of the kingdom' (Goody 1982:105–106). Chinese gourmets used to argue about whether there should be three, four, six, or eight major high cuisines in China, but the post-modern food scene in China, including Hong Kong and Taiwan today, has obscured all the boundary markers, because of migration, innovation, modern communication, creolization and globalization. Maybe the question of what Chinese cuisine is can be answered more satisfactorily today in the foreign, global, or transnational context, when our studies show Chinese cuisine is more readily identified in Australia, the Philippines, Indonesia, Japan, or the US (Chapters 3, 8, 9, 10, and 11).

We can apply Hannerz's (1990) point to a modern Chinese regional cuisine, when he remarks on world culture today: no more ideal type of local, and no cosmopolitan versus local distinction any more. In an article entitled 'Cosmopolitans and Locals in World Culture', Hannerz (1990:237) mentions that:

> No total homogenization of systems of meaning and expression has occurred, nor does it appear likely that there will be one any time soon. But the world has become one network of social relationships, and between its different regions there is a law of meanings as well as of people and goods.

In his investigation of a social history of national cuisine in Belize, Wilk (1999:248) observed that the 'global cultural process finds tendencies toward both homogenization and heterogeneity'. In Chapter 7 here, the author discusses the creation of a distinct Macanese cuisine and a reinterpreted identity that supports Wilk's point. We will find in this volume more evidences of how global manifestation in the local and vice versa. The above theoretical thoughts reflect new awareness in anthropology about the changing concepts of culture. The agency of change rests on the practice, not a rational collective thinking (Foster 1991). The centre, or a nation, is no longer thought to be the producer of culture, as our ethnographic cases demonstrate.

The Fujian and Guangdong Connection: Chinese Diaspora(s) in Overseas Trade and Migration

We wish to emphasize that globalization of Chinese foodways cannot be studied in separation from the migration of the Chinese population. As we propose in this volume, the flow of material culture, specifically a cuisine, in the global process must be studied together with the movement of people; the objects of study should be not merely transference of idea, technology, and organizational principles, as other discourses of globalization like to emphasize. The Chinese diaspora around the world, especially during the past five centuries in East and Southeast Asia, has contributed to the spread and indigenization of Chinese foodways.

Several of our chapters address the issues of Chinese experiences overseas, including 'international' trade of food items as commodities (Chapter 1 by Dai and Chapter 2 by Yusoff), and transnational migration and overseas Chinese cuisines (Chapter 3 by Wu, Chapter 9 by Tan, and Chapter 11 by Fernandez). There are also the interesting phenomena of Chinese living in the peripheral of the Chinese world (i.e. Hong Kong and Macau, see Chapter 6 by Cheung and Chapter 7 by Augustine-Jean), in the port cities where Chinese also experienced Western colonial culture, and where eager emigrants awaited ship to go abroad. Once abroad and settled on foreign land the Chinese may live a non-Western mode of cosmopolitan life, as their eating habits exhibit (Chapter 5 by Wu, Chapter 6 by Cheung, and Chapter 8 by Tam). These peripheral or overseas Chinese experiences fulfil Clifford's (1997) portrayal of the existence in the late twentieth century of a transnational culture at the intersection of East and West contact; or in Rey Chow's (1993) Chinese diaspora existence.

The more we trace back to history in earlier dates, as did Dai in Chapter 1, the more significant we could see the Fujian and Guangdong connections with the overseas trade and globalization of Chinese food and cuisine. The major port cities of the Minnan and Guangdong people, to be explained below, have historically served as centres for foreign trade, emigration and foreign labour recruitment for the nineteenth century European plantations in Southeast Asia, Oceania and North and South America.

During the past two centuries, the so-called Chinese cuisine established outside of China comes predominately from only two regional traditions – Guangdong (Cantonese) and Southern Fujian (Fukien or Hokkien). Most of the Chinese food and cuisine known in Southeast Asia (and described in this volume) derives from Southern Fujian, or Minnan, cooking. (The word *Min* is a short form in Chinese for the province of Fujian that pronounced in Mandarin; *nan* means south. However, outside of China, Minnan people call themselves Hokkien, in their own vernacular.) We will learn in Chapters 9 and 11 that Southern Fujian cuisine has penetrated Indonesia and Philippines' local cooking and daily meals for 500 years. It is interesting to note that in the homeland of China, Minnan cuisine warrants no mention when gourmets describe regional high cuisines, be it three, six, or eight cuisines (Liang 1985). The majority of the early emigrants from Southern Fujian had been labourers of peasant background; they introduced overseas their common dishes or snacks, which eventually became adopted in the Philippines and Indonesia (as described in Chapters 9 and 11).[2]

The Cantonese influence in the global scene of Chinese cuisine came much later, since the nineteenth century, mainly in North America and Australia, where Chinese restaurants served Cantonese cuisine (or *Yue cai*, a short form for Guangdong dishes, as explained in Chapter 5). It is a peasant style variation brought in by Chinese labourers who predominantly came out of four counties, or Siyi (in Mandarin, or See Yap in Cantonese, or Su Yup, in their vernacular), of the Guangdong province. They invented the 'chop suey' dishes, which dominated the food style served in the Chinese restaurants in North America until about the 1970s (see Chapter 3). In the 1960s to 1970s, the second wave of Chinese immigrants brought new cuisines of other Chinese regions, from central and north China. In the 1980s and later, there came the third wave of global spread of Hong

Kong style Cantonese cuisine (see Chapters 5, 8, and 10). The majority of the Chinese restaurant foods found in London, for instance, belong to this new Cantonese of Hong Kong variation (Watson 1975). In fact, when visiting London, we both found that this Cantonese domination was strong enough to change the taste of those few that claimed to serve Peking or Mandarin dishes.

Chinese cuisine is often perceived as representative of Chinese culture, or an authentic cultural marker. Authenticity of Chinese cuisine, whether at home or overseas, is not an objective criterion, however; it is socially constructed and linked to expectations (Lu and Fine 1995). We shall further elaborate on the point with regard to internal divisions and (sub-)ethnicity among the Chinese diasporas.

Food as Marker and Breaker of Ethnic Identity

Most of the chapters in this volume in essence are addressing issues of identity and social relations, rather than food itself. As we can understand, food here becomes powerful lenses through which the authors are able to gaze into the formation and destruction of linguistic, ethnic and national boundaries. Recent thoughts in anthropology once again prove to be relevant in our own case studies of Chinese food and cuisine. Williams (1989) points out the anthropological awareness of ethnicity to be different from other categories of identity (e.g. race or nationality), and adds that: 'To understand what these concepts label, and what place these labels mark in the identity-formation process, we must identify the assumptions underlying the linkages among their lay, political, and scientific meanings' (Williams 1989:402). In Alonso's (1994) words, peoples in contact establish clear ideas about the differences in culture, such as food, taste and cuisine that symbolize ethnic and 'national' identity. In China eating mutton and selling mutton on the street practically testifies Muslim identity. In Beijing, mutton, kebab, pilaf, spice and tomato on rice, all became ethnic markers distinguishing the Uygur sojourners of Xinjiang Autonomous Region of Northwest China from the Han Chinese. Our Chapter 4 about construction of the concept of exotic ethnic groups (nationalities) among the Beijing residents depends on their tasting the new Xinjiang and Tibetan food and experiencing the ethnic restaurants by witnessing exotic costumes of the service personnel (including hired Han waitresses), unfamiliar ambiances inside and outside of the restaurants, and foreign taste of the food. In Hawaii, a popular Chinese restaurant was built according to stereotypic 'Chinese' architectural design, which few Chinese from China today would recognize as Chinese. A foreign, exotic 'Chineseness' attracts non-Chinese customers. So the dishes were improvised foreign inventions rather then imitation of authentic Cantonese traditional cuisine (see Chapter 3).

Friedman (1990) argues that goods are building blocks of self-worlds and further emphasizes that: 'The different strategies of identity, which are always local, just as their subsumed forms of consumption and production, have emerged in interaction with one another in the global arena'. On the other hand, Wilk (1999:244) has made special remarks on the recent resurgence of interests in the issues of identity in the anthropological study of food, because 'food is a particularly potent symbol of personal and group identity, forming one of the foundations of both individuality and a sense of common membership in a larger bounded group'. We cannot agree more with Wilk's finding (1999:246) that 'many issues that were once seen as localized, ethnic, and even familial are now "integrated" in a global context'.

In the global world of Chinese cuisine, as chapter after chapter here testifies, many local cultures become interconnected, in Hannerz's words (1990:237), 'without a clear anchorage in any one territory'. Chinese food and cooking methods are identified, tasted, conceptualized, recreated, and accepted as Chinese cultural and ethnic markers, but after decades or centuries of adoption and creolization, the Chineseness disappeared and fused with many local, indigenous foodways, becoming part of the other's national identity in the foreign land.

When Chinese meet fellow Chinese overseas, consciousness of regional cultural, linguistic and social distinctions among fellow Chinese are pronounced. Among the diasporas who left Fujian or Guangdong, further sub-ethnic differences were so pronounced that they cut across commercial, occupational, cultural, residential and social status groups within the old overseas communities. These social divisions can best be analysed in terms of ethnic identity.

Corresponding to the local, sub-regional cuisines, are ethnic (and sub-ethnic) classifications among the Chinese diasporas that emigrated from different ports along the Chinese southeast coast. Several port cities from whence emigrants exodus are also centres of major ethnic/language categories: namely, Xiamen (Amoy), Quanzhou (Zaitong), Shantou (Swatow), Guangzhou (Canton) and, after the eighteenth century, Xianggang (Hong Kong). Xiamen and Quanzhou historically were important seaports of South China where the local language is Minnan (or Hokkien). Shantou (or Swatao) is the major city of the Chaozhou (Chaozhou in Mandarin, and Teochew in their own vernacular) dialect region. Located on the far east of Guangdong Province bordering Fujian, Chaozhou people are considered a distinct ethnic group, although they have no problem communicating with the Minnan (Hokkien) people in their respective speeches. The descendents of Chaozhou emigrants concentrate in Thailand today. In Hong Kong, Chaozhou (or Chiuchow in Cantonese term) cuisine enjoyed, and still enjoys, a high status in the restaurants (see Chapter 6). For Yue, or Cantonese, speaking people,

Guangzhou, the capital city of Guangdong, and Hong Kong are the two largest urban centres. Among the Chinese diasporas overseas, there is another distinct ethnic group called Kejia (or Hakka, meaning the 'guest people', a northern Chinese dialect group residing in the hilly areas of Guangdong, Fujian, and Taiwan. The Hakka, unfortunately, had historically enjoyed a lower status, and were discriminated against by other Chinese, both at home and overseas. Their 'simple' cuisine is nowadays deemed unsuitable for restaurant consumption, but was once popular in the cosmopolitan city of Hong Kong, especially in the 1960s (see Cheung's Chapter 6).

Eating Out, Taste for Distinction, and Modern Consumerism

Another theoretical issue closely related to the concerns of identity, as our food materials reveal, is dealing with how individuals or a group of people use their taste in food, and their particular way of eating, to demonstrate social standing. Status consciousness and acting out through choice of food and cuisine reflect a strong motivation that is associated with social stratification and group affiliation, whether they are ethnic, political, or even national. Often applied in several chapters of our discussion of food and social hierarchy is the classic theory of Bourdieu (1984) on taste and social distinction. Goody used extensively Chang's (1977) classic collection of Chinese food discussions to stress the differentiation of high and low cuisine in ancient China that in essence is still relevant to our cases in modern times. We also found relevance in our Chinese cases the similar desirability of and imitation in consumption of foreign (for the Chinese may mean other regional) cuisine as described in Tobin's (1992) collection of Japanese 'domestication' of Western commodities and food. The importation and consumption of trepang and bird nests described in Chapters 1 and 2 demonstrate how since ancient times Chinese have ranked foreign import and exotic food items as the highest of refined ingredients; as are abalones and shark fins highly ranked in modern Chinese dishes in Hong Kong, Taipei, Yokohama, Manila, or Jakarta. Other examples revealed in our studies are the internal differentiation and hierarchy among different Chinese regional cuisines due to more recent geo-political and economic developments. Food for distinction explains the emergence of *Yue Cai* or Cantonese cuisine in Taiwan (Chapter 5), the changing status of Hakka cuisine in Hong Kong (Chapter 6), and popularization and domestication of Hong Kong style *yumcha* in Australia and elevated status of *yumcha* in Japan (Chapters 8 and 10).

In contrast to meals at home, 'eating out' in modern times deserves further theoretical discussion. Restaurants emerged very late in the West, in London and Paris. Sociologists, such as Finkelstein (1989), perceive 'eating out' as a modern, cosmopolitan life of (Western) civility. They ignore the fact that the Chinese in their cities had more than a thousand years of history in wining and dining in restaurants. The modern practice of 'eating out', however, is different from the ancient customs of feasting and banquets, in that it involves people of all classes including, especially women who have joined the labour force. In the US by the end of the twentieth century, people eat out at least two meals a day (Finkelstein 1989; Fieldhouse 1995). People eat out, Finkelstein theorizes, for pleasure, for the enjoyment of social participation and for showing off knowledge of restaurant culture and manners. The pleasure and civility argument is overstretched; however, it neglects as a factor the necessity of eating out in modern, urban life. As we observed in Beijing, Hong Kong, Sydney, Taipei and Yokohama, most mobile urbanities do not have the luxury of cooking at home, while restaurants of all kinds provide both convenience and a variety of tastes to serve and please different palates and budgets. We would rather agree with Beardsworth and Keil (1997:121) that 'eating in' and 'eating out' are a continuum, 'linking domestic food events at one end and public food events at the other'. However, in a place like Hong Kong where more than 20,000 public eating places exist, even the continuum or the usual understanding of 'eating out' becomes meaningless, when the majority of the urban dwellers have all three daily meals consumed outside of their homes, and most social events are held in restaurants.

Conspicuous consumption in restaurants has created fashion chasing, making a powerful association between *nouvelle* (Chinese) cuisine and social status as described in Chapters 5, 6, and 10. The post-modern taste has become subject to media publicity and cultural construction, defusing many local Chinese traditions and incorporating global elements. For instance, outside China, the most common, daily eating out style of 'drinking tea', or *yum cha*, of olden day Guangzhou as well as modern Hong Kong, has become a global phenomenon as mentioned in several chapters and elaborated in Chapter 8. And yet, *yum cha* menu absorbs 'global' elements from Japanese, Southeast Asian, and European cuisines as well.

Another point about the globalization of Chinese food which is worth our attention is the differentiation between 'low' and 'high' Chinese cuisines in the presentation of Chinese food in other countries where it has been adopted. We note what we learn from this volume that the expensive and refined Cantonese cuisine, along with the manner and ambiance for Chinese banquets, have recently appeared in the luxury hotel restaurants in Manila and Jakarta, as reported by our authors in Chapters 9 and 11. Globalization of Chinese high cuisine is in fact a recent development, in contrast to the Chinese home cooking or sidewalk (Chinese-inspired) stall food that had been absorbed in local food scenes in Southeast Asia. In the Philippines, we learn, Chinese-style noodles and fried rice dishes are suitable for domestic consumption only, whereas

Spanish, colonial-influenced dishes carry a high prestige and are considered festivity and banquet food. Similar cases of eating Chinese food for convenience and economic reasons can be observed in Australia, England, Japan, and the US; it is usually a cheap way to dine, eat in Chinese restaurants or to eat take-out Chinese food at home. However, during the past decade, the *nouvelle* Chinese cuisine of a globalized Chinese migration history, with localized flavour and style (see Chapter 10 about Yokohama Chinatown in Japan), no matter what regional Chinese tradition it claims to adhere, has caught up with the high end of consumption conscious eaters around the world. Once again, this demonstrates Hannerz's (1996) ideas of connectedness of people, culture and places in the globalized, post-modern world.

Prologue to the Chapters

In the last part of this introduction, we shall highlight the main point in each of the chapters, with emphasis on additional background information that connects the individual chapters to others and to the overall theoretical concerns as well.

Chapter 1 by Dai, 'Food Culture and Overseas Trade', looks into local tax records in Fujian and Guangdong to tell the story about international trade and smuggling between South China and Japan and Southeast Asia. Using trepang as an example of a food item as imported commodity, we can see the structural change over time of its value as a scarce and luxury good to an inexpensive food item for popular consumption, when Chinese monopolization of South Seas trade increased the volume of imports. We learn how Chinese locally produced trepang ranked inferior to the foreign variety when imports from the exotic South Seas increased. One important point ties to our earlier discussion of the Fujianese connection is their trading activities in and migration to the South Seas, including today's Southeast Asian countries (and Taiwan as well), since the documented official records of the seventeenth century. The Minnan seamen, smugglers, traders and adventurers (many of peasant background) based in Xiamen (Amoy) sailed regularly and frequently to the region, as the Qing official records and individual travel logs show. Though it is hard to document the secret of the Minnan domination in the trepang trade and their monopoly after the eighteenth century, anthropological studies of the overseas Chinese indicate their strong, ethnic-based organizations such as guilds, kinship and hometown (and dialect) associations. These solidarities helped the Minnan merchants and their overseas Minnan partners (many possibly being fellow lineage members) establish a chain process of trepang fishing, processing, buying, transportation and marketing (also see Lee (1976) for a discussion of Chinese merchants in Sabah). The same could be said about the collection and importation of bird nests from Borneo to

China by Chinese merchants mentioned in Chapter 2, even though Yusoff has concentrated more on the indigenous side of the social organization of swifts' nests collection.

Yusoff in Chapter 2, 'Sacred Food from the Ancestors' details the most expensive ingredient for Chinese high cuisine – the bird nests: from their special medicine power and social prestige as food in China and Hong Kong to harvesting in Eastern Sabah by indigenous Idahan producers who follow the wisdom of traditional social and environmental control and stand up for clan rights and supernatural beliefs. Other than harvesting, which is difficult and life threatening, the buying, sorting by grades, pricing, middlemen handling, export to Hong Kong, and marketing are all in the hands of Chinese traders. When the nests sold at prices higher than gold, it reminds one of the all-familiar world system economy repeated in the old Chinese world of globalization.

Wu in Chapter 3, 'Improvising Chinese Cuisine Overseas', brings his ethnographic observation of Chinese restaurants from Port Moresby to Honolulu to portray the recreation and creolization of Chinese culture, identity and social life overseas. This chapter serves as an example in applying what Mintz calls a comparative study of the East and West, and echoes Ulf Hannerz's idea of a global ecumene of (Chinese) culture as networks of networks of meanings. The author observed how a 'Chinese cuisine' and related symbols of local, national, and global meanings of Chinese culture evolved on foreign land (Lash and Urry 1994). For the sake of survival, Chinese immigrants in the frontier societies in the Western world provide local, peasant style, dishes in the restaurants to satisfy a global idea of authentic Chinese cuisine (also see Lu and Fine 1995).

In Chapter 4, 'The Development of Ethnic Cuisine in Beijing', Zhuang tells the story of the emergence of a Xinjiang community in a northeast suburb of the Chinese capital city, and of how the minority sojourners play with ethnic identity in restaurant, language, and religion. The Uygur and other ethnic minorities of the Xinjiang Autonomous Region and Xizang (Tibet) used their 'cultural' capital in creating an 'ethnic' food street to uphold their identities, reinforcing the official conception of Chinese nationalities, and profiting from layers and levels of systems of cultural symbols and meanings. The trans-locality of Xinjiang, Uygur, or Xizang (Tibet) makes the meaning of minority cuisine multi-local and multi-vocal. Three important points can be raised here to illuminate some background information. First, the 'ethnic' restaurants are urban squatter buildings set up along the boundary (a lane outside of its cement fence) of the Central Nationality Academy compound (now the Central University of Nationalities), where for more than 40 years hundreds of minority students were recruited around the country each year and trained here to be official cadres of their home government. The development of a minority community in the neighbourhood (and restaurants right outside its compound) of a congregational, residential and institutional ethnic compound was no accident. Second, because Xinjiang is the largest nationality region in China, where ethnic unrest and 'nationalist' agitation occur frequently, authorities have for years tolerated this squatter community in Beijing (and other Xinjiang street (mutton kebab) vendor community in Quangzhou, for instance) for awareness of their powerful solidarity and for fear of stirring up trouble and embarrassment in the Capital City. Third, and most significantly, China has an official policy of a fixed number (55) of officially recognized minorities. Indoctrination of officially endorsed criteria of minority culture as fixed, concrete properties (such as costumes, custom, food, psychological character, and cultural symbols), with no variation or fluidity allowed, has become deeply rooted in the mind of the majority Han Chinese. Therefore, in the 'ethnic' restaurants the Uygur (or others who imitate the Uygur) or Zang owners can capitalize on and profit from the Han customers (and exploit their fixed ideas about the ethnic and exotic) by displaying the correct ethnic things to evoke authenticity of their cuisine – hence ethnic identity.

In Chapter 5, Wu analyses the recent emergence of 'Cantonese cuisine (Yue-Cai) in Taiwan and Taiwanese (Tai-Cai) Cuisine in Hong Kong'. Situating his discussion in the geo-political economy and consumption theory of distinction, Wu tells how the post-1949 economic development and changes in the political and cultural relations among Taiwan, Hong Kong and mainland China are reflected in changes of food culture and preferences in public eating. The development, after 40 years of Nationalist rule, of a 'national' identity has resulted in a 'true' creolization of Taiwanese food culture, indigenized Mainland China, Japan, and Hong Kong styles, coupled with a 'revivalism' of a local, *nouvelle* Taiwanese (Southern Fujian or Minnan) cuisine. Similarly to the findings in other chapters, the case of Taiwan demonstrates how cultural globalization does not necessarily abolish national or local differences, but may rejuvenate such particular identities (Lash and Urry 1994; Watson 1997).

Sidney Cheung in Chapter 6, 'Food and Cuisine in a Changing Society: Hong Kong' provides analysis of the socio-economic history in a manner similar to the previous chapter, and portrays the resulting transformation of food culture, restaurant styles, the meaning of regional Chinese cuisines, and popular eating patterns in Hong Kong since the 1950s. This chapter also tells us more about the issues of Hong Kong identity formation that are relevant to public eating styles and taste variation, and also cross-cuts the material culture, including lifestyles, consumption and social development, in Hong Kong during the past half century.

In Chapter 7, Louis Augustine-Jean presents a survey study into the meaning of representation of a local cuisine in Macau – 'Food Consumption, Food Perception and the Search for a Macanese Identity'.

On the eve of Macau's returning to China from the Portuguese rule of 450 years, a small (creole) minority, known for hundreds of years as the Macanese, felt threatened when the majority Chinese residents also began to call themselves Macanese. Although the food scene in Macau had been quite similar to that in Hong Kong, there was a sudden increase of 'Macanese' and 'Portuguese' restaurants shortly before the change over. Augustin-Jean surveyed different groups' perception of 'eating out' to locate a distinct Macanese identity and Macanese cuisine in the reality of creolization and reinvention.

Another view is taken of Hong Kong people going overseas and using food to maintain their identity, Maria Siumi Tam in Chapter 8 gives a detailed ethnographic account in '*Heunggongyan* Forever: Immigrant Life and Hong Kong Style *Yumcha* in Australia'. It tells an important modern-day Chinese predicament of the late twentieth century of being uprooted, compelled to immigrate to a foreign land for personal security and political sanctuary. Food symbolizes the Chinese diaspora's sense of 'border' and 'borderless', when 'authentic' Hong Kong style eating out of *yumcha* was re-established in Sydney, Australia for the home-longing new immigrants. This piece of research answers to James Clifford's question: 'How do diaspora discourses represent experiences of displacement, of reconstructing homes away from home? What experiences do they reject, replace, or marginalize? How do these discourses attain comparative scope while remaining rooted/routed in specific discrepant histories' (Clifford 1997:244). Tam's investigation in Australia into the Chinese diaspora's eating pattern provides a good model for future research in many other contemporary Chinese diaspora communities in North America.

Chapter 9, 'Chinese Dietary Culture in Indonesia Urban Society', is Mely Tan's field investigation of Chinese influence in local food, cuisine and language over hundreds of years. It gives us a good example of globalization in the Chinese world of food that we have proposed and discussed above. Pork, a must ingredient in Chinese home cooking, separates the 'ethnic' Chinese and the majority Muslim indigenous population. Yet Chinese loan words in the Indonesian language, 84 per cent of which are of Minnan origin, are not only mainly related to food and cooking, they also show effects on the local perceptions about health and healing. It is further interesting to find that the most popular dish in Indonesia in the name of '*pangsit*' – soup-based Chinese dumpling – retains an ancient Chinese term for the modern version of 'wonton' (in Cantonese, it is becoming a household name in English; which in north China is called '*huntun*' in Mandarin). The word *Pangsit* tells how the Minnan language preserves pronunciation of ancient North China, where the Minnan ancestors emigrated to the south. Later, ancient Chinese food terms found its way to Indonesia with Minnan traders and immigrants.

Despite long-term interaction with and assimilation into indigenous Indonesian culture, as many ethnic Chinese did (becoming *peranakans* – going native) and as the food scene demonstrates, continued and escalated violence against 'ethnic' Chinese is evident today. Although food has proven to break through cultural barriers, food cannot heal modern day political ill, nationalism and economic inequality that ignite ethnic violence against the Chinese diaspora.

Sidney Cheung in Chapter 10, 'The Invention of Delicacy: Cantonese Food in Yokohama Chinatown', gives new evidence of indigenization of Chinese food and cuisine in Japan. In *Re-made in Japan*, Tobin (1992) coined the word 'domestication' in order to show how Western goods, practices and ideas have been Japanized in their encounter with Japan in various respects. Instead of focusing on the final appearance of those borrowed cultures and imported modernity from the West, a look at the socio-historic change that has occurred in an ethnic (Chinese) neighbourhood reflects the other side of the picture. By studying the emergence of Yokohama Chinatown as a centre for discovering the real and authentic in contemporary Japanese society, Cheung suggests that Cantonese cuisine was mostly reinvented to meet different social interests in the modern Japanese context.

The last one, Chapter 11, on 'Chinese Food in the Philippines: Indigenization and Transformation' is our final testimony of the global world of Chinese foodways. Once again we have to emphasize the Southern Fujian or Minnan connection, as the author, Doreen Fernandez, remarks on her pleasant surprise in finding familiar food when she visited that part of China where the majority of the Chinese diaspora of the Philippines originated. When the first writer of this introduction visited Manila he was also surprised to find many childhood dishes (of rural Taiwan where he grew up, but almost completely disappeared from Taipei today) readily available in small restaurants selling dishes he recognized as 'Chinese'. In Manila, he had no problem conversing with elder Filipino Chinese in the Minnan dialect. Here we wish to further indulge ourselves in offering an alternative interpretation of the original meaning of the most popular dish in the Filipino homes – *Pansit*. While Fernandez speculated its Minnan semantic being 'convenient food', we would like to point out the ancient (Tang or Song Dynasty) Chinese word '*bensi't*' (in Minnan pronunciation, or *bianshi* in Mandarin) to mean either a noodle dish or 'wonton' (Chinese dumpling). When the Filipino word '*pansit*' is compared with the Indonesia word '*pangsit*' it is possible to say that they both derived from the one and same Minnan term of '*bensi't*'.

With the arrival in the past decade of thousands of Taiwanese entrepreneurs and investors in Manila, it is again no surprise to learn in this chapter that Chinese high cuisines and new style of Chinese restaurant food have invaded the foodways of the Philippines.

To conclude this introduction we would like to single out one Chinese food item that gives more layers of cultural meanings and local variations in the sense of globalization and creolization. The term *'lumpia'* is almost universally known in Southeast Asia, and is mentioned in both Chapters 9 and 11 for the Philippines and Indonesia. It is cooked vegetables wrapped in a piece of paper-thin rice pancake, garnished with smashed peanuts, and served cold. The food originated in South Fujian, called *'lumbia'* (meaning moist-cake) in Minnan language, and used to be a festival food specially prepared at home and eaten at lunchtime on the occasion of Spring Festival. Now it is readily available at street-side vendors in Fujian or at carparks – 'hawker food centres' in Singapore. *Lumpia* is about four times larger than the fried 'spring roll' (with meat fillings) that can be found in most Chinese restaurants in the West. Mely Tan in Chapter 8 mentioned this type of fried spring roll as *'Lumpia*-Shanghai' in Indonesia, and which exemplifies well the differentiation in China according to regional/ethnic division – the Shanghai-style spring roll (*chunjuan* in Mandarin) is fried and served hot; while *lumbia* in the Minnan region or in Taiwan is non-fried and served cold.

In the US or in Europe if one wished to taste *lumpia* one could find such a dish in a Vietnamese restaurant, listed on the menu as 'summer roll'. The first author has lived for four years in Australia. While he enjoyed the Australian steak and lamb chops (which were served even at breakfast), he found two mundane food items distasteful: meat pie and 'egg roll'. An egg roll has the appearance of a Chinese spring roll, yet is five to ten times larger (and with a thicker skin). After one bite he lost his appetite and never returned to try another! From his own experience, as a person impartial to food of any ethnic or national origin, he does not blame the overseas *Heunggongyan*'s desire for the Hong Kong style *dim sum*, which include tiny, crispy Shanghai spring rolls.

Notes

1 We are grateful to the three anonymous reviewers of this book manuscript. In writing this Introduction, we have incorporated their useful suggestions and literature citations. We wish also to thank the C.C.K. Foundation in Taipei for funds to cover editorial cost in preparing our manuscript. The funds are part of the project on 'Food Culture in Taiwan: Study of Indigenization and Globalization of Cultural Tradition and Identity Through Food and Cuisine', with David Yen-Ho Wu as the Principal Investigator.

2 Regarding different cuisines in the Fujian area, the northern, or Minbei, cuisine, centred on the provincial capital city of Fuzhou (Foochow in the vernacular), is often ranked among the best of the high cuisine in China. However, Fuzhou cuisine has never spread to the South Seas, as the Minbei emigrants are minorities in terms of number, wealth and power among the overseas Chinese in Southeast Asia. Although Fuzhou people in reality came from the same Fujian province, they were not considered Hokkien or Fujianese, the term was reserved exclusively for the Minnanese.

References

Abu-Lughod, Lila (1997) 'The Interpretation of Culture(s) after Television', *Presentations* 59:109–134.

Anderson, Eugene (1988) *The Food of China*. New Haven: Yale University Press.

Anderson, N. Eugene and Marja L. Anderson (1977) 'Modern China: The South', in K. C. Chang (ed.) *Food in Chinese Culture: Anthropological and Historical Perspectives*, pp. 337–381 New Haven: Yale University Press.

Alonso, Ana M. (1994) 'The Politics of Space, Time and Substance: State Formation, Nationalism, and Ethnicity', *Annual Review of Anthropology*, 23:379–405.

Appadurai, Arjun (ed.) (1986) *The Social Life of Things: Commodities in Cultural Perspective*. Cambridge: Cambridge University Press.

Appadurai, Arjun (1988) 'How to Make a National Cuisine: Cookbooks in Contemporary India', *Comparative Study of Society and History*, 30 (1):3–24.

—— (1990) 'Disjuncture and Difference in the Global Cultural Economy', *Public Culture*, 2 (2):1–24.

—— (1996) 'Consumption, Duration and History', in A. Appadurai (ed.) *Modernity at Large: Cultural Dimensions of Globalization*, pp. 66–85, Minnesota: University of Minnesota Press.

Beardsworth, Alan and Teresa Keil (1997) *Sociology on the Menu*. London: Routledge.

Bourdieu, Pierre (1984) *Distinction: A Social Critique of the Judgment of Taste (translated by Richard Nice)*. London: Routledge & K. Paul.

Chang, Kwang-chi (ed.) (1977) *Food in Chinese Culture: Anthropological and Historical Perspectives*. New Haven: Yale University Press.

Chow, Rey (1993) *Writing Diaspora*. Bloomington: Indiana University Press.

Counihan, Carole and Penny Van Esterik (eds) (1997) *Food and Culture: A Reader*. New York: Routledge.

Clifford, James (1997) *Routes: Travel and Translation in the late Twentieth Century*. Cambridge, MA: Harvard University Press.

Fieldhouse, Paul (1995) *Food and Nutrition: Customs and Culture*. London: Chapman and Hall.

Finkelstein, Joanne (1989) *Dining Out: A Sociology of Modern Manners*. Cambridge: Polity Press.

Foster, Robert J. (1991) Making National Cultures in the Global Ecumene, *Annual Review of Anthropology* 20:235–260.

Friedman, Jonathan (1990) Being in the World: Globalization and Localization, *Theory, Culture and Society* 7:311–328.

—— (1994a) 'The Past in the Future: History and the Politics of Identity', *American Anthropologist*, 94 (4):837–839.

—— (1994b) *Cultural Identity and Global Process*. London: Sage.

Goody, Jack (1982) *Cooking, Cuisine and Class: A Study in Comparative Sociology*. Cambridge: Cambridge University Press.

Hannerz, Ulf (1988) 'The World in Creolisation', *Africa* 57(4):546–559.

—— (1989a) Culture between Center and Periphery: Toward a Macroanthropology, *Ethnos*, 54 (3–4):200–216.

—— (1989b) Notes on the Global Ecumene, *Public Culture*, 1(2):66–75.

—— (1990) 'Cosmopolitans and Locals in World Culture', *Theory, Culture and Society*, 7:237–251.

—— (1996) *Transnational Connections, Culture, People, Places*. London: Routledge.

Lee, Edwin (1976) *The Towkays of Sabah*. Singapore: Singapore University Press.

Lash, Scott and John Urry (1994) *Economies of Signs and Space*. London: Sage.

Liang, Shi-chio (1985) *Ya-she Tan-chi* [My Experience of Food]. Taipei: Jiuge.

Lu, Shun and Gary A. Fine (1995) The Presentation of Ethnic Authenticity: Chinese Food as a Social Accomplishment, *Sociological Quarterly* 36 (3):535–553.

Marcus, George (1995) 'Ethnography in/of the World System: The Emergence of Multi-sited Ethnography', *Annual Review of Anthropology*, 24:95–117.

Mintz, W. Sidney (1985) *Sweetness and Power: The Place of Sugar in Modern History*. New York: Viking.

—— (1994) 'The Changing Roles of Food in the Study of Consumption', in John Brewer and Roy Porter (eds) *Consumption and the World of Goods*, pp. 261–273. London: Routledge.

—— (1996) *Tasting Food, Tasting Freedom*. Boston: Beacon Press.

Simoons, Frederick (1991) *Food in China: A Cultural and Historical Inquiry*, Boca Raton: CRC Press.

Tobin, J. Joseph (ed.) (1992) 'Introduction', in J. J. Tobin (ed.) *Re-made in Japan: Everyday Life and Consumer Taste in a Changing Society*, pp. 1–41 New Haven: Yale University Press.

Watson, L. James (1975) *Emigration and the Chinese Lineage: The Mans in Hong Kong and London*. Berkeley and London: University of California Press.

—— (ed.) (1997) *Golden Arches East: McDonald's in East Asia*. Stanford: Stanford University Press.

Wilk, Richard R. (1999) '"Real Belizean Food": Building Local Identity in the Transnational Caribbean, *American Anthropologist* 99:244–255.

Williams, Brackette F. (1989) 'A Class Act: Anthropology and the Race to Nation Across Ethnic Terrain', *Annual Review of Anthropology* 18:401–444.

Wu, David Y. H. (1977) 'Chinese as an Intrusive Language', in S. A. Wurm (ed.) *New Guinea Languages and Language Study, Vol. 3*, pp. 1047–1055 Language, Culture, Society, and the Modern World. Fascicle 2, Canberra: Australian National University.

PART I

Sources of the Globe

CHAPTER ONE

Food Culture and Overseas Trade

The Trepang Trade between China and
Southeast Asia during the Qing Dynasty

Dai Yifeng

Traditional Chinese food culture often emphasizes that some animals and plants or their body parts have special balancing or healing functions for the human body. Trepang is a typical example of this theory concerning the relationship between the human body and the outside world. It also sheds light on reasons behind the great demand for trepang in China, especially in South China, during the Qing Dynasty (1644–1911 AD). Chinese traders, most were from Fujian province, went all the way to Southeast Asia to import trepang to China when Chinese trepang could no longer satisfy the Chinese demand (see Figure 1.1). Therefore, in this chapter, I will show how a chain reaction occurs where food culture cultivates consumer needs, needs form a market, and then the market promotes trade, from a socio-historic perspective. Again, it is worth mentioning that the trepang trade between China and Southeast Asia in the Qing Dynasty show several interesting characteristics that are closely related to the change of trade pattern in the South China Sea during the time which will be discussed in this chapter.

The Knowledge of Chinese people on Trepang in the Qing Dynasty

Trepang (or, sea cucumber in English; *haishen* 海参 in Mandarin) is an echinoderm living in coastal waters; it belongs to Holothuroidea in zoology and shows a great variety in terms of shape and colour. Apart from its biological nature, the Chinese have inherited a rich knowledge about trepang because of its close relationship with traditional Chinese food culture. In Chinese literature the earliest record about trepang came from a book called *Miscellanies of Five Items* (*Wuzazhu*), written by Xie Zhaozhe, a successful candidate in the highest imperial examinations in 1602, during the reign of Emperor Wanli in the Ming Dynasty. He wrote:

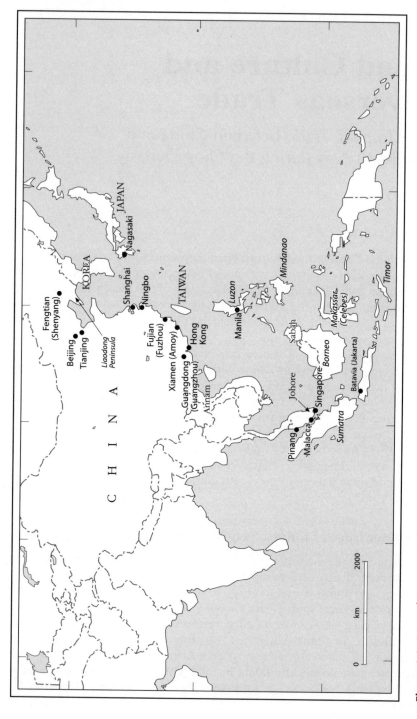

Figure 1.1: Map of Trepang Trade between China and Southeast Asia

There was *haishen* along the coast of *Liaohai*. It was also called sea man (*Hai Nanzi*) because it is shaped like the penis of a man. Its function which is mildly invigorating to the body of man, is equal to ginseng (Ren shen). That is the reason it is called *haishen* (Xie 1959:259).

Starting from the Qing Dynasty, records about trepang in Chinese literature were more and more extensive. Zhou Lianggong, a provincial judge and financial officer of Fujian province during the early Qing Dynasty, described Fujianese trepang: 'The trepang living in Fujian is white with some bamboo pink accents. It is as large as palm and different from the kind in *Jiaozhou* and *Liaohai*. Its taste is bad' (Zhou 1985:36). Moreover, among various records about trepang, the most complete description may be the one from *Miscellanies of Everything in the Qing Dynasty (Qingbi Leichao)*, written by Xu Ke. It roughly mirrors common knowledge about trepang in the Qing Dynasty.

Trepang is an echinoderm. Its former name was *shaxun* and the name of *haishen* was used for dried trepang. However, its general name is *haishen* today. The length of trepang is five or six *cun* (one cun = 3.333 cm). Its body is round and soft, and its color is black. There are more than twenty tentacles around its mouth. Some of its feet take the shape of a piece of uneven baked stone, and others are arranged in three lines on its abdomen. There are sucking discs on its feet, and its intestine is long. There are some separated tubes near the anus, the shape is like a branch, and the function is to breathe, they are called water lungs, and are also called tree of breath. The male and female are different. Trepang lives in coastal areas. They can be used as food after being dried in the sun. The finest live in *Fengtian*, they are black have multiple thorns, and they are called *liaoshen* 遼參. Its popular name is *hongqishen* 紅旗參. The second live in *Guangdong*, they are yellow and called *guangshen* 廣參. The third live in *Ningbo*, they are white and called *guapishen* 瓜皮參. Neither *guangshen* nor *guapishen* have no thorns. Another kind living in Fujian, is white, has thorns, and is called *guangshen* 光參. However, trepang is also imported, in great quantity, from India and Japan every year (Xu 1986:5709).

This record gives a very informative and comprehensive description of trepang and its characteristics. First, it tells us the name of trepang in Chinese – *haishen* – which was actually used to signify dried trepang and *shaxun* was used to signify fresh trepang. In addition, there was another popular name for trepang in Chinese literature, sea mouse (*haishu*) which is less common today. Obviously, the names *shaxun* and *haishu* denote the shape and living habits of trepang. However, *haishen* is slightly different as it is based on an analogy with ginseng. In fact, the comparison with ginseng was also mentioned in the record of *Wuzazu* above. During the Qing Dynasty, the Chinese said: 'Living in the land is renshen, living in the water is *haishen*' (Zhou 1985:36). Second, comparing the written record with contemporary knowledge about the shape and living habits of trepang, we can see that people in the Qing Dynasty had a rather exact understanding of trepang. The Qing description is so vivid, indicating that trepang must have been a very common food at that time. Third, the record indicates that dried trepang was edible. More importantly in the same book the writer also introduced several ways to eat trepang.

> For thick soup of trepang: Break the trepang into pieces. Then put the broken trepang into chicken soup with bamboo shoots and wild rice.

> For shredded trepang: Pick out a small trepang with prickles, wash off the sand and mire. Then put it into the broth to stew three times. After that, pour meat juice and chicken extract on it. In addition, use some mushrooms and edible fungus because their colour is as black as the trepang.

> For cold shredded trepang: To eat trepang in summer, you should slice trepang and mix it with shredded chicken and mustard into a cold dish (Xu 1986:6369, 6492).

Fourth, the record gives evidence about where trepang was collected. It mentions that trepang lives along most of China's coastal areas, but that the local production of trepang could not meet the demand of Chinese markets, neither in quantity nor in quality. Therefore, China had to import trepang from other countries. Finally, regarding the import of trepang, the *Qingbi Leichao* shows that during most of the Qing Dynasty, trepang was mainly imported from India and Japan. According to Chinese literature, trepang was imported from Japan even earlier than it was from Southeast Asia. The amount of imports grew gradually after the mid-nineteenth century. For example in 1864, based on Chinese customs returns, there were 2,422 *dan* (one dan = 60 kg) of black trepang and 1,930 *dan* of white trepang imported from Japan (CMC 1865). However, I have not found any records about imports from India in the returns and reports of Chinese customs. I suspect that the mention of India was a slip of the pen. In addition, it is very surprising that the writer did not mention imports of trepang from Southeast Asia.

Most surprising, however, is that this record did not mention the use of trepang in nourishment and medicine. In fact, trepang is not eaten by the Chinese for its good taste but rather for its nourishment and for its medicinal qualities. There is much written in the Chinese literature of the

Qing Dynasty concerning trepang's medicinal qualities. For instance, a Chinese medicinal book known as *Renew One of Materia Medica* (*Bencao Congxin*) stated:

> The best trepang live in Liaohai. Some trepang having prickles are known as *Cishen*, others without prickles are known as Guangshen. The medical function of trepang is to invigorate the kidney, to benefit the essence of life, to strengthen the penis of man and to treat fistula (Wu 1958:124).

There are two very interesting stories in *The Collection of Travel Records* (*Langji Congtan*), a book written in the reign of the Emperor Jiaqing (1796–1820) of the Qing Dynasty:

> When I was a government official in *Guangxi* province, I found that *Xing Jingsan*, an official in charge of the prefecture (*Fu*) of *Guilin*, had a very strong body and never drank wine. He told me that when he was about twenty years old, he had been ill and nearly died due to excessive drinking. Someone taught him to eat two trepangs every day to treat his illness. Also for more than thirty years, he had stopped drinking.... One of my assistants was more than eighty years old. What he told me about the function of trepang was very inconceivable. He said that he was born in a poor family and had no money to buy trepang. When entertained by his relatives or friends, he often ate all the trepang. He kept this habit for forty or fifty years. His relatives or friends all knew his habit and always got trepang ready for him when they entertained him. Some people also sent trepang to him. Therefore he was never ill although he never took any other medicine (Liang 1981:133).

How is trepang used as medicine? *Records on Fujian* (*Min Xiao Ji*), a book written in the reign of Emperor Shunzhi (1644–1662) of the Qing Dynasty, recorded an important description given by one doctor:

> Ginseng can benefit man. The taste of trepang is bitterer than ginseng. Its effect seems different from ginseng. However, both can warm and invigorate men. That is how trepang got its name. People consider the kidney like the sea. Trepang live in the salty waters of the North Sea, and its colour is also black. People use it to invigorate the kidney because they are similar.... Ginseng is like man, trepang is especially like the penis of a man. Trepang's function for man is not weaker than ginseng's ... (Zhou 1985:36).

Formation and Development of the Trepang Trade between China and Southeast Asia

When did the trepang trade between China and Southeast Asia begin? There are no exact records in Chinese literature, but Chinese literature and research show that imported commodities from Southeast Asia were usually luxury goods destined to increase the enjoyment of the royal court or rich and powerful people. Items such as rhinoceros horn, elephant tusk, jadeite, pearl, agalloch, gold and silver were traded over a very long period after the establishment of trade relations between China and Southeast Asia (Li and Liao 1995:1–54). During the Song and Yuan dynasties (960–1279 AD and 1279–1368 AD), the maritime trade between China and Southeast Asia went through a period of rapid development. More than 50 countries and areas established trade relations with China. Consequently, the trading commodities between China and Southeast Asia were both varied and structurally changed.

According to records included in the *Collection of Important Documents in the Song Dynasty* (*Song Huiyao Jigao*) and *The History of South China Sea* (*Nanhai Zi*), during this period, more than 300 distinct products were imported from Southeast Asia to China by sea routes. These goods can be divided into eight classifications as follows: perfume, medicine, treasures, piece goods, fur, handicrafts, food and raw materials for the handicraft industry. Among these perfume and medicine comprised a multitude of items and made up the largest percentage. The proportion of imports comprised treasures such as rhinoceros horn, elephant's tusk, jadeite and pearl were large but not of primary importance. Imports of handicrafts, food and raw materials for the handicraft industry were relatively small. During that period, it has been shown that the market for imported commodities began to slowly transform from luxury goods for upper class society to ordinary goods to meet the demands of the ordinary people, even though the majority of imports were still of luxurious items and significant structural transformation was not obvious. Among the imported foods, most were fruits of all kinds such as betel palm, pineapple, coconut palm and grape. Seafood was not mentioned in the records (Chen and Wu 1981:46–50).

Since the great development of Chinese private trade in the Ming Dynasty (1368–1644 AD), a structural transformation among imported commodities became more crucial and evident. According to the record of *Investigation of East and West Oceans* (*Dongxiyang Kao*), there were 116 types of goods requiring duty in the tax regulations. Among them, about 25 per cent were goods for daily use. More noticeable is that there were various ordinary foods such as betel palm, pineapple, coconut palm, rice, sugar, edible seaweed, shark's fin and shelled shrimps; however, among these, trepang was not mentioned (Zhang 1981:140–147).

From the Qing Dynasty records concerning the trepang trade between China and Japan can be found in Chinese literature. In 1660, during the reign of Emperor Shunxhi, the Qing government caught some maritime traders from Fujian, Guangdong and Zhejiang provinces in the coastal area of Fujian, and charged them with violating the ban on maritime trade or intercourse with foreign countries. These maritime traders came back from Japan. Included in their cargo were more than 40 *dan* of Japanese trepang from Nagasaki (ZKY 1951:258–259). I could not find any records of the trepang trade between China and Southeast Asia until the fifth year of the reign of the Emperor Yongzheng (1727), where in a memorial to the throne from Gao Qizhuo, the governor-general of Fujian, he said:

> Based on the check, there are a large number of Junks that went to Southeast Asia but declared to *Annam* (present-day Vietnam). Now, according to reports from some government officers in *Xiamen*, there are two junks that came back to *Xiamen*. They declared that they would go to Annam, but went to *Kelapa* (present-day Jakarta in Indonesia). From *Kelapa*, they brought trepang, padauk and 300 *dan* of rice (GBY 1982:524).

This would probably be considered the earliest record about trepang trade between China and Southeast Asia. Of course, it does not mean that the trepang trade between China and Southeast Asia began in the reign of Emperor Yongzheng (1723–1736). In fact, in the second year of the reign of Emperor Yongzheng (1724) trepang is listed as an item among imported goods for duty in the tax regulations. The tariff rate on trepang was three *qian*[1] of silver for one hundred *jin*[2] (Zhou 1996:168*)*. This shows that the trepang trade between China and Southeast Asia must have begun before the reign of the Emperor Yongzheng. However, it is only after the reign of the Emperor Yongzheng that we find records on trepang trade in Chinese literature. Some examples follow:

> In 1735, the thirteenth year of the reign of Emperor Yongzheng, Wang Jin, a commander-in-chief (*Tidu*) of Fujian province, reported that due to the poor harvest in Luzon, a junk brought 200 *dan* of rice, 700 *jin* of trepang and 2,000 *liang*[3] of silver to Xiamen. Traders want to buy 2,000 or 3,000 *dan* of wheat in Xiamen (Zhonghua Shuju 1985:926).

> In 1755, the twentieth year of the reign of Emperor Qianlong, Xinzhu, a general of Fuzhou and concurrently supervisor of *Min* Customs reported one foreign junk from Luzon to Xiamen with three litter boats and 139 persons. They carried 10,000 *dan* of rice, 50 *dan* of indigo, 50 *dan* of trepang, and so on (GBYWG 1930:360).

In 1760, the twenty-fifth year of the reign of Emperor Qianlong, Xi Labu, an officer of the Xiamen Customs reported that one junk for tribute trade came from Sulu with 7754 *jin* of trepang, 26900 dried of dry snail, 231 *jin* of clam shells wanting to trade in Xiamen (Qian 1988:85).

In 1783, the forty-eighth year of the reign of Emperor Qianlong, a trader, Lang Wanlei, came to Xiamen with more than 50 boatmen. They carried trepang, rice, padauk, betel palm, and dried venison to sell and they purchased clothes, china, umbrella, paper, medicine, cassia bark, and graphite, etc. (Zhou 1996:142).

In 1811, the fourteenth year of the reign of Emperor JiaQing, one trader, Lang Mianyi, came from Luzon with more than 60 boatmen. They carried 140,000 *yuan* (silver) and some goods such as trepang, betel palm, dried shrimps, deer muscles, edible bird's nest, rice, cattlehide, etc. And purchased clothes, tea, flaxen thread, crystal sugar, medicine, umbrellas and others (Zhou 1996:142–143).

Beginning in the reign of Emperor Daoguang (1821–1850), the records concerning the trepang trade between China and Southeast Asia increased constantly. For example, according to a record in the *Singapore Daily*, eight junks of Chinese traders came to Singapore in 1829. Among them, there were three junks from Xiamen and five junks from Guangzhou. These junks carried Chinese goods to sell and they purchased trepang, edible bird's nest, shark's fin and others on then return to China (Yao 1962:66–67). Another record from the *Chinese Repository* shows that during the 1840s, several hundred junks from Fujian and Guangdong shipped trepang from Southeast Asia to Shanghai each year. A part of that trepang was then transported from Shanghai to Tianjin, Liaodong and other places in North China (Yao 1962:554–556).

We cannot exactly know the quantity of trepang traded between China and Southeast Asia before the mid-nineteenth century due to a shortage of records in the literature. Based on the piecemeal materials, however, we can infer that from several hundred to more than one thousand *dan* of trepang were imported from Southeast Asia to China every year during the reigns of the three Emperors, Yongzheng, Qianlong and Jiaqing (1723–1820). From the reign of Emperor Daoguang (1821–1850), the number of imported trepang rose very quickly. Each year several thousand *dan* of Southeast Asia trepang were imported into China (GBYWG 1930:360; Yao 1962:66–69; GBY 1982:524; Zhou 1996:142–143).

After the reign of Emperor Xianfeng (1851–1860), the trepang trade between China and Southeast Asia went into a period of stable development. According to Chinese Custom's statistics during the period

1861–1872, about 15,000 *dan* of trepang were imported into China every year. And about 20,000 *dan* of trepang were imported every year after 1873. After 1886, annual imports of trepang rose to 30,000 *dan*. In 1892 and 1893, the imports increased to over 40,000 *dan*, and in 1896 reached their highest point with 44,142 *dan* imported. Of the trepang imports 80–85 per cent were from Southeast Asia. As for the amount of trepang imported into China during the late Qing Dynasty, please refer to Table 1.1.

Trepang Production and Export Areas in Southeast Asia

The earliest record about trepang collecting in Southeast Asia in Chinese literature is also from the reign of Emperor Yongzheng. In *Records of What One Sees and Hears in Countries over the Sea (Haiguo Wenjian Lu)*, which was written in 1730, there is a record as follows:

> In southeast of Legaspi, there are five islands: Panay, Oton, Cebu, Zamboanga and Mindanao. Chinese have junks going to and coming from these islands for trade. The people living in these islands are all Malayu. The products in these areas are the same as in Luzon, such as deer or muntjac, cattle hide, muscles or breast, ebony, padauk, edible bird's nest, trepang, etc. (Chen 1980:143– 144).

The writer of *Haiguo Wenjian Lu*, Chen Lunjiong, was born in Tong'an, in the southern part of Fujian province. During his early childhood, Chen often travelled with his father between China and Southeast Asia; he was selected as an imperial bodyguard of Emperor Kangxi when he grew up. His early travel experience allowed him to understand different kinds of customs and traditions, moreover, his job also gave him a very good opportunity to read books of all kinds about Southeast Asia that ordinary people had no chance to read at all. Furthermore, after taking up an official post in the coastal areas of Southeast China, he was in touch with many foreign merchants. Thus, based on what he saw and heard, he wrote the book called *Haiguo Wenjian Lu* which is now useful for us to use to understand the trade network of China at that period.

Haiguo Wenjian Lu recorded areas where large amount of trepang could be collected, especially areas around the Philippines. Due to its geographic propriety, Chinese traders, especially the maritime traders of Fujian, went to the Philippine Archipelago for business from quite early. *Dongxiyang Kao*, which was published in 1617 during the reign of Emperor Wanli, recorded that a large number of trade junks from southern Fujian went to Luzon Island because it was so near to Zhangzhou in southern Fujian (Zhang 1981:89). According to another record, from the late sixteenth century to the early seventeenth century, there were about 30 to 40 Chinese junks going to the Philippines for trade. However, until the reign of

Table 1.1: Imported trepang of China in the Qing Dynasty (1867–1900)

Years	Quantity (*dan*)	Volume (H.K. Tls)
1867	18924	312972
1868	18198	313692
1869	15661	327524
1870	14692	305540
1871	11350	249236
1872	17983	389085
1873	22086	*
1874	23909	450358
1875	22110	385251
1876	19155	340812
1877	20031	402088
1878	23089	426838
1879	19667	383580
1880	19819	474529
1881	27034	616854
1882	26180	635055
1883	28239	550834
1884	22204	475266
1885	28547	529331
1886	33156	592086
1887	35575	681185
1888	32199	656000
1889	33150	863674
1890	*	*
1891	36065	854954
1892	40353	1030905
1893	41518	1052993
1894	35344	853028
1895	30864	837287
1896	38108	766982
1897	44142	1091557
1898	37047	987275
1899	37581	1064987
1900	29561	683474

*No details available
Source: Chinese Maritime Customs: Trade Returns (1867–1900)

Emperor Yongzheng in the Qing Dynasty, there were no records about trepang or trepang trade between China and the Philippines. It was following the *Haiguo Wenjian Lu*, that more records were found in Chinese literature. Some examples follow:

The local products of Luzon are gold, ebony, padauk, and trepang. In its northeast there is a mountain over the sea, called Yeli, belonging to Luzon. The people living here are like the Chinese. Its product is trepang (Xie 1980:144).

Luzon Island, belonging to Spain, is located far away, several thousand miles from the Fujian sea. Its population is more than several hundred thousand and its local products are gold, pearl, hawksbill, borneol, edible bird's nest, trepang, ebony, padauk, fish and salt. An advantage to its products is that they are the best over the seas ... (Huang 1980:147).

Chinese traders often go from *Shanghai* to Luzon for trade. The only local products they can purchase are padauk, ebony, edible bird's nest and trepang. Other goods come from other countries and are not worth buying (Ye 1980a:155).

Sulu is also one country located over the southeast sea. Its local products are edible bird's nest, trepang, pearl, borneol, ebony, padauk, and coral tree (Ye 1980b:219).

Regarding the trepang trade between China and the Philippines Archipelago, I suggest that the amount of trade could have been about 200–300 *dan* per year during the early eighteenth century, and that furthermore, the scale of trepang trade was continuously and incrementally rising. Up to the mid-nineteenth century there were 3,000–4,000 *dan* of trepang imported from Manila to Shanghai every year. And in Xiamen, about 2,000–3,000 *dan* of trepang were imported from Manila every year. For example, in 1864, according to returns of the Xiamen Customs there were 2,698 *dan* of trepang imported from Manila (CMC 1865).

Another important trepang collecting area in Southeast Asia is the Indonesian Archipelago. The most exhaustive record in the Chinese literature comes from *Anecdote of the Island over the Sea* (*Haidao Yuzhi*), written by Wang Dahai. Some records from it follow:

Bugis live in Makassar. Its local products are *Youbu* and trepang, which are the finest in *Xiyang*.

Miaoli located in eastern *Banyuwangi*, the end of the east of Batavia. All its sides are seas. Islands spread out. There are so many stone holes on these islands. Its local products are edible bird's nest, edible seaweed, shark's fin and trepang.

Boton is located in the south of Makassar, near Buton. Its local products are rattan, padauk, trepang and ambergris.

Timor is located at the end of the east of Weichen. Its local products are ebony, cloves, padauk, trepang and edible seaweed.

31

Ambon is located in the southeast of Batavia. Its local products are trepang, cloves, parrots, flower oil and honey.

Banda is located at the end of the southeast of Batavia. Its local products are trepang, hawksbill turtle, gold, pearl, etc. It has many dependent islands.

Ternate is located at the end of the southeast of Batavia. Its local products are trepang, hawksbill turtle, gold and pearl. It has seven dependent states (Wang 1790s:483–5).

The author, Wang Dahai was born in *Rongxi* in the southern part of Fujian. In the late eighteenth century, he went to Indonesia with fellow villagers after he failed an imperial examination, and stayed there for almost ten years. During that period he travelled to many islands and ports in Indonesia. *Haidao Yuzhi*, published at the end of the eighteenth century, recorded what he saw and heard when he stayed in Indonesia. More interesting is that Wang Dahai described the appearance, kinds and processing of trepang in his book as follows:

Trepang is one kind of insect living at the bottom of the sea. Its appearance is like a long pillow. Its length is more than one *chi*.[4] It is as soft as cotton wadding. Boil it with salt and then dry it in the sun until its length is two or three *cun*. The deeper the sea, the more and the finer the trepang is. The kinds of trepang are many, but the finest are *Ciseng* and *Wuzhou* (Wang 1790s:489).

From descriptions of producing areas, appearance, kinds and processing of trepang in Indonesia we can estimate that the trepang trade between China and Indonesia must have been frequent. There is further evidence from the results of Sutherland's research. This research shows that for most of the eighteenth and nineteenth centuries, the Chinese were certainly playing a central role in the Makassar trade network. As Sutherland (1995:139) points out: 'Commercial contacts were long-established, but the boom came from 1730 on, with the tremendous growth in Chinese (Amoy[5]) imports of sea and forest products (trepang, rattan, wax, agar-agar), and their exports of earthenware, ironware, porcelain, and silk'. However, the exact amount of trepang trade during that period is unknown. Moreover, it was only in the mid-nineteenth century that Chinese Customs' returns show the amount of trepang imported into China was about 6,000–7,000 *dan,* especially in Xiamen where the amount of trepang imported from Indonesia was 4,729 *dan* in 1865 (CMC 1865).

The Malay Peninsula was also one of the important trepang collecting areas of Southeast Asia. The Chinese literature of the Qing Dynasty recorded that the products of *Johore* were spice, ebony, rice, borneol, trepang, pepper and edible bird's nest (SY 1936:7464). After Singapore was occupied in 1819, English colonial authorities tried to increase business activities with China based on the former trading network established in Southeast Asia. Among the local products transported from Singapore to China were large amounts of seafood, including trepang. For instance, during 1829 and 1830, 28 junks from Xiamen and Guangzhou went to Singapore and carried trepang and shark's fin back to China (Yao 1962:68–69). One statistic shows that from the 1820s to the 1850s the number of Chinese trade junks to Singapore rose very quickly, from 20–30 junks to more than 200 junks per annum (Wong 1960:122–123). From these statistics we can estimate that the trepang trade between China and the Malay Peninsula became a large-scale development, although, we are unable to know the exact quantities involved.

Up to the middle of nineteenth century the number of trepang imported from Straits Settlements to China was more than 1,000 *dan*, worth 60,000 *liang* of silver. For example, in 1864, 991 *dan* of trepang, worth 27,850 *liang* of silver, were imported from the Straits Settlements to Xiamen, including 434 *dan* of black trepang, worth 30,350 *liang* of silver and 557 *dan* of white trepang, worth 27,850 *liang* of silver. In 1865, 564 *dan* of trepang were imported to Xiamen, worth 21,820 *liang* of silver, including 245 *dan* of black trepang, worth 12,250 *liang* of silver and 319 *dan* of white trepang, worth 9,570 *liang* of silver. In the same year, there were 592 *dan* of trepang imported from Straits Settlements to Shanghai, including 14 *dan* of black trepang, worth 216 *liang* of silver and 578 *dan* of white trepang, worth 8090 *liang* of silver (CMC 1865 and 1866). It is worth noting, however, that among the exported trepang from Singapore to China a small amount was transported by local traders, such as the Bugis, from the east of the Indonesian islands to Singapore.

The Import Ports and Trepang Traders

During the eighteenth and nineteenth centuries Xiamen and Shanghai were the two most important Chinese ports for the trepang trade between China and Southeast Asia. Xiamen, located in the southeastern part of Fujian province, is at the mouth of Jiulong River as it meets the South China Sea. It has served as a strategic military point for coastal areas of southeast China since the Yuan Dynasty. In 1394, during the reign of Emperor Hongwu, Zhou Dexing, an official in charge of Xiamen, built the city wall, and the city was named Xiamen. During the late Ming Dynasty and the early Qing Dynasty, Xiamen developed quickly with the increase in overseas trade and took the place of the Zhangzhou port in importance. It became a centre of trade in southeast China and was regarded as one of the best ports on the coast of China (Dai 1996a:172–173). In 1727, during the reign of Emperor Yongzheng, the Qing government officially ended its ban on shipping to Southeast Asia, and named Xiamen the only port open for trade between China and Southeast Asia. This action enhanced Xiamen's trade position with Southeast Asia. Thus, more than 10,000 junks were berthed in Xiamen during the reign of Emperor Yongzheng. They traded in Southeast Asia ports such as Jakarta, Semarang, Bandjarmasin, Siam, Johore, Nakhon Srithamarat, Songkhla, Kuala Trengganu, Sebu, Sulu, Annam and Luzon, etc. A large number of businessmen gathered in Xiamen for trade and general merchandise was collected there (Zhou 1996:138–141, 512). So, in the early period of trepang trade, Xiamen was almost the only port open to trepang imports. Until the reign of the Emperor Tongzhi (1862–1874), more than 6,000 *dan* of trepang were imported to Xiamen every year, with the highest figure over 9,000 *dan* in 1867. After that, the number of imported trepang fell to only about 5,000 *dan* in most years, with the number reading over 6,000 *dan* in only a few years. Xiamen's trade position was declining (see Table 1.2).

Shanghai, located in the centre of the eastern coast of China, is at the mouth of the Changjiang River as it meets the South China Sea and has large area inland. It formed a town (*zhen*) in the Song Dynasty and a county (*xian*) in the Yuan Dynasty. At that time, Shanghai developed quickly and became a trade port, where junks gathered. In 1685, during the reign of Emperor Kangxi, the Qing government set up a maritime customs, called Jianghaiguan 江海關 in Shanghai which became a collecting and distributing centre on the eastern coast of China (Zhang 1990:37–42). Compared to Xiamen, Shanghai had little foreign trade, contributing mostly to domestic trade before the reign of Emperor Daoguang (1821–1850). Sometimes a few junks from Japan, Kerio, Annam and Siam arrived, but the scale of its trade with Southeast Asia was far inferior to that of Xiamen (Dai 1996b:161–162). Later, however, Shanghai gradually became another important port for imported trepang. In the late 1840s, about 3,000–4,000 *dan* of trepang were imported into Shanghai every year (Yao 1962:556). Up to the mid 1860s, the number rose to about 7,000 *dan*. In 1869, the amount of trepang imported through Shanghai, more than 10,000 *dan*, exceeded the amount that went through Xiamen. From that time, Shanghai became the largest port importing trepang. In most years during the reign of Emperor Guangxu (1875–1908), the number of trepang imported through Shanghai was over 15,000 *dan* per year. In 1897 for example, 20,157 *dan* were imported, which was the highest amount for Shanghai during the Qing Dynasty (see Table 1.2).

It is necessary to note that trepang imported through Xiamen was mostly consumed in the southern part of Fujian province and mostly in Xiamen. Yet, in Shanghai most of the imported trepang was re-exported to the Changjiang River valley, north China and Hong Kong. According to the returns of the Shanghai Customs, the re-exported trepang in Shanghai made up 45–50 per cent of the total amount imported every year during the 1870s, and 60–70 per cent during the 1880s. The year with the highest

Table 1.2: Imported trepang of Shanghai and Xiamen (1865–1900)

Ports	*Shanghai*		*Xiamen*	
Years	Quantity (*dan*)	Volume (H.K. silver)	Quantity (*dan*)	Volume (H.K. silver)
1865	6950	115942	9347	342070
1866	*	111466	6429	156683
1867	6932	136613	9521	187251
1868	*	*	6974	115225
1869	10271	256772	4060	70446
1870	7370	193732	6648	126662
1871	8002	202636	7427	112639
1872	10715	288270	6063	113628
1873	14559	400284	5494	116077
1874	*	*	*	*
1875	12600	283913	4828	37245
1876	10593	256363	3957	35467
1877	11840	294099	4611	54431
1878	12230	293945	5456	59224
1879	12462	305801	4337	42437
1880	9668	373376	4274	39910
1881	16542	519871	4703	48919
1882	15806	519635	5462	50910
1883	15717	375764	5972	61041
1884	11497	339332	5228	54152
1885	15127	366776	4737	48442
1886	15709	376134	6512	65994
1887	17319	421681	5319	51410
1888	14473	359203	4365	53384
1889	16097	574942	4824	65691
1890	17236	619836	5156	71558
1891	16174	478525	5475	87443
1892	17729	595186	7259	108993
1893	18495	612448	*	*
1894	16864	508554	4955	80159
1895	17542	538242	2997	49080
1896	18866	347907	6787	104409
1897	20157	567860	7067	108957
1898	15625	462976	6857	96001
1899	15819	462862	6236	95896
1900	11983	222575	5972	92523

*No details available
Source: Chinese Maritime Customs: Trade Returns, (1865–1900), *Shanghai* and *Amoy*.

re-export was 1883, with 78 per cent. This shows that Shanghai had become a transfer port for imported trepang from Southeast Asia in the late nineteenth century (see Table 1.3).

Now, let us discuss the traders of trepang. The most important characteristic of the trepang trade between China and Southeast Asia in the

Table 1.3: The re-export of trepang from Shanghai and Xiamen (1870–1900)

Ports	Shanghai		Xiamen	
Years	Quantity (*dan*)	Volume (H.K. silver)	Quantity (*dan*)	Volume (H.K. silver)
1870	3498	109673	803	14594
1871	4194	127785	518	7848
1872	5196	160880	1523	29536
1873	6613	221491	595	13165
1875	6342	163674	213	3180
1876	5744	151917	176	1557
1877	7055	202549	344	1419
1878	6023	176371	202	2927
1879	7640	221142	34	527
1880	6965	254686	19	270
1881	9765	362774	69	1026
1882	9269	352228	26	383
1883	12296	326293	10	195
1884	8150	267295	27	488
1885	8754	239953	42	634
1886	9441	260494	–	–
1887	10022	278875	23	273
1888	9205	259145	–	–
1889	9948	415305	–	–
1890	10711	442078	3	55
1891	10605	356046	44	617
1892	10656	428750	–	–
1893	10535	420894	–	–
1894	11286	376893	25	437
1895	11980	402953	–	–
1896	11655	235716	3	106
1897	11524	386138	1	33
1898	9563	319832	93	1397
1899	10604	333790	–	–
1900	7600	150178	20	300

Source: Chinese Maritime Customs: Trade Returns, (1870–1900), *Shanghai* and *Amoy*.

Qing Dynasty was that it was mostly controlled by Chinese traders, especially from Fujian Province. Wang's *Haidao Yuzhi*, mentioned above, vividly described the Indonesian Archipelago as teeming in trepang in the late eighteenth century when Fujian traders plied the Southeast Asian trade routes. From incomplete statistics, there were about ten Chinese junks travelling between the coast of China and Batavia (present-day Jakarta) every year during the eighteenth century. Chinese traders went to Batavia with chinaware and tea, and came back to China with trepang and other goods (Qian 1989:87). Between China and Sulu, another place which was also teeming in trepang, the trepang trade was completely managed by Fujian traders in the eighteenth century. For a very long period there were three or four Fujianese junks travelling between Xiamen and Sulu. Among all the goods that Fujian traders carried back to Xiamen, one of the most important was trepang (Qian 1988:85).

Starting from the nineteenth century, records show that Chinese merchants traded in trepang more and more frequently. For instance, according to the records of British Parliamentary Papers in the early part of the nineteenth century, there was large scale junk trade between China and Southeast Asia. A lot of Chinese junks went to Java, the north and northwest of Borneo, the Sulu Islands, Makassar of Celebes Island and Sumatra Island. There were a large number of Chinese overseas living on these islands. Chinese traders carried chinaware, silk, tea, furniture and other goods. They returned to China with tin, sugar, pepper, edible bird's nest, trepang, cane and rattan, etc. (Yao 1962:75). In the 1820s, many Chinese junks went to Singapore to trade local products, including trepang. And in the middle of nineteenth century, there were 300 junks from Fujian and 400 junks from Guangdong travelling to Shanghai from Singapore, Malacca, Pinang, Java, Sulu, Sumatra and Borneo, transporting pepper, shark's fin, trepang, edible bird's nest, sugar, padauk, etc. to China. Among these 520,000 *dan* of sugar, 25,000–30,000 *dan* of padauk, 1,950 *dan* of trepang, 1,700 *dan* of shark's fin, and 1,500 *dan* of edible bird's nest were imported from Manila. If one adds goods from smuggling, the number of imported trepang would be 3,000–4,000 *dan* (Yao 1962:66–69).

Up to the late nineteenth century, many Chinese Customs reports show that the trepang trade was mostly managed by Chinese traders. For example, in the 1860s, the commissioner of Xiamen Customs noted in his trade report that in Xiamen Chinese traders were independent, and were engaged in large scale trade with foreign traders (CMC 1864–1869). He mentioned the trade was of local products between China and Southeast Asia, including the trepang trade. In1881, F. E. Woodruff, another Xiamen Customs commissioner reported that in Xiamen there were 50 Chinese trade firms engaged in Southeast Asian trade. Among them, eleven firms for Straits Settlements, fifteen firms for Makassar, Batavia, Semarang and

Surabaya, fifteen firms for the Philippine Islands, and nine firms for Siam and Cochin China (CMC 1881). Why did Chinese traders mostly control the trepang trade and some other Southeast Asia local product trades? George Hughes, an English commissioner in Xiamen Customs, at that time explained that foreign traders were not interested in these goods (CMC 1874). The fact was not so simple. It was due to a closed relation with the change of trade pattern in South China Sea, which will be discussed in the following section.

Trepang Trade and the Changing Trade Patterns in the South China Sea

In order to answer this question, it is necessary to understand socio-historic changes in trade patterns in the South China Sea. As we know, maritime trade between China and Southeast Asia has a long and complicated history. Before European traders expanded their trade routes into Southeast Asia, Chinese traders had for a long time set up business networks with geographical superiority and well-connected communication systems. However, beginning in the sixteenth century, trade patterns changed because of several factors. In the past, prevalent historical argument was simply framed as: the West conquers the East and the East is subordinate to the West. Many western scholars often exaggerated the function and the influence of European traders on changing trade patterns in the South China Sea. While Chinese scholars, despite exposure to European colonial aggression and plunder, also adopted the same mode of thinking that Chinese traders were driven away because of a different trade pattern. This mode of thinking overlooked not only the abilities of Chinese traders to change despite their activities over such a long period, but also the inherent continuity and complex nature of the well-developed Chinese trade network.

I do not deny the influence of European traders on changing trade patterns in the South China Sea; likewise, I would consider influences from two directions. First, the coming of European business power stimulated the development of Chinese trade networks as European traders used this network to maintain and expand their business. Europeans also destroyed Chinese trade networks by butchering Chinese to safeguard their business dominance. However, one also cannot overlook other important factors affecting the development of trade in the South China Sea.

First, in Southeast Asia, Chinese communities emerged and spread widely over Southeast Asia. The scale of these communities also grew significantly. By the late eighteenth century, the population of these Chinese communities exceeded 500,000; at the same time, various Chinese voluntary associations emerged in succession in Chinese communities (Purcell 1965:123; Yen 1993:679–716). These Chinese communities set up a good business infrastructure and created external economies for Chinese trade networks (Zhang 1988:355–358). For example in Xiamen, customs reports show that Xiamen was a highway of commerce between China and the southern markets of the Indian Archipelago, such as: Bangkok, Singapore, Malacca, Penang, the ports in Java, Sumatra, Borneo and Macassar. Most of the Chinese in Java, Siam, and the Strait Settlements were Fujianese, who naturally desired to trade their manufactured and native produce; hence there existed a large trade. All such trade was controlled by Chinese merchants (CMC 1865).

Second, as trade rapidly expanded in this period some Chinese maritime merchant groups emerged. These maritime merchant groups were organized by family ties and regional ties. They possessed large-scale management capability and had close relations with each other. Meanwhile, with the rise of maritime merchant groups, some new trade ports emerged along the coast of South China, such as Xiamen, Haicheng, Shantou, Nan'ao, Macao and Zhapu (Ng 1983; Lim 1987; Liu 1993). These ports kept very close relations with those trade ports scattered in Southeast Asia. Clearly, the emergence of regional maritime merchant groups and central trade ports enhanced regional ties in the Chinese trade network.

Third, the rise of local business power and confrontations between leaders of indigenous inhabitants and European colonialists in Southeast Asia largely restricted the sphere of European influence, and formed vast peripheral areas, where the colonial superstructure was obscure. That gave Chinese traders a very good opportunity to develop their business there. For example, according to the reports of the British Parliamentary Papers, in the waters of the Sulu Sea and the Celebes Sea, Chinese traders easily traded with local people and engaged in coastal trade among the islands after gaining the tacit understanding of the inhabitants. These places not only refused to receive any Europeans, but it was very dangerous for Europeans even to contact these inhabitants (Yao 1962:75).

It is worth noting that such peripheral areas were exactly the most important places of trepang production in Southeast Asia. Therefore, it is not surprising that most trepang trade was managed by Chinese traders. For instance in the Sulu Islands, before 1876 when Spanish colonialists occupied *Helo* Island, the sultan of Sulu controlled this island and other surrounding islands. The trade between China and Sulu was controlled by Chinese traders, most of whom were Fujianese. The Chinese traders gained rich and generous profits from their trade. In Sulu, the price for one *dan* of black trepang was fifteen *yuan* (silver), and in China it could be sold for thirty *yuan*. For white trepang, it was ten *yuan* in Sulu and twenty *yuan* in China. The profit margin was 100 per cent. In addition, many Sulu traders also made use of Chinese traders' junks to have a hand in such trade, sometimes in the name of tributary trade (Qian 1988:85–92). And in the Celebes Islands, for most of the eighteenth and nineteenth centuries,

Dutch business power was marginal to Makassar's trade network because it could not compete with the Chinese traders and indigenous merchants. Thus, when Chinese, Malay and indigenous commerce was flourishing in Makassar, the Dutch East India Company trade was in decline (Sutherland 1995:138–140).

With the development of trade overseas Chinese communities in these peripheral areas also quickly expanded during this period. In Helo Island, up to the middle of eighteenth century, there were more than 4,000 Chinese, who established a Chinese community like one in Manila (Qian 1988:91). And in Cebeles Island there were more than 6,000 Chinese (most were Fujianese) in the mid-nineteenth century. Most of them were gathered in Makasar and also established a Chinese community under the dominance of Chinese Capitan. In 1868, the Chinese built a Fujianese memorial temple, called Yong Xi Tang (Salmon 1991:84–85).

To summarize, it is very clear that the formation and development of trepang trade between China and Southeast Asia had a close relation not only with Chinese food culture but also with changing trade patterns in South China Sea, which also reflected the complex nature and continuous of this socio-historical change. We should approach this problem seriously when re-constructing Asian history.

Notes

1 1 *qian* =5g.
2 1 *jin* =0.5kg.
3 1 *liang* =50g.
4 1 *chi* = 33.33 cm.
5 In English literature Xiamen was called Amoy based on its dialect.

References

Chen, Gaohua and Wu Tai (1981) *Song Yuan Shiji de Haiwai Maoyi* [The Overseas Trade in the Song and Yuan Dynasties]. Tianjin: Tianjin renmin Chubanshe.

Chen, Lunjiong (1980) '*Haiguo Wenjian Lu*' [Records of what one sees and hears in countries overseas], in *Zhongshandaxue Dongnanyan Lishi Yanjiusuo* (eds) *Zhongguo Guji zhong Youguan Feilubin Ziliao Huibian* [Collection of Materials about the Philippines in Chinese Literature], pp. 142–144. Beijing: Zhonghua Shuju.

Chinese Maritime Customs (CMC) (1864–1900) *Trade Reports and Returns*. Shanghai: Statistical Department of the Inspectorate General of Customs.

Dai, Yifeng (1996a) '*Xiamen yu Zhongguo Jindaihua*' ['Xiamen and the modernization of China'], in Zhang Zhongli (ed.) *Dongnan Yanhai Chengchi yu Zhongguo Jindaihua* [Cities in southeast coast and the modernization of China], pp. 172–219. Shanghai: Shanghai Renmin Chubanshe.

—— (1996b) 'Overseas Migration and the Economic Modernization of Xiamen City during the Twentieth Century', in L. M. Douw and P. Post (eds) *South China: State, Culture and Social Change during the 20th century*, pp. 159–168. Amsterdam: Royal Netherlands Academy of Arts and Sciences.

Gugong Bowu Yuan (GBY) [National Palace Museum] (eds) (1982) *Yongzhengchao Gongzhongdang Zhouzhe* [Secret palace memorial of the Yongzheng period]. Taipei: Gugong Bowu Yuan.

Gugong Bowu Yuang Wenxian Guan (GBYWG) (1930) *Shiliao Xunkan* [Journal of historical material]. Beijing: Jinghua Yinshu Ju.

Huang, Kechui (1980) *Luzon Jilie* [A Short History of Luzon], in *Zhongshandaxue Dongnanyan Lishi Yanjiusuo* (eds) *Zhongguo Guji zhong Youguan Feilubin Ziliao Huibian* [Collection of Materials about the Philippines in Chinese Literature], pp. 146–147. Beijing: *Zhonghua Shuju*.

Liang, Zhangji (1981) [1847] *Langji Congtan* [The collection of travel records]. Beijing: Zhonghua Shuju.

Li, Jinming and Liao Dake (1995) *Zhongguo Gudai Haiwai Maoyi Shi* [History of Chinese overseas trade in ancient times]. Nanling: Guangxi Renming Chubanshe.

Lim, Renchuan (1987) *Mingmo Qingchu Siren Haishang Maoyi* [Private maritime trade during the late Ming dynasty and the early Qing dynasty]. Shanghai: Huadong Shifan Daxue Chubanshe.

Liu, Xufeng (1993) *'Qingdai de Zhapu Gang yu Zhongri Maoyi'* ['Zhapu port and the trade between China and Japan in the Qing Dynasty], in Zhang Bincun and Liu Siji (eds) *Zhong guo Haiyang Fazhanshi Lunwen Ji* [A collection of the history of China's ocean development] 5, pp. 187–244. Taipei: Zhongyang Yanjiuyan Zhongsan Renwen Shehui Kexue Yanjiu Shuo.

Ng, Chin-keong (1983) *Trade and Society: The Amoy Network on the China Coast, 1683–1735.* Singapore: Singapore University Press.

Purcell, Victor (1965) *The Chinese in Southeast Asia.* London: Oxford University Press.

—— (1967) *The Chinese in Malaya.* Kuala Lumpur: Oxford University Press.

Qian, Jiang (1988) *Qingda Zhongguo yu Sulu de Maoyi* [The trade between China and Sulu in the Qing dynasty], *Nanyang Wenti Yanjiu* (Studies of Southeast Asian issue) 1:85–92.

—— (1989) *Shiqi zhi Shiba Shiji Zhongguo yu Sulu de Chiqi Maoyi* [Chinaware trade between China and Sulu during the seventeenth and eighteenth centuries], in *Nanyang Wenti Yanjiu* (Studies fn Southeast Asian issue) 1:80–91.

Salmon, Claudine (1991) 'A Debate on Etiquette and Custom of Fujian Gongdetang in surabaya Area during the Nineteenth Century' ['Shijiu Shiji Yinni Sishui Diqu Weirao Fujian Gongdetang de Lishuzhizhen'] (A Chinese translation), *Maritime History Studies*, 2:84–85.

Shangwu Yinshuguan (SY) (1936) *Qingchao Wenxian Tongkao* [Collection of the Qing Dynasty's literature]. Shanghai: Shangwu Yinshuguan.

Sutherland, Heather (1995) 'Believing is Seeing: Perspectives on Political Power and Economic Activities in the Malay world 1700–1940', *Journal of Southeast Asian Studies*, 26 (1):133–146.

Wang, Dahai (1790s) *Haidao Yuzhi* [Anecdote of the island over the sea], in Wang Xiqi (ed.) (1891) *Xiaofangfuzhai Yudi Congchao*. Shanghai: Shanghai Zhuyitang.

Wong, Lin Ken (1960) 'The Trade of Singapore (1819–69)', *Journal of Malay Branch of the Royal Asiatic Society*, 33 (4):121–126.

Wu, Yiluo (1958) [1757] *Bencao Congxin* [Renewal of material medicine]. Shanghai: Shanghai Kexue Jishu Chubanshe.

Xie, Qinggao (1980) *Hailu* [Records of Sea], in *Zhongshandaxue Dongnanyan Lishi Yanjiusuo* (eds) *Zhongguo Guji zhong Youguan Feilubin Ziliao Huibian* [Collection of materials about the Philippines in Chinese literature], pp. 144–145. Beijing: Zhonghua Shuju.

Xie, Zhaozhe (1959) [1616] *Wuzazhu* [Miscellanies of Five Items]. Beijing: Zhonghua Shuju.

Xu, Ke (1986) [1917] *Qingbi Leichao* [Miscellanies of everything in the Qing dynasty]. Beijing: Zhonghua Shuju.

Yao, Xiangao (1962) *Zhongguo Jindai Duiwai Maoyishi Ziliao* [Collection of historical material of Chinese foreign trade]. Beijing: Zhonghua Shuju.

Ye, Jiangyong (1980a) *Luzon Jilie* [A Short History of Luzon], in *Zhongshandaxue Dongnanyan Lishi Yanjiusuo* (eds) *Zhongguo Guji zhong Youguan Feilubin Ziliao Huibian* [Collection of materials about the Philippines in Chinese literature], pp. 147–155. Beijing: Zhonghua Shuju.

—— (1980b) *Sulu Jilie* [A Short History of Sulu], in *Zhongshandaxue Dongnanyan Lishi Yanjiusuo* (eds) *Zhongguo Guji zhong Youguan Feilubin Ziliao Huibian* [Collection of materials about the Philippines in Chinese literature], p. 219. Beijing: Zhonghua Shuju.

Yen, Ching-hwang (1993) 'Early Fukienese Migration and Social Organization in Singapore and Malaya before 1900', in Zhang Bincun and Liu Siji (eds) *Zhong guo Haiyang Fazhanshi Lunwen Ji* [A collection of the history of China's ocean development] 5, pp. 679–740. Taipei: Zhongyang Yanjiuyan Zhongsan Renwen Shehui Kexue Yanjiu Shuo.

Zhang, Binchun (1988) *Shiliu zhi Shiba Shiji Huaren zai Dongya Shuiyi de Maoyi Youshi* [Overseas Chinese superiority of trade in the waters of East Asia], in Zhang Yanxian (ed.) *Zhongguo Haiyang Fazhanshi Lunwen Ji* [A collection of the history of China's ocean development] 3, pp. 345–368. Taipei: Zhongyang Yanjiuyan Zhongsan Renwen Shehui Kexue Yanjiu Shuo.

Zhang, Zhongli (ed.) (1990) *Jindai Shanghai Chengshi Yanjiu* [A study of the history of modern Shanghai]. Shanghai: *Shanghai Renmin Chubanshe*.

Zhang, Xue (1981) [1617] *Dongxiyang Kao* [Investigation of East and West Oceans]. Beijing: Zhonghua Shuju.

Zhongguo Kexue Yang (ZKY) (ed.)(1951) *Ming Qing Shiliao* [Historical material of the Ming and Qing dynasties]. Shanghai: Shangwu Yinshu Guan.

Zhonghua Shuju (1985) *Shizong Shilu* [Records of Emperor Shizong]. Beijing: Zhonghua Shuju.

Zhou, Kai (1996) [1839] *Xiamen Zhi* [History of Xiamen]. Xiamen: Lujiang Chubanshe.

Zhou, Lianggong (1985) [1644–1654] *Min Xiaoji* [Records of Fujian Province]. Fujian: Fujian Renmin Chubanshe.

CHAPTER TWO

Sacred Food from the Ancestors

Edible Bird Nest Harvesting among the Idahan

Mohamed Yusoff Ismail

The Idahan of Sabah have long been known for their involvement in the harvesting of edible bird nests. Although they are major producers of the nests, they are not really the consumers. Instead almost all the nests harvested are sold to middlemen who in turn supply them to traders in Singapore and Hong Kong. The nests made by birds of the swiftlet species are not really an essential part of the Idahan diet; it is the lucrative cash return they get from selling the produce to traders that makes bird nesting activities an important, and indeed jealously guarded, occupation. So far as the Idahan are concerned this gift of food handed down from the great ancestors is just too valuable, and perhaps too sacred, to be consumed as part of ordinary everyday meals.

In this chapter I wish to discuss the nature of bird nest production among the Idahan, an indigenous minority group in eastern Sabah.[1] Bird nest harvesting has become synonymous with their ethnic identity because the Idahan are about the only group which has a permanent claim on the harvesting rights of the nests in four specific locations. What makes the relationship between bird nesting and the Idahan really special is that since ancestral times they have devised a way to ensure the survival of the swiftlet species which produces the nests. Because of this there is a continuous supply of nests coming from Madai and three other caves even though harvesting has now increased from two to three times a year. The key to their success is embedded in the method of ecological and social control which regulates, through intricate kinship arrangements, access to the nesting chambers.

As a rule, harvesting is carried out only after the fledging period, thus letting the bird complete the full term of its breeding cycle. Secondly, harvesting rights are distributed among members of the larger Idahan kinship group through a rotation system which means that permanent ownership of nesting chambers is denied to any single individual.

Collection rights therefore rotate among clan members; access to these chambers is communally controlled. It appears that the concept of private ownership is not the norm among the Idahan when it comes to bird nesting rights.

The Idahan approach to ecological management contrasts with that of the residents of other places known for nesting activities. Because of the lucrative returns many of the traditional habitats of the species in other parts of Southeast Asia have been plundered, causing either the extinction or the migration of the birds. There are also nesting caves in other parts of Sabah, but collection rights are farmed out by the relevant government agencies to the highest bidder in an open tender system. More often than not this also leads to over-harvesting and exploitation of the caves. In view of this, it is no surprise that total production of bird nests has been reduced quite significantly in the past decade. Undoubtedly this decline has also led the Idahan to be among the most important producers of the nests.

Although the Idahan do not have any direct influence on Chinese culinary and eating habits, they do however know that the bird nests which they collect find a ready market once they are harvested and brought down to the foot of the hills. There is very little post harvest processing that needs to be done since the nests do not require any special drying or any other forms of treatment except in the case of nests which contain too many impurities. But this task has now been taken over by middlemen with the hope of increasing the market value of the nests.

The edible part of the nests, taken by itself, does not have any distinctive taste. But the intense desirability of bird nests among the Chinese perhaps can be explained by what E. F. Schafer (quoted in Goody 1982:108) termed the obsession with emphasizing social differences between rich and poor through cuisine. Commenting on the cultural behaviour of the rich during the Tang period (618–907 AD), Schafer mentions that the importation of spices from Indonesia and elsewhere was an important social indicator: rich households were generally addicted to foods from abroad; 'foreign food (to say nothing of foreign clothes, foreign music, and foreign dances) were rigorously required at tastefully prepared banquets and this necessarily included dishes cooked in the Indian style' (quoted in Goody 1982:108).

Perhaps it should also be added that bird nests represent materials of relative scarcity. Not only that, the actual harvesting of the nests, as any Idahan will testify, involves some degree of physical and ritual danger. Since they are items of rare origin they are therefore viewed as culturally and socially prestigious. Their transportation over long distances, together with the risks involved, makes the trade in bird nests even more exalted, so that by the time they reach the shores of China and Hong Kong the commercial value of the nests will have increased many fold.

Bird Nest Economy and Trade

The hills of Madai in Lahad Datu district, where this study was conducted, are among the four localities in which the Idahan lay claim to traditional rights of nest collecting. The trade in the product probably started in or before the early fifteenth century when the Chinese frequented the region in search of various tropical products (Harrisson and Harrisson 1970:33).[2] The following two or three centuries saw the trade between China and the region prosper, 'bringing considerable wealth and impact to the east coast... Chinese stonewares and porcelains, iron, glass beads and textiles were obtained and traded inland, often in exchange for edible nests' (ibid.:35). It was also mentioned that Admiral Cheng Ho, the Muslim eunuch serving the Ming court, was responsible for inaugurating the trade in edible bird nests when he made his first voyage to the Sulu region around 1405 AD (ibid.:229). The Idahan claim that their ancestors first traded the bird nests to a powerful Chinese group further north across the Sulu Sea, just about the time Islam was introduced, around 1408 AD (ibid.:26).

In any case, the trade itself had a humble beginning since the supply of bird nests during the last century was quite plentiful. Only during the latter half of this century has the price of the nests increased drastically due to short supply aggravated by the extinction of the species in other places.

It is related by the Idahan that at first bird nests had little commercial value until their ancestors showed them to Chinese traders. The Chinese were already familiar with the product which they had previously known from elsewhere. They asked if more could be gathered and promised to return regularly to trade them for Chinese goods. According to the Idahan, upon realizing that the Chinese had a keen interest in the nests, their ancestors were cautious not to disclose the exact locations of the nesting caves, but rather assured them of a continuous supply if the Chinese agreed to wait on the coast.

The use of the bird nests among the Chinese can be traced back to the Ming Dynasty (1368–1644 AD). The nests were considered to have magical 'cure-all' quantities. Even today they are supposed to work various wonders, 'from improving the complexion to warding off influenza, to cleansing the body of toxins, aiding digestion, and are recommended for those suffering from lung problems like bronchitis, tuberculosis, asthma, etc.' (Tan 1995:7). The Chinese book of medicine, *Zhong Yau Da Ci Dian 1978* (*Big Dictionary of Chinese Medicine 1978*), recommends bird nests for purifying the blood and lungs (quoted from Tan 1995:7). At banquets the bird nests are served as a popular soup of prestigious value, reputed to revitalize internal organs and promote a smooth complexion (Tan 1995:7). The Chinese also believe that the nest acts as an aphrodisiac, another factor which accounts for its large demand and high prices (Smythies 1981:186).

45

The collection and sale of the nests seem to be a very lucrative economic activity indeed. The price in September 1995 was US$357.50 (or RM893.75) per kilogram for black nests, while the price for white nests was US$1,621 (or RM4,062.50) per kilogram.[3] It is reported that the price of bird nests in Hong Kong in September 1995 was around US$45 for about 50 grams. A kilogram of nests of premium quality can fetch up to US$3,756 with the vendor making about US$1,000 in profits. According to the World Wildlife Fund Organization, Hong Kong seems to be the world's largest importer of bird nests, with a total import value of about US$2.2 million in 1992. A large proportion of the nests eventually find their way to China (Lim 1995:22).

The edible nest is made from the dried saliva of a number of swiftlet species, which belong to the Micropodidae family; the most common are the *Collocalia maxima* and *Collocalia vestita*.[4] In the Malay language the species is known as *layang-layang*, or *lelayang*. More specifically, the species that builds its nests in limestone caves is called *layang-layang gua*; in Indonesia this species is referred to as *burung walet*. The Idahan term for the bird is *kelimpisau*.

The saliva is primarily used to cement down feathers in the construction of the nest, the typical size of which is eight centimetres long, five centimetres wide, and three centimetres deep. 'It is half-saucer shaped, the flat side against the cave wall, buttressed at the side with two thickened feet, which are the main support of the nest' (Smythies 1981:187). These nests are built in clusters in rock recesses or chambers some 30 metres or more above the cave floor. Each chamber, known as *pesui* in the Idahan language (Malay: *lubang gua*), may contain a large number of nests, depending on its size and location.

The *Collocalia maxima* species takes about two months to build the nest, with a minimum of 40 days needed. Incubation takes 28 days with a fledging period of about two months. Therefore, the rearing time of a single brood is between five to six months (Smythies 1981:187).[5] It is most crucial that the nests are collected immediately after the fledging period, otherwise they drop to the ground and are eventually eaten by wild pigs, rats, and insects which thrive on the birds' dung. Nests that fall to the ground appear to have no commercial value at all. Only mature nests plucked from the walls of the nesting chambers are worthy of collection for sale to the middlemen and traders.

There are two types of edible nests. The more expensive ones, the white nests (*sarang putih*), are made entirely of the bird's saliva. These are normally produced by the Collocalia vestita. The other type, the more commonly available black nests (*sarang hitam*) contain a considerable portion of saliva as well as down feathers plus some other vegetable materials, usually grass and small twigs. These are produced by the *Collocalia maxima*.

The Idahan People

The Idahan are indigenous to Lahad Datu district. Now numbering between 5,000 and 6,000, they claim ancestry to a mystical hero, Besai, who originated from the Kinabatangan river. According to their creation myth, the seventh generation of ancestral figures after Besai laid the foundation for the Idahan's claim to the harvesting rights of edible nests. Thus the Idahan's involvement in the harvesting of these nests is traced back to ancestral times through legends and myths which re-affirm their claims to harvesting rights.

Of these ancestors, a man by the name of Apoi,[6] and his dog, Siod Rapat, discovered a number of caves while chasing a golden deer in a legendary hunt that took them to various places where the swiftlets were known to thrive. Bird nests found in these caves have ever since been declared the tribal property of the Idahan. The following excerpt is part of the creation myth which underscores the Idahan's claim to harvesting rights in the various limestone hills around Lahad Datu:

> After a while Siod Rapat said, 'Brother, I want you to remember this hill. Its name is Madai. In the future you and your children will find riches here.' Gomorid said: 'Yes.' After a wild and fruitless chase Siod Rapat stopped on top of Baturung Hill and waited for his brother, who caught up hours later. Siod Rapat then said: 'Brother, remember also this hill. Its name is Baturung. In the future it will give you and your children riches.' As before Gomorid replied: 'Yes.' They looked again for the golden deer. The two brothers grew tired and they rested on top of Tapadong Hill. Here, as on top of Madai and Baturung Hill, Siod Rapat told Gomorid to remember the hill, the name of which is Tapadong. Gomorid, as before replied: 'Yes.' (Orolfo 1961:271)

The Idahan have been enjoying these customary rights with respect to four locations: Madai, Baturung, Segarong and Tepadung (see Figure 2.1). These rights were later endorsed by the British administration under the Chartered Company of North Borneo, and subsequently by the post-independence governments. In 1914 the Bird Nest Ordinance was instituted to regulate the collection of the nests in various parts of the state. The ordinance also gives recognition to the Idahan's traditional claim to the caves in the four locations. Since the British colonial period, the Lahad Datu district office has kept a register of claims to the harvesting rights of the nests. The Forestry Department also closely supervises harvesting activities, while at the same time taking responsibility for collecting taxes on the nests. It is estimated that the Madai caves produce a total harvest of one to one point five metric tons annually.

Figure 2.1: Map of the Limestone Caves of Sabah
Source: Harrisson and Harrison (1970:37).

The Idahan live in various settlements in Lahad Datu district, the main one being the village of Sepagaya located on the outskirts of Lahad Datu town. It takes about one and a half hours to drive from Sepagaya to the Madai hills.[7] Most Idahan who are directly involved in nest collection own a second house within the vicinity of the caves, which they occupy during harvesting seasons. In between the seasons the Idahan move back to their respective villages and engage themselves in various occupations. Only a few individuals stay behind to look after the caves.

Social Control for the Bird Nest Harvesting

The Idahan have an ambilineal system of kinship, meaning that people trace their descent through both male and female lines. Because of the tendency among the Idahan to marry endogamously, a person may have multiple claims to bird nest collection rights by virtue of the lineages of both parents. In addition, people who marry non-Idahan do not lose these rights.

The annual right to collect the nests from each chamber (*pesui*) is assigned in rotation between various lineages within the Idahan clan based on established kinship principles. The proceeds of the collection are divided according to pre-determined shares between members of a group of lineages who are assigned to a particular chamber for that year.

The following year the same chamber will be assigned to a different set of lineages. In the meantime, the previous year's lineage group will break up and form alternatives new groups which are entitled to collection rights in other chambers. It takes from two to five years before the rotation comes full circle, depending on how many groups of lineages are entitled to a particular chamber. The rotation ensures the cohesion of the Idahan as a kinship-based corporate group. For one thing, no single chamber belongs to any lineage permanently. It is the rights to collect the nests that are annually rotated while the chamber itself remains the communal property of the Idahan. Most of these chamber rights are normally shared between people who originate from the 'discoverer-lineages', namely those ancestors who first came across these chambers. The actual number of people in the lineage, and the number of lineages sharing the chamber, determine the share of the harvest eventually received by individuals. In cases where the lineage membership is large, an individual may receive not more than two or three Malaysian *ringgit*, that is, after deductions are made for the costs of labour and equipment used in the harvesting of the nests.

Since the sizes of the chambers vary, the total harvest for an individual lineage also varies. The rotation therefore ensures that every lineage has a fair chance of benefiting from a number of chambers irrespective of their size and harvest capacity. Because there are at least 116 known chambers within the Madai cave complex, and a few hundred more in the other three hills of Baturung, Segarong and Tepadung, no one lineage goes entirely without collection rights for a particular year. In most years a lineage should have multiple rights in various chambers.

One of the control mechanisms used in the management of the cave's resources can be seen in the way the Idahan organize themselves collectively as a cohesive social group. Leadership is based on kinship seniority and elders decide on matters related to disputed claims. They are highly respected for their intricate knowledge of Idahan genealogy and because of this they have the final say in verifying entitlements and claims to harvesting rights. Overlapping claims do occur from time to time, but most are settled through their intervention.

There is a fifteen-member committee called 'The Committee of Inheritors to the Bird Nests of Madai, Baturung, Segarong and Tepadung' (*Jawatankuasa Pewaris Sarang Burung Madai, Baturung, Segarong dan Tepadung*) which looks after the interests of the Idahan people in terms of the ecological management of the caves, the most important of which is deciding on the harvesting times. The post of chief harvester (*ketua pemungut*) is crucial because among other things, his responsibility is to co-ordinate the work done by the teams of harvesters. His other job is to keep intruders away from the caves, especially during breeding seasons. For this purpose a group of able-bodied Idahan men find ready employment as security guards who conduct regular patrols of the caves to ward off thieves.

Harvesting of the Nests

The nests are harvested by specialized climbers, known as *tukang pungut*, using intricate systems of guy ropes, rattan ladders and bamboo poles. The work is by no means easy since it requires advanced acrobatic skills to reach the chambers, which are often as high as 30 metres. Because of this, harvesters have to work as a team; one person climbs to the highest point possible and then using the specially plied rattan ladders, he manoeuvres his way down into the rock chambers to get to the nests. Other members of the team keep the rattan ladders steady by means of long bamboo poles and guy ropes.

Because of the danger involved and because of the specialized skills needed, not every Idahan man is qualified for the profession. Moody and Moody (1990:144) mention that nest harvesting is 'an activity that cannot be done safely without a support team to hold the rattan cables used for guying the ladders, and to help with the raising and lowering of ladders and collection baskets, etc. Thus, it is a group activity whereby fathers and sons or brothers become co-labourers, often in the company of more distant relatives and friends.' All in all, it is the experience gained early in one's life which constitutes the most important part of the profession.

It appears that among the Idahan themselves skilled groups of people have emerged, who receive training from childhood to do the dangerous task of scaling the rock surface. They work for others during harvesting seasons and are paid handsomely, depending on the degree of difficulty and danger involved. In fact, for certain parts of the cave, no other people are able to reach the chambers except for a few known teams of harvesters. Their services are highly demanded during peak periods and they are in a position to charge more than the going rate for their kind of neck-breaking job, one that others are unwilling to do.

The daily rates paid to harvesters vary between US$12 (RM30) and US$20 (RM50) per person depending on the difficulty of the job. In places where extra equipment is needed, the cost of acquiring such apparatus is recovered from the sale of the nests for the year. Therefore, a considerable amount of the proceeds may go towards defraying labour and equipment costs.[8]

There used to be only two harvesting cycles during the year, *papas* (from March to June) and *penango* (from September to November) (Moody and Moody 1990:144). But in 1995 the number of harvesting seasons was increased to three, namely *papas* (20 April to 5 May);

penengah or *penango* (15 August to 10 September) and *ekor* (15 November to 15 December).[9]

The change to three seasons may have been prompted by an increase in the price of bird nests on the world market, perhaps due to a reduction in supply resulting from the destruction of traditional sources in other areas. In fact, in some parts of Southeast Asia over-harvesting is a real problem. Under unregulated conditions harvesters have done significant damage by collecting nests still bearing unhatched eggs and fledglings. As a result some caves are known to have been permanently abandoned by the species in favour of other places.

Despite the change to three seasons, there appears to have been a relative increase in the actual harvest of the nests from some chambers. For instance, a chamber by the name of Balok Kajong in Madai produced a total harvest of 30 kilograms in 1994; but in 1995 the harvest had increased significantly to about 40 kilograms.

Another important consideration pointing to the sustainability of the swiftlet species is related to the fact that the Idahan tend to regard the caves with great respect and deference. There exists a body of belief among the Idahan concerning taboos related to bird nest harvesting. The observation of these taboos helps to keep their location secluded during non-harvesting seasons, leaving the nesting chambers and fledglings in peace.

Deference to the guardian spirits of ancestral times may take the form of various offerings – perhaps similar to what has been described by Harrisson and Harrisson (1970:44, 84) – including the use of yellow rice, white fowls, ceramic jars and goats. Although present-day Idahan no longer placate the guardian spirits in a very rigorous way, they nevertheless harbour a considerable store of respect for the sanctity of the caves as ancient burial grounds and dwelling places of their ancestral spirits. Hence, a marked change of behaviour, which only a true Idahan can explain, is expected of a person whenever he enters the cave.

Recent Changes

Accessibility to the caves in the old days from Sepagaya and other Idahan settlements was not an easy matter. One had to travel by sail boat for at least one day and one night followed by another two hours of trekking by land. Poor accessibility in the past meant that the caves were likely to be left alone for most of the year. Nowadays a gravel road leads right up to the caves' entrance, thus providing easy access to the nesting sites. Such access brings more people to the caves, including intruders and thieves.

Second, a number of people, especially youths, are unemployed and it is most tempting for them to sneak into the caves to steal the nests even if they are not yet matured. This temptation is further fuelled by the high price of the nests and the availability of ready buyers on the black market.

It also appears that many non-Idahan brokers have been injecting money into the bird nest economy by making advance purchases of the harvest from the rightful claimants years ahead of their turn. Large sums of money from Singapore and Hong Kong have reportedly been used to secure such sales. Although not fully approved by the committee of Madai inheritors, some shady arrangements appear to have taken place. To what extent these deals will influence the effectiveness of the Idahan's traditional method of social control of shared cave resources remains to be seen.

In many cases, the actual collection of the nests has now been entrusted to professional harvesters. This means that the rightful claimants can now wait in the comfort of their homes for their share to be delivered to their doorsteps; they need not bother going to the cave site themselves. This contrasts with past harvesting seasons, when gathering for a harvest provided a valid reason for members of the larger Idahan clan to get together. It was on these occasions that bird nesting activities underscored the real meaning of being an Idahan, when existing kinship ties were re-validated and re-emphasized on a regular basis. Certainly the gathering of relatives from various lineages at the caves appeared to enhance the communal solidarity of the Idahan as a corporate kinship group.

Over the years another trend has emerged to affect the bird nest economy; the final shares of the harvest received by individuals have tended to diminish, despite the high prices the nests now fetch at market. Since the membership of the lineage has increased considerably, a larger number of people must share the same harvest. In addition, the operating costs involved in the collection of the nests have increased dramatically, thus cutting further into the profit margin.

Conclusion

Among the Idahan, bird nest harvesting seems to centre around two main points of contents. First, the collection of the nests is regulated by traditional social controls dating back to ancestral times. It is based on intensive ecological observations of the species of birds producing the nests. Their observation of the behaviour and life cycle of the species over a long period of time has equipped the Idahan with a body of indigenous knowledge most relevant to the management of these natural resources. Despite the high demand for the bird nests, the Idahan have not yet succumbed to the temptation of collecting them during breeding seasons. In so far as the dictates of the market economy have not destroyed the Idahan's ingenuity concerning traditional conservation techniques, the survival of the swiftlet species is guaranteed.

Second, the social organization of the Idahan, which is based on kinship affiliation, is another mechanism which directly contributes to the continuing survival of the swiftlet species. Because of their rotation system, the rock chambers and the nests are not in actual fact the perpetual property of any single person. While harvesting rights rotate on an annual basis to be shared by several lineages, the caves themselves remain the communal property of the Idahan.

The system of resource allocation practised by the Idahan can perhaps, for the lack of a better term, be referred to as a form of usufruct, where the rights over animals or the produce are given greater importance than the rights to alienate the land – on which the resources are found – in the form of private ownership. Hence a system has to be instituted to determine in what manner the resources could be fairly distributed among members of the group. For the Idahan the social control of the harvesting is done at clan level. As such the concept of custodianship seems to be more appropriate than that of individual ownership in ensuring effective management and distribution. Had the chambers been designated as individual property, then they might have experienced untold damage from over exploitation.

The caves which provide economic sustenance to the Idahan are always considered sacred grounds, a factor which keeps people away most of the time, except during harvesting seasons. This sacralization of space directly benefits the swiftlets, which are left alone to breed for most of the year, thereby perpetuating the survival of the species.

Conservation techniques used by the Idahan have definitely made full use of three important elements found in most traditional societies: indigenous ecological knowledge, kinship organization and belief systems. Perhaps the kinship element should be given another special mention here. It underscores an important aspect of Idahan ethnicity and their minority position in the larger society of Sabah: since bird nesting rights are exclusive to the Idahan, and membership in the clan is meaningful only through kinship relatedness, Idahan identity and the bird nesting economy are intertwined. As long as they continue to identify themselves as Idahan and remain a cohesive corporate group, they are assured of their traditional claim to the harvesting rights of the nests. And in so far as Idahan identity and bird nesting activities remain synonymous, connoisseurs of Chinese cuisine can be certain that their supply of these delicious nests will always be available in the future.

Notes

1 I wish to thank the following people for making my fieldwork among the Idahan of the Madai caves most interesting and fruitful: Datuk Lamri Ali of Sabah Parks (who kindly introduced me to the Idahan people), Encik Kasuari Ariff (*Ketua Daerah* of Lahad Datu), Haji Ongah Langadai (*Ketua Anak Negeri*, Lahad Datu and Chairman of the Committee of Inheritors of the Bird's Nests of Madai, Baturung, Segarong and Tepadung), Tuan Haji Imam Injir bin Panjang Ahmad, Datu Asibi bin Datu Agasi, Encik Abdul Karim Gurau, Encik Hamid

Aong, Encik Mohamad Yunus Kuyong (Chief Clerk of *Mahkamah Anak Negeri*, Lahad Datu), and Haji Manap OK Usah (Chief Harvestor of Madai Caves). I am most grateful for the research grant provided by the Asian-Pacific Center, Fukuoka, Japan. Thomas P. Gill, Visiting Research Scholar at the Department of Cultural Anthropology, Kyoto Bunkyo University, read and gave valuable comments on a draft of this paper, but the normal disclaimer applies.

2 According to Harrisson and Harrisson (1970:25), the earliest authenticated record of Sino–Borneon contact is 631 AD. It began with the arrival of a deputation from the capital of the Brunei sultanate located in Kota Batu south of present day Sabah, to the court of the Tang Emperor in Ch'ang-an. After the seventh century, there was a further increase in the contact, although it was rather erratic.

3 The quoted price was paid by brokers who bought the nests directly at the Madai cave site. The actual price of the nests once delivered to Chinese middlemen in the town is much higher, at least 15 to 20 per cent more. RM (for *ringgit Malaysia*) is the Malaysian unit of currency; according to the exchange rate in 1995, one US dollar was equivalent to about RM 2.50 when this research was conducted.

4 There are other species of swiftlets that build edible nests. Beccari (1989:57) reports that in the limestone hills around the Serambo area in Sarawak, the species *Collocalia nidifica*, also produces edible nests. Another species, known as *Collocalia fuciphaga*, produces 'white nests', but birds of this species build their nests in the crevices of sandstone cliffs along the sea coast (Smythies 1981:189) and are not cave dwellers. Swiftlets, often referred to as swifts, are to be differentiated from swallows, despite the fact that the two share many similar physical features. 'Swifts are aerial insect-feeders and spend the greater part of their time in the air... true swifts have very weak legs, and never perch like swallows on wires, branches or rooftops, but cling to vertical surfaces' (Holmes and Nash 1990:23). A common feature of these swiftlets is 'their remarkable ability of finding, not only their way, but their own individual nest amongst hundreds of others in *total darkness*' (Smythies 1981:186; emphasis in the original). The species relies on echo-location, some sort of avian radar to guide them in flight (Holmes and Nash 1990:23).

5 The fledging period of other species of swiftlets may vary. For instance, in an observation of another species of the *Collocalia*, the *C. esculenta*, Burgess (1961:265) notes that the '...approximate time from the laying of the egg to the fledging of the young is about five weeks'.

6 The culture hero of the Idahan, Apoi, seemed to have another name in other versions of the creation myth. Orolfo (1961) refers to this hero as Gomorid (see quotation from the following myth below). An interesting point about the trilogy of the culture hero, his dog and the golden deer is that they are blood brothers. This theme seems to be quite common not only among the Idahan, but also among other indigenous ethnic groups in Borneo.

7 Idahan settlements are also found in Tabanak, Sagangan, Binuwan, Bikang, Terusan, Diwata, Segama and Kampung Ipir. For a concise description of the village of Sepagaya and the kinship system of the Idahan, see Moody and Moody (1990).

8 For instance, in the case of a chamber by the name of Tagbatu, the price of the harvest in September 1995 was US$4,800; however after deductions for labour and equipment costs, only US$1,200 remained. This amount had to be split into eight shares because for that particular year the chamber was claimed by eight different lineage groups. The final share had to be further distributed to

the individual members of the respective lineage. This made the net amount eventually received by an individual very modest indeed, especially when the lineage membership is large.

9 I am not sure of the ecological implications resulting from this decision. Because of the shorter break between harvests, the hatchlings may not have enough time to grow to full maturity before the third harvest takes place. However, more systematic studies need to be done on the life cycle of the particular species of swiftlets nesting in the Madai caves.

References

Beccari, Odoardo (1989) [1904] *Wanderings in the Great Forests of Borneo.* Singapore: Oxford University Press.

Burgess, P. F. (1961) 'Breeding of White-bellied Swiftlet (*Collocalia esculenta*) in North Borneo', *The Sarawak Museum Journal,* 10 (17–18):264–268.

Goody, Jack (1982) *Cooking, Cuisine and Class: A Study in Comparative Sociology.* Cambridge: Cambridge University Press.

Harrisson, Tom and Barbara Harrisson (1970) 'The Prehistory of Sabah', *Sabah Society Journal,* 4:1–272.

Holmes, Derek and Stephen Nash (1990) *The Birds of Sumatra and Kalimantan.* Singapore: Oxford University Press.

Lim, Peter (1995) 'Bird's Nests: Target of New Crime Wave', *The Sun,* September 20, p. 22. Kuala Lumpur.

Moody, David and Marsha Moody (1990) 'The Ida'an', in Sherwood G. Lingenfelter (ed.), *Social Organization of Sabah Societies,* pp. 133–158. Kota Kinabalu: Sabah Museum and State Archives Department.

Orolfo, P. (1961) 'Discovery of Bird's Nest Caves in North Borneo', *The Sarawak Museum Journal,* 10 (17–18):270–273.

Smythies, E. Bertram (1981) *The Birds of Borneo.* Kota Kinabalu: The Sabah Society.

Tan, Bee Hong (1995) 'Nests of Goodness', in *New Sunday Times (Sunday Style),* September 14, p. 7. Kuala Lumpur.

▪ CHAPTER THREE ▪

Improvising Chinese Cuisine Overseas

David Y. H. Wu

Chinese restaurants can be found in almost any city around the world. The image of Chinese food and cuisine, especially in the past, has been invariably associated with the image of Chinatown. This brief chapter will focus on how a still-changing, overseas Chinese cuisine has evolved, and how Chinese restaurants in overseas communities have spread, and have manifested the change in the cuisine. The discussion is based on field data collected at two field sites, Papua New Guinea and Hawaii, where fieldwork was conducted in the early 1970s and, for Hawaii, in the summer of 1997. For the case of Chinese in Hawaii, I also speak from my own experience of living in Honolulu for more than 30 years.

In reference to an emerging discourse in the social sciences about globalization processes of foodways around the world, the main point of my argument is that although Chinese cuisine overseas has been globalized for almost a century, it did not follow the rules suggested by current globalization theories. It is not a result of the often-assumed global process of a direct flow of cultural traditions from the centre to the periphery; nor is it characterized by the diffusion of capitalized cooking industry pushed from the Chinese homeland by professional chefs and restaurateurs. Rather, Chinese cuisine overseas demonstrated re-creation, invention and representation of cooking, especially in restaurants. Immigrants who are self-taught cooks improvise both cooking materials and how they present dishes, to satisfy the imagination of a Chinese eating culture comprising both Chinese migrants and host (non-Chinese) populations. Especially in the last half a century, the development of Chinese cuisines overseas, or the representation of a great tradition of Chinese culinary arts illustrate a globalization process that has been largely overlooked by political economists who are influenced by current Western theories associated with multi-national capitalistic domination, commercialization, industrialization, and international trade.

The Globalization of Foodways

Ethnogastronomy, the study of culinary culture, nutritional anthropology, and the anthropology of food are but some of the names that denote an established sub-field of cultural anthropology dealing with the issues of food and eating (Messer 1984). Since the 1960s, human concepts and classifications of food in terms of linguistic meanings, structural symbols and myths have been popular topics in anthropology (Douglas 1972; Chang 1977; Wu 1979; Anderson 1988; Ohnuki-Tierny 1993). During the past decade, students of anthropology also have been stimulated by a new approach to study the complicated relationship between food and economic development (Mintz 1985,1996), between eating and socio-political context (Goody 1982), and between changing taste and global trade (Terrio 1996).

Globalization of food and taste in the late twentieth century has recently become a popular topic of study among social scientists, especially among political scientists and political economists. Frequently-quoted terms such as 'Coca-Colanization' and 'McDonaldization' indicate world-wide economic domination of simple food tastes and fast styles of eating. These terms imply a homogenizing force of taste through political and capitalist domination, as well as a commercialization of cultural ways of eating across national boundaries (Befu and Stalker 1996; McQueen 1997). The global presence of Chinese restaurants in many urban centres has been a continuous phenomenon since the last half of the nineteenth century. This old Chinatown-centred Chinese cuisine, and the restaurants where this cuisine has been promoted represent either Cantonese style or that of the 'old overseas Chinese'. Since the 1950s another, homogenizing 'new' style Chinese cuisine has reached every corner of the world because of new waves of Chinese emigrants from China, Hong Kong, Taiwan, and Southeast Asian countries that have reached North America, Australia, Europe and, more recently, Oceania and Central and South America.

In this chapter, I will explore the globalization of Chinese restaurants and cuisine along the line of inquiry proposed by Appadurai (1986, 1988) in treating food, diet and food consumption in public as alive, and as having a social history that need to be better documented. By analyzing a social history of 'traditional' food in overseas communities, the process of cultural construction and the changing socio-political meanings of Chinese national, regional and local identities in the diaspora can be revealed. To illustrate, I shall draw examples from Hawaii and Papua New Guinea. The Hawaiian case reflects an overall pattern regarding the American experience of Chinese food and cuisine. The Papua New Guinea case demonstrates how a 'Chinese' public eating place evolved in a remote and underdeveloped region.

Chinese Restaurants in Papua New Guinea

Chinese restaurants in Papua and the Territory of New Guinea in the early 1970s represented a kind of frontier encounter between Chinese cuisine and a colonized, indigenous people from a non-industrialized society. When I arrived there in the early 1970s, a few thousand Chinese residents, mostly second generation local-born, maintained a diet and home-style cooking that was still influenced in some ways by the Cantonese peasant culture brought to New Guinea by their forefathers. My first Chinese dinner in a Chinese restaurant in Port Moresby in 1971 was, however, quite an eye opener about what 'Chineseness' could be.

The 'Chinese' restaurant, located in a new shopping area developed by Chinese who came from Rabaul during the 1960s, was considered one of the more fancy restaurants in town, frequented by expatriates (or Europeans, as the white were called at that time) in Port Moresby. Both the exterior and the interior decor were 'Western'. Once inside, especially in the evenings, the lights were so dim that many square tables were barely visible; and each table could seat only two or four guests. There were no large, round tables usually found in Chinese restaurants. On one side of the large restaurant was a piano bar, and at dinner time an Indian-looking pianist played Western music. In my opinion, the dishes served, and the taste of the food, were barely and tolerably 'Chinese', but not in the desirable 'Chinese' flavour one might have expected. Of course, my own taste and expectation (or standard) of Chinese flavour combined three experiences: my growing up in Taiwan with Taiwanese-style Fujian dishes and Peking-style food at home; restaurant cuisines representing the best of Chinese cuisine of all the regional traditions brought from mainland China to Taiwan since the late 1940s; and overseas Chinese cuisine served in the Chinatowns in Honolulu, San Francisco, and Sydney. Comparing my memory of dishes I had in the past, the Port Moresby Chinese restaurant dishes failed to pass the test of my eclectic palate.

In the early 1970s in Rabaul, the New Guinea town with the largest Chinese population of more than a thousand since the First World War, had two Chinese restaurants (Wu 1982) in the old 'Chinatown' area. One was operated in the Kuo Min Tang Club in a cafeteria style that served only set meals – usually either roast chicken or pork chops. The other Chinese restaurant, with a slightly more extended menu, had a proprietor known to be part-Chinese. Both restaurants were patronized by an expatriate and a Chinese clientele. Their cooks and kitchen helpers were either Chinese of mixed blood or native *niuginians*. None of the dishes served were familiar or desirable to our palate. My wife and I stayed in Rabaul for more than a year, but we ate in these two Chinese restaurants no more than three or four times; not by choice, but as part of fieldwork.

In the small town of Kavieng, on the northern tip of New Ireland Island, where we spent about two months studying the Chinese community of about one hundred families, there was no restaurant. The small hotel provided only room and board to hotel guests. The Europeans and élite Chinese could go to the Kavieng (country) Club to drink and eat, where only Western food was served. During our stay in the Chinese quarter (about half a square mile in size), we witnessed a Chinese restaurant in the making. A very enterprising Chinese woman, who operated a truck company for her family, started to experiment with serving Chinese dishes commercially at home on Saturday evenings. According to her, the reason for starting the experimental restaurant was the many requests from her European friends who had heard that she was a good cook. Whether this enterprising young lady was, in fact, a good cook of Chinese dishes was anyone's guess, but she was born and raised in the 'bush', or *sanpa* in Cantonese, a term used by Rabaul people to refer to remote plantations on the islands or mountains. Rabaul people sometimes were sarcastic about Kavieng Chinese, saying that these bush Chinese were coarse and did not know Chinese costume and culture. Then how could a 'bush' lady be qualified to open a Chinese restaurant? The point I am trying to make here is that Chinese believe that Chinese food is superior than any other type of food, and no professional training is required for a Chinese to open a restaurant. Actually, one of the most important factors prompting her decision to start a 'restaurant' was 'economy'. By the 1970s Chinese merchants on the Bismarck Archipelago had branched out to the new urban centres on the New Guinea highlands. They introduced and successfully produced new varieties of 'Chinese' vegetables, such as turnip and cabbages that could only be grown in a mild climate. This Kavieng woman imported and sold Chinese vegetables that her relatives on the highland sent to her air-freight. She could use the leftover vegetables to cook new dishes that were not available before.

This lady's experimental restaurant served no more than four or five couples, by reservation only. Yet, it was the beginning of a restaurant and catering business. Curiously, the Chinese in Kavieng for a long time were known to have supplied salty fish, smoked wild pigeon and smoked flying fox (giant bat) to relatives in Rabaul. They were considered Chinese delicacies. At one time in the early part of this century, Kavieng was also known to have produced sea slugs, which required special skills, such as lengthy smoking and sun-drying, and which were mainly exported to China. However, the Chinese and European population in Kavieng, until then, was not large enough to support and sustain a Chinese restaurant.

Hawaiian Chinese Restaurants and Chinese Immigration

Legend has it that the first Chinese arrived in Hawaii on a European ship more than 200 years ago, but large-scale immigration by Chinese did not begin until the middle of the nineteenth century. Both Chinese restaurants and Chinese cuisines reflect changing representation (and presentation) of a variety of Chinese ethnic and language groups that came to the islands in waves. During the late nineteenth century, Chinese plantation workers, mainly from Xiangshan (later called Zhongshan) of Guangdong, in the Hawaiian Kingdom formed a growing Chinatown in Honolulu. Many Chinese restaurants were concentrated in a few blocks of Chinatown during the first half of the twentieth century. Country-style Zhongshan and Siyi dishes were served in Chinatown restaurants until the 1960s. Most of them used the word 'chop suey 雜碎' to name a restaurant, as a clear indication of its Chineseness. Chop suey, or a mixed plate of Chinese food, was an American invention. It was understood by the host population to represent Chinese dishes served in Chinese restaurants. By the late 1960s the Chinese community in Hawaii included an increasing number of new Chinese immigrants coming from Hong Kong, Taiwan, and, in much smaller numbers, Korea. The later waves of Chinese immigrants, from different parts of China, brought with them both new cuisines and new styles of restaurants, spreading from Honolulu's Chinatown to all commercial areas in the Hawaiian islands. Unlike the previous Cantonese or American Chinese 'chop suey' establishments, by the 1970s Honolulu had witnessed the mushrooming of many new restaurants that represented the cuisines of Peking, Shanghai, Tianjin, Hunan, Sichuan and, later, Hakka, Mongolia and 'Hong Kong'. Several so-called Beijing restaurants and Beijing noodle places were opened by overseas Korean Chinese immigrants, whose families originally came from Shandong Province. Other Chinese regional restaurants – Hunan, Shanghai, or Sichuan – were opened by new immigrant families who had sojourned in either Hong Kong or Taiwan. By the 1980s ethnic Chinese who had arrived from Southeast Asia added Thai and Vietnamese cuisines to Honolulu's new 'oriental' restaurants. This was also the decade when Hong Kong style 'yam cha 飲茶' lunch and 'swimming (live) seafood' were introduced to the islands.

Representation and Symbols of Chinese Culture and Chineseness

Both from interviews and from my own observation during the past 30 years I have learned that many restaurant owners opened a restaurant to make a living and to support a growing family. They often emphasized to me that cooking Chinese food was easy and required no special training, although many owners worked for a while as waiters or waitresses prior to opening their own restaurant. Those engaged in either the cooking and/or serving business have tended to stay in the same line of restaurant business; sons would follow their fathers' trade, even though a restaurant's business might rise or fall, and the ownership might change hands frequently.

In the early days in Chinatown, small Chinese restaurants that could seat as few as a dozen, or as many as a few dozen customers were usually operated by either a family or a few immigrant partners. They also relied on take-out services. This pattern is still repeated for newly arrived immigrants. However, many successful operators expanded their restaurant's business to accommodate banquet parties and weddings. Customers consisted of all ethnic groups on the islands. After the Second World War, large and luxuriously decorated Chinese restaurants were developed in major shopping centres and commercial streets by partners of wealthy Chinese businessmen and politicians in Hawaii. The chop suey places, although they were down-graded to second or third class restaurants, continued to serve cheap American (Cantonese) style food. This development coincided with the rising social status of ethnic Chinese both in wealth and in political power. By the 1960s, a new generation of Chinese professionals emerged in Honolulu and some Chinese began to move into the most expansive and exclusive residential areas (such as Kahala) that were formerly occupied exclusively by the *haoles*, or whites.

Generally, Chinese restaurants in the United States, and in Hawaii in particular, are seen to play the role of cultural ambassadors. Restaurants, by their presentation and advertising, emphasize a stereotype of Chinese culture, by virtue of how they market 'authentic' Chinese cuisine, how they decorate and furnish the places where that cuisine is eaten, and in how they dress the employees who serve that cuisine. The story of one legendary Chinese in Hawaii, P.Y. Chong, is one key example. In his lifetime (1920s to 1954) Chong claimed to have opened and closed some twenty restaurants in Honolulu. The now deceased Mr. Chong in the 1940s owned a restaurant in Waikiki, Lau Yee Chai (留餘齋), which was advertised to be the 'largest and most beautiful Chinese restaurant in the whole world'. This famous cook and legendary restaurant owner also reinforced a long-lasting stereotyped image about 'Chinaman' and 'Chinese culture' through his self-advertising phrase in pidgin English – 'me P.Y. Chong, Namba (number) One China Cook.' Photographs of him in newspaper advertisements often had him in the stereotyped Chinaman cap and Manchu jacket. The restaurant and night club was opened in 1940 with a capital of US$5,000 (an equivalent of perhaps US$50 million in today's value) for the construction of a 'Chinese Utopia (*taohuayuan* 桃花源)' with a pagoda, a large dining hall (claimed to be able to accommodate 2,000 guests at a time), fish ponds and landscape. The entire place formed a familiar image of 'China' to the educated *haoles* (hundreds of thousands of whom were arriving from the US mainland) because the image conformed to the Western paintings of a stereotyped Chinese mansion found on blue and white Chinese porcelain (or French wallpaper) exported to Europe in the seventeenth century.

The new and luxurious Chinese restaurants that opened in Honolulu at the beginning of the 1960s, whether owned by local Hawaiian Chinese or by those newly arriving from Hong Kong, would almost definitely use dragon-patterned ceiling tiles, red or hard wood furniture, and other Chinese paintings or murals to decorate the interior. By the 1960s the fancy names of these new restaurants, such as Ming Palace, King's Garden and Winter Garden, replaced those of the less-elegant X or Y Chop Suey House. The image of Chinese culture as seen through Chinese restaurant architecture, interior design, artifacts and names seemed to confirm the stereotypical and popular view of Chinese culture. The stereotype seemed to satisfy the customers; even though decorations and dishes served were of local invention or adaptation. During the 1980s several local-born Chinese businessmen made a special effort to elevate both their investment and representation of Chinese culture by introducing (and inventing) fancy and large Chinese restaurants. One introduced a 'Hong Kong style' floating Chinese restaurant. Another introduced the 'Great Wok' restaurant where the chef cooked in front of the customers at individual tables (an apparent imitation of the American invention of Japanese *teppan yaki*). Both were short-lived and suffered heavy losses.

Mrs Alice Wong, Career Waitress and Chop Suey Owner

Among the restaurant owners and professional restaurant workers we have interviewed in Hawaii, the story of Mrs Alice Wong (pseudonym) stands out, as her career spans some 40 years and involves two of the most popular chop suey houses – the Lau Yee Chai and McCully Chop Sui. The latter one was still in operation in the year 2000. Alice's story will help us to get some insight into the Chinese restaurant business in the US during the main part of the twentieth century.

When Alice's father died in 1939, a difficult family situation prevented this island-born young woman from going to the University of Hawaii. Instead, she was hired as a part-time waitress at Lau Yee Chai in Waikiki. In 1941 she joined the House of P.Y. Chong as a full-time waitress. She considered herself lucky to have such a job because as she put it, 'I was a Chinese woman without marketable skills'. She received, in her own perception, an attractive income primarily from generous tips.

According to Mrs Wong, she and all her fellow workers at both the Lau Yee Chai restaurant and the House of P.Y. Chong were Cantonese from the Chung Shan District (or Zhongshan County of Guandong Province today). Zhongshan people constituted the majority of the plantation workers and small traders who came to Hawaii during the nineteenth century. Mrs Wong reminisced about how busy it was at lunchtime when 'servicemen and local people would line up to order P.Y. Chong's fried chicken or steak plate'. One recent article in the *Honolulu Advertiser* (1997) wrote about the best steak one could get in town, at the House of P.Y. Chong. At dinner, she recalled that the customers were mostly local people, and Chinese dishes such as roast duck, roast chicken, pot-roasted pork, and spare ribs were typically served.

Asked about how P.Y. Chong, the '*Numba* One China Cook', trained and became a famous chef, Mrs. Wong replied that he had not acquired his skills from any formal training. She said, that in those days, young aspiring chefs learned by observation and by working as 'prep cooks'. Such apprentices do basic tasks in the kitchen, including peeling and chopping vegetables, chopping meats, deep frying, wrapping dumplings, and cooking noodles and dumplings. Mrs Wong claimed that preparation of many of the popular dishes 'was easy', and that she herself had prepared them. Dishes like stuffed duck, roast duck, roast chicken, and *shoyu* (soy sauce) chicken were pre-made by the prep cook or other staff and that the chef merely re-heated the dish and prepared the sauce at the time the order was placed. As a matter of fact, in Chinese restaurants in the old days, most of the waitresses not only waited on tables, but also did most of the preparation duties, including wrapping won ton and cleaning vegetables. Women sometimes substituted for the chef and though quite capable, women, according to Alice Wong, were always 'stuck doing the dirty work' and were never able to advance to the level of chef. The following accounts of Alice's experience testify to her restaurant work life in her 'husband's restaurant'.

In 1946 Alice married one of the cooks, Mr Mun Tin Wong (pseudonym) at the House of P.Y. Chong. The following year they left the House, and with three partner workers (all Zhongshan emigrants), they opened a new restaurant in Chinatown, named Lau Heong Chai (House of Lingering Fragrance), which could seat more than 100 customers. When the lease expired two years later, the partners went their separate ways. Alice said her husband then became 'sole proprietor' of a smaller restaurant 'Lau Heong Inn' that he opened in Chinatown. Over the next twelve years, her husband opened and closed three other restaurants. He finally gave up the idea of owning 'his own' restaurant after almost twenty years, and became a cook at a restaurant until his death in 1970.

Although a good cook is perhaps the most important element in a successful Chinese restaurant business, our interview with Alice Wong revealed that a supportive wife is even more important. She worked as a cashier, a waitress, a prep cook, and as a mother who raised a family of four children while working in the restaurant. Alice recalled how her daily routine began at 8.00 a.m. and ended at 2.00 a.m. the following day. When her children were old enough to work, they also helped as cashiers, took telephone orders, wrapped won ton, and peeled vegetables. All four children received their education at the University of Hawaii; one became president of a construction company and two became company managers and the last became an administrator. By the time Mun Tin opened his second restaurant, Alice also had her sister working in their restaurant as a waitress. After her husband gave up his restaurant and returned to work as a cook in another restaurant, in 1963 Alice was recruited to work as a waitress (and prep staff) at the newly opened McCully Chop Sui, where her sister was a 'silent partner'. The job was meant to be part-time and temporary, but it lasted 25 years until the restaurant was sold to a new owner in 1988 and Alice decided to retire. Although she never claimed to be a restaurateur, chef, or owner, she actually retired from McCully Chop Sui as its partner-owner, prep chef, waitress, and sometime cashier. McCully Chop Sui is still in operation today. It is perhaps the oldest surviving chop suey house that still serves dishes similar to those served when it first opened in the 1960s and claimed to serve 'authentic Cantonese food'.

In the late 1960s, my wife and I spent many nights eating late suppers at the McCully Chop Sui after long hours writing seminar papers (we were both graduate students at the University of Hawaii). Even in 1990s, the menu was quite the same and the prices were inexpensive, fitting the budget for college students and working class customers. By then, only a handful of Chinese restaurants in Hawaii still bore the name of chop suey.

Discussion

Since the beginning of the twentieth century, the 'old' overseas Chinese (Huaqiao 華僑) community in Honolulu often stressed the cultural and political proximity between Hawaii and China. Hawaii does occupy a special place in the history of modern Chinese history, as evidenced by how Dr Sun Yat-sen and his followers mobilized the Chinese community in Hawaii to support his revolutionary causes in China. It is interesting to note that a Chinese restaurant in Hawaii played a role in the memory of Dr Sun, who is reputed to have frequented one of the most popular Chinese restaurants in Chinatown, Wo Fat (or *he fa* 和發, peace and prosperity), paying a dime for a meal in the early twentieth century. Wo Fat lasted for almost a hundred years, only to be finally closed down in the early 1990s. The episode of Dr Sun in Hawaii serves to legitimize both the claim of continuity of Chinese culture and political connections between China and the overseas Chinese community in Hawaii, and the claim of authenticity of Chinese dishes. By the 1960s when I first ate at Wo Fat, I realized that the dishes represented the standardized local Cantonese food. To the local Hawaiian Chinese, dishes served in Wo Fat represented traditional Chinese cuisine and symbolized authentic Chinese culinary art. To someone who had just arrived from Taiwan, it tasted different, though quite delicious. To me the dishes did not represent a refined cuisine of China; instead, they reflected a kind of overseas version of rural Cantonese food.

In Hawaii, or elsewhere in other overseas Chinese communities, many dishes became standardized even though they were local inventions.

Examples of dishes in the pre-war period in Hawaii were frog leg noodles, duck leg noodles, lobster noodles, and cake noodles. To this day, the dinner banquet of seven or nine courses in Hawaii includes lemon chicken or fried (crispy skin) chicken, pot roast pork (dyed red), and taro duck. These banquet dishes represent the 'high' Chinese (Cantonese) cuisine that has become standardized in Honolulu. Local invention and standardization of Chinese dishes also showed variation under the influence of new waves of Chinese immigrants. By the early 1980s, for instance, chicken salad (lettuce tossed with cooked and shredded chicken, a dish unknown in China), pot stickers (actually fried dumplings), or hot and sour soup somehow appeared on the menu as the standard first course or appetiser in restaurants claiming to serve Beijing, Sichuan, or Shanghai (i.e. non-Cantonese) food. Most of the cooks and restaurant owners in Chinatown before the Second World War came from peasant or working class backgrounds. They had little education. After the 1960s, especially after the change of US immigration laws in 1995, many Chinese restaurant owners became more highly educated and entered the food business as an alternative way of making a decent living. Among the owners we interviewed, several arrived first in the US as graduate students. One owner who had come from Hong Kong had worked previously as an engineer. Since he could not find an equivalent job in Honolulu, he decided to open up a small take-away restaurant to support his family. The business was profitable and he was able to take over a larger restaurant and specialize in a combination of 'Peking' and Cantonese food. These new owners had no prior training in cooking or management when they opened their family-style restaurants. By the 1970s, another type of restaurant owner who came to the islands included millionaire Hong Kong investors who could import professional cooks to serve 'authentic' Hong Kong dishes in the fancy and large Chinese restaurants. These new restaurants did not last very long, for the cooks would often abandon their patron and opened up small restaurants themselves. As these restaurants were large and had high overhead costs, when the food deteriorated in taste customers did not return. In contrast, only the small to middle-sized Chinese restaurants operated by family members could survive for years or decades, especially when they continued to serve standardized, locally-invented dishes to satisfy both local Chinese clients and a larger number of non-Chinese customers with non-exclusive palates.

Whether these restaurants symbolize Chinese culture or regional ethnicity – such as certain districts of Guangdong, Cantonese, north China, or Shanghai – their popularity was dependant on dishes that were, and are, familiar to the overseas community. These dishes or cooking styles will likely continue to be subject to local invention, adaptation, advertising and popular imagery about what Chinese food and culture are supposed to be.

Acknowledgement

The author wishes to thank The Chinese University of Hong Kong for a 'Summer Studies Grant' from the Faculty of Social Science that supported his fieldtrip to Hawaii in 1997.

References

Anderson, N. Eugene (1988) *The Food of China*. New Haven: Yale University Press.

Appadurai, Arjun (1986) *The Social Life of Things*. Cambridge: Cambridge University Press.

—— (1988) 'How to Make a National Cuisine: Cookbooks in Contemporary India', *Comparative Study of Society and History*, 30 (1):3–24.

Befu, Harumi and Nancy Stalker (1996) 'Globalization of Japan: Cosmopolitanization or Spread of the Japanese Village', in H. Befu (ed.) *Japan Engaging the World*, pp. 101–120. Japan: Center for Japan Studies at Teikyo Loretto Heights University.

Chang, Kwang-chi (ed.) (1977) *Food in Chinese Culture: Anthropological and Historical Perspectives, New Haven: Yale University Press.*

Douglas, Mary (1972) 'Deciphering a Meal', *Daedalus*, 101:61–82.

Goody, Jack (1982) *Cooking, Cuisine and Class: A Study in Comparative Sociology.* Cambridge: Cambridge University Press.

McQueen, Humphrey (1997) 'Repressive Pluralism', in David Wu, H. McQueen, and Yamamoto Y. (eds) *Emerging Pluralism in Asia and the Pacific*, pp. 3–27. Hong Kong: HKIAPS, Chinese University of Hong Kong.

Messer, Ellen (1984) 'Anthropological Perspectives in Diet', *Annual Review of Anthropology*, 13:205–249.

Mintz, W. Sidney (1985) *Sweetness and Power: The Place of Sugar in Modern History.* New York: Viking.

—— (1996) *Tasting Food, Tasting Freedom.* Boston: Beacon Press.

Ohnuki-Tierney, Emiko (1993) *Rice as Self: Japanese Identities through Time.* Princeton: Princeton University Press.

Terrio, J. Susan (1996) 'Crafting Grand Cru Chocolates in Contemporary France', *American Anthropologist*, 98 (1):67–79.

Wu, Y. H. David (1979) *Traditional Chinese Concept of Food and Medicine.* Singapore: Institute of Southeast Asian Studies #55.

—— (1982) *The Chinese in Papua New Guinea*, Hong Kong: Chinese University Press.

PART II

Chinese Food and Food for Chinese

CHAPTER FOUR

The Development of Ethnic Cuisine in Beijing

On the Xinjiang Road

Zhuang Kongshao

Many taxi-drivers know that there is a Xinjiang Road at Weigongcun (lit.,Weigong Village – Weigong is a homonym of Uygur) in the Haidian District of Beijing, but they do not like to drive there for reasons unknown. The east end of the road leads to the Baiyi Road (a new name for the Baishiqiao Road). On the northern side in the middle section of the road there are about ten Xinjiang restaurants. Some of them have been operating for a dozen years. For example, the Avanti Restaurant has been running since the late 1970s; it is one of the three Xinjiang restaurants that have the longest history there. Over the past twenty years so many people from Xinjiang have moved to this road that it has been called Xinjiang Road. A number of other ethnic restaurants have been opened over the past few years, so some people say that the term Xinjiang Road is no longer correct. The media generally call it Ethnic Food Street, although the term is not popular. Today it is officially named Northern Road of the Central University for Nationalities. Will this name replace the unofficial term Xinjiang Road once and for all? One purpose of this chapter is to answer this question.

Why do Uygur people like to operate Xinjiang restaurants at Weigongcun? It seemed difficult to find an answer to this question. I found accidentally a record about the Uygurs in the Yuan capital from some six or seven centuries ago, and became more interested in digging into historical records of the Yuan dynasty in order to see whether the present site is related to that past dynasty and how it is related. The record indicates that there was a Uygurcun (Uygur Village) located to the northwest of Dadu, the capital of the Yuan dynasty in the twelfth and thirteenth centuries (Wang Gang 1996:108).

The village got its name from the Uygurs who lived there in compact communities and the place was later renamed in Chinese as Weigongcun (lit. Weigong Village; 'Weigong' in Chinese might refer to 'Uygur' because of its homophony). Some local elderly people said there was a temple called Weigong Temple here in the past, and a big Chinese scholar tree standing by the side of it. The temple cannot be found today; it exists only in oral tradition. Whether it was a tiny temple housing a village god or was a Uygur mosque needs further study. Many scholars have suggested that there would have been many more mosques in China during the Yuan Dynasty (1279–1368); some records mentioned: 'There are about ten thousand mosques in the capital city and the seats of all the circuits, for people worshipping the heaven westward' (quoted from the *Record of Rebuilding the Mosque at Dingzhou*). Therefore, I would like to put an emphasis upon how the emergence of ethnic food business in this ancient 'Uygur Village' as well as the present 'Weigong Village' shows the socio-historic development of Beijing City.

The capital city of Dadu in the Yuan dynasty represented an urban and rural scene of mixed communities of members from various ethnic groups. The Qidans (Khitans) and Nüzhens from the northeast, Mongols from the north and Uygurs from the northwest lived in mixed communities with Han people. As a result of the three westward expeditions launched by the Mongols and the overlordship of the Yuan emperor in the four khanates in Central and Western Asia, there were many immigrants from central Asia in the city of Dadu. They were called the Semus, consisting of Kanglis, Qinchas (members of the Golden Horde Khanate), Russians, Asurs, Turks and Iranians, etc. Commonly, they were also called the Huihui. There were 2,953 Huihui households in Zhongdu Circuit alone (Wang Yun n.d.). This shows that there were a great number of immigrants from the west and north. In the later years of the Yuan Dynasty, the Uygur in Dadu suddenly decreased significantly. This was probably because a number of high-ranking Semu officials lost favour in the imperial court and lost their positions (History Department of Peking University 1990:132).

Other than the decline in numbers of households reflected by historical archive, it is almost impossible to see any constant community of Uygurs over the years. Some six or seven centuries later, at the beginning of the 1980s a few Uygurs began to move into Weigongcun to open restaurants. In mid-1980s, the number of restaurants increased to about ten. The narrow lane where the restaurants were located began to be referred to as Xinjiang Road. There were two questions regarding its historic development. One question was how the 'significant history' held by one ethnic group could be activated and spread out across different space-time continuums under certain appropriate objective conditions (Najam 1990). And the other question was the process of the historical extension and changes to its significant history, as Gilbert (1988) mentions: 'The new situation is not simply added to the old one; the new is interrelated and interacts with the old one, adapts to it and even modifies it'. Furthermore, the rebuilt location and space has been redefined by social culture, and is quite suited for a definite living practice and a pattern of interaction. By looking at the night market in Taiwan society, Yu (1995:396) suggests that space is media which involves participants in a set of social relations, and even lets them adapt to the local sentimental situation; the process of cognition of space is also the process of perceptual knowledge.

Two Kinds of Xinjiang Restaurant

As far as I know, some young Uygurs were selling mutton barbecues at Weigongcun some twenty years ago. They grilled barbecues along the roadside, fanning the coal fire while calling out for customers. They wore gorgeously coloured small floral caps all year round, even in the cold winters. Now twenty years later, there are still Uygurs selling barbecues there, but the street scenes have long changed greatly and their small floral caps are not often seen.

In the 1970s many of the Uygurs selling barbecue resided in the area were traders involved in the costume business between Xinjiang and Beijing. At the beginning of the 1980s, some Uygurs earned money by selling *lamian*, a kind of special Xinjiang flavoured noodle. Among them was a Mr. Litipur, who opened the first *lamian* eating house on the Xinjiang Road. He was the pioneer of the Xinjiang restaurants in Weigongcun. Soon afterwards, seeing that there was a market among many Uygurs living at Weigongcun, another Uygur named Aniware decided to open a Xinjiang restaurant there. On his menu was not only *lamian*, but also other special Uygur dishes. Owing to its good location, and by serving regular dinner and supper dishes in addition to *lamian*, the restaurant took the upper hand in the *lamian* eating-house trades. Recurring competitions between the two earliest restaurants were so fierce that they were unable to reach a compromise until the public security personnel and the Biding Office of Xinjiang came to mediate between the two parties. The keen competition forced Litipur, owner of the first noodle house, to close his Uygur eating-house and leave the Xinjiang Road. Apart from this earlier type of eating-house, I would like to draw your attention to the following one which emerged in the 1990s.

T restaurant, opened in 1990, is now the largest Xinjiang restaurant in Weigongcun. When we went to the restaurant to investigate, the owner together with his wife had gone back to Xinjiang to observe the Corban Bairam, leaving the owner's sister in charge of the restaurant during his absence. She proudly told us that the restaurant enjoyed a good reputation and increased earnings. The restaurant has an outer hall, a middle hall and three inner rooms. The outer hall is next to the road, with an Islamic proverb pasted on the window. An Arabic verse from the Koran with a Chinese translation is on the wall of the middle hall. It says: 'With Allah's help, you will overcome all difficulties'. I actually felt a strong Islamic atmosphere in the outer and middle halls. However, the inner rooms were different. They were decorated with a few Chinese-style portraits of Uygur women by Uygur artists. Although the pictures portrayed the rich flavour of Uygur life, their representations do not exactly tally with Islamic doctrine. In any case, the dominant Uygur Islamic aspect for visitors is clear. Several nearby Uygur restaurants display conspicuous signboards and Uygur men tend to stand outside the door to solicit customers. So, in the eyes of passers-by, these restaurants first are more symbolic of an ethnic group and its cuisine than they are symbolic of a religion of Islam.

The T restaurant was established, the owner told me, when he left his family in Xinjiang and came to Beijing with a recommendation letter from the Xinjiang Industrial and Commercial Management Bureau after the launch of China's Opened Door policy. As there was a preferential policy for Uygurs and members of other minority ethnic groups, his restaurant business was successful. He said: 'As we are now here in Beijing instead of our hometown, we have to do our best to make adequate arrangements for the daily life of our shop helpers.... The name Uygur means "unity" or "alliance"'. The Uygurs are accustomed to living in compact communities. According to our investigations, the Uygurs at Weigongcun like to rent and share a house jointly.

He has hired six ethnic Han women for his restaurant: two serve as waitresses in the front hall, two cut up vegetables and slice meat, and the other two do odds and ends. They came from Henan and Sichuan provinces. They are allowed to prepare cold dishes, but hot dishes must be done by Uygur cooks. One of the reasons that Uygur restaurants hired ethnic Han waitresses was that there were few Uygur women in Beijing. A second reason was that Uygur women in Beijing did not speak fluent Putonghua and so they could not communicate very well with Han customers. Also, some Uygur youths did not know how to make out bills or write receipts. However in another restaurant interviewed, they hired an ethnic Han young man named Wu. While he was employed by the restaurant, he was required to abstain from non-Islamic food, as a condition of his employment. Also, he was not permitted to bring non-Islamic food into the restaurant. His duties included doing odds and ends in the restaurant, but he was not allowed in the kitchen.

Despite the competition among the Uygurs in the Weigongcun Xinjiang restaurants, they still help supply each other's needs and their ethnic consciousness and religious beliefs are probably the main source of cohesion among the Uygurs in the area of Weigongcun. As one mentioned:

> The Xinjiang Road and the areas around it are places where we usually meet, so our style of life and religious beliefs can be easily preserved. Men go to the mosque to worship Allah and abstain from drinking alcohol every Friday. There are no Moslem clergy in

Beijing. When somebody dies, a funeral is carried out for the dead in accordance with the customs of their homeland. A Nezir ritual is performed to call back the spirit of the dead. Generally, the dead are buried in the Muslim cemetery; only a few rich families are able to transport the body to its hometown in Xinjiang. The Uygurs in Weigongcun help each other even when they are not of the same religious sect. They like to get together with their townsmen, especially when they go to mosque on Fridays.

Wayiti, head of the Uygur in Weigongcun, has no registered permanent residence in Beijing. He said:

> A temporary resident permit is enough for a Xinjianger. I have no intention of staying in Beijing for long. Now I have many friends in Beijing and I have close contacts with the Xinjiang Office in Beijing, the State Nationalities Commission and all the related government departments of the Weigongcun community. When we run into trouble, we prefer to settle the disputes in private, because we have the ability to mediate between two parties. But to serve as the 'chief' of the Uygurs in Weigongcun is not easy, because in doing the work it is likely to offend people.

Xinjiang Road is under the rule of the local neighbourhood committee; the position of a 'chief' has even been set up in the Uygur residential area. The chief should be a man who enjoys great prestige among the masses; he is appointed by a leading body of a higher level. His duties include convening conferences and settling disputes among the Uygurs, and those between Uygurs and members of other ethnic groups. As it was mentioned by one aged owner of a house located in Xinjiang Road

> Uygurs have rented my house. My family has been living here for several generations already. Our relations are not bad. I only wish that they would not turn on their loudspeaker so loud and would not take drugs. Several of them live in a room. Their boss pays for their lodgings and board. They all came from Xinjiang to serve as helpers in the restaurants and they like to live together.

In most cases the Uygurs use their own language, which decreases the chances for them to mix with and communicate with the Beijing Han residents. Thus, food serves as the tool of communication between the two ethnic groups. In this case, the Uygurs like to add a strong-flavoured seasoning called *ziran* (cumin in English) when they bake or stir-fry mutton. At first Beijingers were not accustomed to the taste, but now many Beijingers cannot do without it. To Beijingers' taste, some Uygur dishes are a little too sour, and have too much tomato. On the restaurant menus, only three Xinjiang cold dishes, plus *zhuafan* (a special Uygur dish eaten with

73

the fingers, which is made of mutton, sheep fat, carrots, raisins, onions and rice) and *lamian* (a kind of fried noodles with mutton and sheep fat) are marked 'Uygur-style' in English.

Xinjiang Restaurants on Xinjiang Road

The purpose of investigating the Xinjiang Road is not simply to make a comparison between Xinjiang cuisine and that of other places, but also to explore the reasons why members of the Uygur ethnic group emigrated such a long distance. Historic relations and relevant inheritances, no matter whether they are material or ideological or other, surely would affect and modify present-day social relations, and furthermore the inheritances of present-day social relations will in turn have an effect on the future relations (Zunz 1985). The Weigongcun phenomenon is a rare case that extends over a geographical separation and time difference.

In the mean time, even though I am not able to provide any evidence explaining the re-appearance of the Uygur community, certain aspects of their lifestyles show continuity for further considerations. In particular, I was reminded that members of the same ethnic group continue their same lifestyle across both a great distance and over a great interval of time. Doubtless, Uygur habits and customs, and the roles played by the different sexes continue in Beijing. None the less, Uygur men keep on doing business outside their hometown, in this case Beijing, and once they have gained a foothold in Beijing, they bring their family there when they are fully settled. It is, as a rule, the men who run the restaurants, with only a few exceptions. This phenomenon shows that the Uygurs have duplicated their original family system in the place they have moved to. The Uygurs have a strong sense of collectivism, which is reflected in their entertainment activities such as dancing and singing and religious assemblies.

The Weigongcun phenomenon has shown the degree to which this collectivism exists. The original meaning of the word 'Uygur' is 'alliance', 'help', or 'cohesion' (Feng *et al.* 1981:4). For instance, the restaurant helpers usually live together. Their strong ethnic bonds help them face the challenges of a new environment. They benefit from group contacts in finding a place to live, establishing a business, enlarging the stage to display their ethnic culture, bringing up and educating the younger generation, fostering individual and group development. Individuals profit from group cohesion stemming from their culture.

Here, let me use food as an example for showing the complicated ethnic relations. Pancakes made of wheat flour such as Nan and the fried-roasted meat (seasoned with *ziran*) are popular and widespread in Northwest China and Central Asia. However, it is clear that the quality and processing methods of even common foods vary in different places. Even a small variation may serve as a symbolic sign for the differentiation of ethnic group identity. In some cases, as mentioned above, the kitchen may be taboo for members of another ethnic group, food and the kitchen may bar cultural exchanges between different ethnic groups, because of a pre-existing meaning (e.g. the principles of taboo). But in other cases, for instance, under the control of commercial principles, ethnic identification and religious identification may be flexible. This has become a strategic behaviour of small ethnic groups for both their cultural development and preservation (to be explained in the ensuing paragraphs).

The locale of Weigongcun has ignited meaning, feeling and enthusiasm of Uygur people. They have chosen their own patterns of behaviour, and entered the social-interacting space of Weigongcun. This social space provides a 'small atmosphere' for cultural consciousness, cultural intuition and cultural symbolism. Nowadays, the unitary Uygur community is mixed up with other ethnic cultures. The so-called Xinjiang Road has always been under the influence of commercial principles and the interactions of other ethnic groups. In the case of present day Beijing, development can indeed separate the present from the past. Vast urban projects are able to destroy any semblance of history in an area.

Besides a few Xinjiang restaurants there are now restaurants where many different dishes of various ethnic groups are served, owing to the arrival of members from different ethnic groups. All these might imply that the name Xinjiang Road is no longer appropriate. Obviously, re-creation is always going on historically and geographically. An area is not a fixed division of territory, but a changing social creation (Johnston 1991). Therefore, dealing with the social re-construction of Xinjiang Road is a significant problem that the members of every ethnic group need to consider.

The restaurants of other ethnic groups have opened in the Xinjiang Road because the Xinjiang restaurants were going downhill due to poor management. This provided other ethnic groups with an opportunity to display their culture's cuisine. Since the quality of the cuisine in the neighbouring restaurants was poor and their neighbours did not enjoy a good reputation in the community, the Dongxiang people decided to build up their own ethnic image. Having witnessed the decline of many restaurants in the Xinjiang Road, they understood that to ensure their prosperity they must provide good quality dishes with a special ethnic flavour. The monopoly formed by Xinjiang restaurants at the beginning of the 1990s was now irreversibly giving way to multicultural cuisine.

Dongxiang Food on Xinjiang Road

There is another kind of Xinjiang restaurant which is run by members of the Dongxiang people, whose relevant culture is usually misread by customers. Consider the following example: The 'Friendship Restaurant' is a big restaurant located in the east section of the Xinjiang Road. At the top of the front door are the words 'Xinjiang Flavour', and 'Islamic Restaurant' in Chinese and Arabic. Nevertheless, my students and myself were were quite puzzled when we learned that the owner of the restaurant and his family were members of the Dongxiang ethnic group from Gansu province and whose family originated in the Dongxiang Autonomous County of the Linxia Hui Autonomous Prefecture. The family could not speak the Uygur language. That they should advertise that their cuisine was of Xinjiang flavour was surprising.

The owner's wife spoke fluent Putonghua and Dongxiang. When she was studying at the Northwest College for Nationalities at Lanzhou, she was selected by the Central Nationalities Song and Dance Ensemble and later came to Beijing to study. At a memorial meeting for the late Chairman Mao, she refused to wear a mourning armband and kowtow to Mao's portrait because of her ethnic and religious customs; consequently she was discharged from the Ensemble and sent back to her hometown in Dongxiang County. Fortunately, she was not discriminated against there. Later she organized the first local Dongxiang theatre troupe and the local people received it favourably. Her earlier dismissal was redressed some years later and she was transferred back to Beijing. Later, after her retirement from service, she was joined by her husband, who had been engaged in construction in Lanzhou. They settled on Xinjiang Road and opened their restaurant.

At present, in addition to the owner, his wife and their three daughters, there are two ethnic Dongxiang waitresses, three ethnic Hui waitresses from Linxia, a Hui waitress from Shandong, and a Han waiter working in the restaurant. During the interviews, they all received us very warmly and answered any questions asked.

The restaurant owner's wife was asked: 'Why didn't you open a Dongxiang restaurant?' She answered: 'Because most of the restaurants in the Xinjiang Road are Uygur restaurants and the customers come here to taste Xinjiang dishes, without them you can't attract customers.'

We had several meals at the Friendship Restaurant, and we found its menu was a little different from that of a Xinjiang restaurant. Of the 103 items on the menu, there were 38 meat dishes, of which 13 were Dongxiang dishes or Northwest Hui dishes, such as *suanla-liji* (tenderloin cooked with vinegar-pepper), *baishui-shouzhua* (mutton stewed in water and eaten with the fingers), and *yang-zasui* (chopped cooked entrails of sheep). The other 25 meat dishes were of Uygur origin, such as roast meat with *ziran*. Of the 24 vegetarian dishes, 7 dishes were of Dongxiang or Hui flavour; the others were Uygur dishes. Of the 5 snacks with a distinctive national flavour, 4 were Dongxiang dishes, only *zhuafan* was Uygur. Of 8 kinds of soups only the 'soup with tomato and minced meat' was of Xinjiang flavour; and none of the 19 cold dishes were Xinjiang dishes.

There were altogether 14 kinds of staple food in the restaurant, 4 of which were of Dongxiang flavour, including *yuantang-yangrou-mian* (noodles boiled in thick mutton soup) and *huajuan* (steamed twisted rolls). The Dongxiang owner ordered all the fried breads to be seasoned with tomato juice and *ziran* was sprayed on all roast meat dishes to give them a strong 'Xinjiang flavour'.

Again, she told us on one occasion:

> At the beginning of the 1990s, this road was called Xinjiang Road just because many Uygurs had come from Xinjiang and opened many Uygur restaurants. Many customers came here just for a taste of Xinjiang Uygur dishes. If we had named our shop a 'Dongxiang Restaurant', you may be sure that very few people would have come to us.

When asking her: 'But now the road has been renamed 'Ethnic Food Street'; will you change the Uygur dishes on your menu to those with a Dongxiang dishes?'

She answered that:

> We've already been serving Dongxiang dishes for a long time. I also intend to let all the Dongxiang girls wear our ethnic headdress and all our male helpers will wear our traditional black sleeveless waistcoat. We'll serve genuine 'Dongxiang banquets' and rename our restaurant as a Dongxiang Restaurant!

The life experience of the restaurant owner's wife can help to form an impression of her motives. Her religion and her ethnicity motivate her ideals and her resolution. She wants to abide by her Islamic faith, showing respect for others, and deserving respect in return. Based on these beliefs, her actions were consistent over the past twenty years. When faced with a conflict between her religious beliefs and political expediency, she acted according to her beliefs. Her work to promote the Dongxiang Theatre Troupe was not really contradicted by her Xinjiang restaurant, because she used the restaurant to promote Dongxiang cuisine. In order to be a commercial success, she compromised by calling the restaurant Xinjiang, while maintaining aspiration to further promote Dongxiang culture.

Shangri-La/Shambhala: the first Tibetan restaurant

Shangri-La Hotels are a 'name-brand hotel' that have been built in many big cities around the world. The term Shangri-La was derived from James Hilton's 1933 work, *Lost Horizon* from Shambhala, the Buddhist name for a mythical kingdom, the geographical location of which is uncertain, but which according to legend lies northeast of India. It is considered the place of origin of the Kalachakra teachings and, with all its associations as a 'source of suspicious', plays a central role in Tibetan Buddhism. A key part of the myth is that the saviour of humanity will come out of Shambhala at a time when the world is dominated by war and destruction. In 1997 people tried to expound and prove that the so-called Shangri-La or Shambhala was located in the Deqen Tibetan Autonomous Prefecture in Yunnan province. The place gained widespread fame with a great number of tourists from both home and abroad going there to sightsee in the following years. Nevertheless, the Tibetans say the holy place is in Tibet.

'Shambhala' is the first Tibetan restaurant in the Xinjiang Road. In the whole of Beijing there are only a few Tibetan restaurants. Now a Tibetan restaurant has moved to the Xinjiang Road. Initially, the restaurant owner named her shop Shangri-La, but later renamed it Shambhala. Obviously this was a reflection of cultural identity. The shop-owner Miss Nyima is not from Tibet; she is a Tibetan from Qinghai. In addition, many other ethnic restaurants (serving Mongolian, Korean, Dai, Hui, Sichuan and the Mao family dishes, etc.) have been set up at the eastern and western ends of the Xinjiang Road; the Xinjiang restaurants located in the middle section of the road have surely felt pressure from such competition.

The author has been to the 'Shambhala' restaurant many times. A yak skull hangs on the right-hand wall within the gate, and a yellow *katag* (ceremonial scarf) hangs on it. At the centre of its forehead is the first word 'Om' of the Mantra of Chenrezi (Avalokiteshvara), which means the Buddha. The dining hall is divided into two parts: an outer hall and a small inner hall. On the wall at the northern side of the outer hall are painted six out of eight religious instruments. There are also two paintings on the southern wall: one is an elephant carrying a religious bell, and the other is a horse carrying a magic bell. Both pictures have auspicious significance. On the wall behind the counter at the eastern side is a shrine, in which a statue of Shakyamuni is in a meditation position. Behind the statue is a painting of an eye; a precious stone is inlaid as its eyeball. This is also an auspicious decoration prevalent among Tibetans. There is also a *tangka* (religious scroll painting) of Pelden Lhamo, the 'Glorious Goddess', who is an object of worship. The goddess is the protector of the hostess's family, and the *tangka* has been handed down from generation to generation. Besides the Tibetan decorations in the outer hall there is a golden model of a junk on which the Chinese propitious phrase *yi-fan-feng-shun* meaning 'Wish you a smooth sailing' is written. It is a gift from a friend on the opening day of the restaurant. The symbols of good wishes of the Han Chinese and the Tibetans stand side by side in one room.

Every time I go there I like to have my meal in the inner hall. On either side of the entrance is a sutra-banner; banners of this kind were used as decorations on the posts in the halls of monasteries. Within the inner hall there is another niche for a statue of Buddha, a white *katag* is hung on it, and three butter-lamps burn in front of the niche. It is worthy of notice that in addition to the statue of Buddha kept in the niche, incense was also burning in front of a photo of the Living Buddha from the shopkeeper's hometown. In addition to the auspicious symbols of Tibetan Buddhism decorating the wall, the shopkeeper's family strictly follow religious ceremonies on the first and fifteenth day of every Tibetan lunar month. The ceremonies begin at dawn of the day when the family kowtow and chant sutras before the statue of Buddha. They make no offerings on ordinary days, but on festival days and on New Year's Day they hold a ceremony called *bsang* (incense-burning ritual) at midnight.

Bsang means burning offerings to gods. In areas where Tibetan Buddhism prevails, on the morning of every first and fifteenth day of the month and on other important occasions, people go up to the hills to burn cypress leaves, throw *tsamba* (roasted barley flour) and highland barley into the fire to worship the gods. In places where there are no hills, the ceremony is held on the flat roof of the Tibetan-style house. First, people light three butter-lamps in front of the niche, then they go up to the roof, where a special place is reserved for this special ceremony. (The shopkeeper also holds the *bsang* ceremony on the roof of Shambhala Restaurant.) For the *bsang* ceremony only the men of the house can go up to the roof, while women must stay downstairs kowtowing to the statue of the Buddha. (By the way, all the Tibetan girls from Qinghai can recite Buddhist scriptures fluently.)

On New Year's Day, fruits, cooked wheaten food and meat are placed before the niche. All the offerings must be fresh. Wine is not included in the offerings. When a person drinks, he first dips his finger in a cup of wine and then flicks the wine-drops off his finger into the sky to show his respect to the gods. In the hometown of the owner of the Shambhala Restaurant, all the offerings would be thrown onto the hillside. However, in the restaurant, the offerings are thrown into the sky on the rooftop. Only the staff of the restaurant participate in this ceremony.

In Beijing, the political centre of China, a restaurant with such a strong religious atmosphere (though in Tibetans' eyes, the above-mentioned ceremony is already greatly simplified) is rarely seen, and it can only exist on the Xinjiang Road. Since commercial interest is their main consideration, the religious rituals are only observed by the owner and the employees of the shop, for their religious faith. Beside the statues of Buddhas, they also put up the picture of the local Living Buddha of their hometown. Neither the Dalai Lama nor Panchen Lama's picture can be seen. Usually the waitresses receive customers in their beautiful Tibetan gowns, behaving with composure and showing a tender and friendly attitude. There is no expression of commercial cunning to be found on their faces. I intended to ask for some *lungta* (prayer flags) hanging on the niche, so I asked my hostess:

'May I take a few of them?'
'Of course. Please.'
'Thank you.'
'Mind you don't step on them. They will bring you good fortune.'
'I won't forget.'

Every time we went there we had our meals before the niche in the inner hall, we quietly enjoyed the auspicious and serene atmosphere of Tibetan Buddhism emanating from this very small space within the secular world. As a matter of fact, one of the pleasures of the newly opened Shambhala is that this Tibetan family has created a distinctively Tibetan atmosphere. While there are many religious objects in the hall such as a prominently placed statue of the family protector god, there are also some women's headdresses used as decorations. These things would never be found in a monastery. However, the Shambhala provides customers with a cultural atmosphere where 'family' is part of ethnic identity in a humane environment. The Shambhala is probably the only restaurant where Tibetans who come from Tibetan areas could find a strong family and folksy atmosphere, which might alleviate their homesickness.

What are Tibetan dishes? Is the diet of ordinary Tibetan herdsmen the same as that in a Tibetan restaurant? First of all, Miss Nyima served us with butter tea. Traditionally butter tea is prepared with a little freshly-brewed brick tea with the tea leaves removed, a lump of butter and a pinch of salt. They are put into the wooden 'tea churn' with some boiling water and then churned for a minute or so until the tea is well mixed. The resulting liquid is poured into a kettle, heated and then served. However, Shambhala prepares butter tea with an electric mixer. In order to suit the Beijingers' taste, Shambhala's tea is not as strong as it is in Tibetan-inhabited areas.

Next we were served sugar-coated ginseng-fruit (a kind of rare local vegetable root). In the past, it was a snack served to aristocrats who could afford to eat it. According to Tibetan custom, butter tea and ginseng-fruit cooked with rice are served only to distinguished guests.

Then Miss Nyima served up a small plate, on which was a square of food. It was made with a brown colour mixed with white colour, with a raised swastika design on the upper side of it. This food with a Buddhist pattern turned out to be a piece of *tsamba*, made of roasted barley flour, butter and *chula* (dry cheese). Traditionally, *tsamba* is made from sun-dried barley, which has been roasted and ground into flour. It is eaten by adding a little of the flour to some butter in a bowl, kneading the mixture into a dough with the fingers, and then breaking off a tiny portion, rolling it into a ball and eating it. However, at the Shambhala restaurant, the cake-like *tsamba* is served on a plate with a small knife, indicating that we should cut it into small pieces before eating it. So we shared the *tsamba* by cutting it into several pieces. The hostess said that they themselves usually eat *tsamba* with the fingers without adding cheese. Customers who have tasted Shambhala's *tsamba* probably think it is the typical food of the Tibetans.

The first main course was *shou-zhua-rou* (meat eaten with the hands). Traditionally, Tibetan herdsmen in pastures boil big pieces of mutton in a cauldron, with little or no salt. When the mutton is done, they cut it with a knife and eat it with the fingers. The mutton served at the Shambhala was bought in Inner Mongolia or Qinghai. In order to suit the Beijing customers' taste, the restaurant cooks the mutton with salt and spices, especially a kind of spice called *huajiao* (Chinese pepper), which is a favourite spice of Beijingers. The meat is served on a big plate with two knives. Customers cut the meat and eat it with chopsticks instead of the hands.

'Mutton soup with pancake' is a speciality of the Salar people in Qinghai and 'stewed mutton' is a speciality of the Hui people in the Northwest. The Shambhala has made some changes to these dishes and made them Shambhala's own specialities. A common feature of these two dishes is that they are taken from other ethnic groups and have become two important items of the Tibetan cuisine served at the Shambhala. What surprised us most was the fish and chicken on the Shambhala's menu. The hostess's brother Tsering explained to us that: 'Many Tibetans do not eat fish because they practise water burial, and they avoid fish as it might have eaten a corpse'. Another reason for the aversion is the Buddhist doctrine about setting free captive animals. Still another reason appeared in *China's Tibet* magazine (Namgyal 1996:21), which said that fish is the incarnation of Lu (dragon); therefore eating fish is not only a violation of the religious doctrine of 'no killing', but also an offence to the water god. Tsering also told us that because the chicken's claws are divided and the toes branch out in different directions, Tibetan Buddhists believe chickens are evil animals and do not like to eat them. He also told us several stories about the aristocrats eating fish. It seems that the restaurant owner has no taboos about chickens and fish. In fact, we found at least a dozen dishes with chicken and fish on the Shambhala's menu, which indicates therefore, that taboos are not always unchangeable. Change is limited by cultural principle (religious or cognitive). Adhering to or modifying food taboos on the Xinjiang Road provides us with an opportunity to observe the co-ordination of commerce and culture.

Of the 117 cold and hot dishes on the Shambhala's menu, 110 of them are non-Tibetan style dishes, while there are only 7 genuine Tibetan dishes. They are butter tea, milk tea, *tsamba*, *shou-zhua-rou* (meat eaten with the hands), yogurt (made of Beijing milk, not of yak milk or dzo milk), sugar-coated ginseng-fruit, and highland barley gruel. Some of the Tibetan local specialities such as yellow mushrooms and Chinese caterpillar fungus are now also used as ingredients in the dishes. As a matter of fact, Tibetans do not use these items in their daily diet. However, their use expanded and enriched the Shambhala's menu.

'The Mao Family's Dishes': Political symbolism in business

Some years ago, not far from the Xinjiang Road, there was a Han Chinese restaurant called Tong-xin-ju (lit. Childlike Innocence Eating-House). It was a common restaurant selling ordinary dishes. Because many restaurants of this kind emerged and their menus were all the same, business was slow. So on July 1 1997, Tong-xin-ju moved to the western end of Xinjiang Road. It reopened with the new name of 'Mao (Zedong) Family's Dishes'. Thus it entered the multicultural community of Xinjiang Road.

The 'Mao family's dishes' serve Hunan cuisine. Why does the owner want to serve dishes Mao liked? She knows the Beijing restaurant business very well. In the past, Hunan restaurants were lagging, but after the first restaurant that served 'Mao family's dishes' opened at Qianmen in downtown Beijing, its business grew and flourished. This led to the birth of a series of Hunan restaurants serving Mao family dishes, with many Hunan restaurants changing their name. The name of the restaurant Tong-xin is a Chinese homonym of Miss Tong Xin, its 29-year-old owner. She is a Beijinger who has never been to Hunan. None of the seven waitresses she hired are from Hunan; but her six cooks are all from Hunan, each having worked for several years for other Hunan restaurants in Beijing.

The Mao Family's Dishes Restaurant became more popular and larger than the original Tong-xin-ju. The area of the dining hall is about 70 square meters. The window screens are made of reed matting, a model of a stream flowing under a bridge, bamboo baskets, and tables and chairs like the ones usually used by farmers, add a strong native Hunan flavour to the room. On the walls of the dining hall there are 13 photos of Mao taken in various periods, one of which shows of Mao and Chiang Kai Shek proposing a toast to each other taken during the Chongqing negotiation in 1945. In another photo Mao is smoking among a group of farmers in Shaoshan in his birthplace in Hunan province. In a corner of the hall Mao's works and the well-known 'little red book' together with a porcelain bust of Mao are on a bamboo bookshelf. Also there is the design of a red heart made from grouping a number of Mao badges together (a symbolic pattern of loyalty to Mao from the Cultural Revolution).

The main courses of Hunan Xiangtan Prefecture are smoked cured meat and steamed foods such as cured rabbit meat with red-hot pepper oil and steamed fish. But the most popular among customers is 'Mao's pork braised in brown sauce'. In addition, the 'Shaoshan Mao family's hodgepodge', 'Mao family's twice-cooked pork', and 'Mao family's bean curd', etc. are among the popular dishes prepared in this restaurant.

The ingredients of these hot dishes are meat balls, vegetables, fermented soya beans, hot pepper, squid and others. All the dishes are very hot, as it is widely known that Mao Zedong was fond of hot pepper.

There are two reasons for the restaurant owner to serve the so-called Mao family's dishes: one is to stress the relationship between the dishes and Mao; and the other is to maintain Hunan local flavour and a familiar atmosphere. For example, the owner put the words 'Mao Family's', 'Mao's', or 'Shaoshan' in front of the original names of Hunan dishes. This was very successful business strategy. It was impossible to imagine in the past that political symbolism could be adopted by business twenty years after the opening up and reform.

With for those who experienced first the heroism and idealism and then the hardships, suffering and confusion of post liberation China, restaurants like 'Mao Family's Dishes' provide ageing former Red Guards and their contemporaries with a place to remember times past with nostalgia. With Mao finally down from the altar of a god, contemporary Chinese who remember several by social incidents, a general mood of remembering times past quietly rose up in the 1990s. This is also the case for the even older generation who remembered joining in dancing parties in the Moscow Restaurant in the USSR Exhibition Hall (present-day Beijing Exhibition Hall) and the people who did the *yangke* dance in the city streets in the 1950s (now they are all over 60 years of age) – all have a kind of nostalgia for their times. Different age groups have different symbolic marks of their own lifetimes.

However, the life experiences of all age groups were, without exception, affected by Mao's domestic social campaigns and foreign policies. Restaurants run by those educated urban youth who worked in the countryside and mountain areas during the Cultural Revolution serve dishes that increase nostalgia for those times as they recall past suffering and renew their old friendships. The gloomy shadow of the Cultural Revolution always follows them. However, restaurants like the 'Mao Family's Dishes' are certainly more than the place for tasting nostalgia, because people also go there mostly out of curiosity about Mao, a human being represented as a god; or they try to experience the lifestyle of a great politician in former times. The 'Little Red Book' and Mao's photos are the most important symbols and 'stage property' in 'Mao Family's Dishes' restaurants. 'Mao's pork braised in brown sauce' is without doubt both a main course and the symbol of the altar.

The commercial adoption of Mao's political symbolism is the part that tends to be overlooked by the research of pure social cultural structure. It involves not only the discussion of symbolism, but also the motivating power of a commercial operation – to what degree this motivating power can modify and reinvent the traditional culture. This is just one of the starting points for the modern market economy to promote socio-cultural changes and for anthropology to make an adaptive renewal of itself. Now the 'Mao Family's Dishes' restaurants with their conspicuous political symbols carry out commercial activities.

Conclusion

The Xinjiang Road is really a multicultural place. It includes political, commercial, ethnic and religious topics, while food is the main line that connects all the topics. This chapter has provided a preliminary discussion on the historical relationship of the re-construction of the Xinjiang Road at Weigongcun in Beijing. It shows: (1) how the 'significant history' of the group of Uygur restaurant operators as social actors might have a great impact on themselves in modern times; and (2) how the present-day Uygurs' Xinjiang Road, which was called Uygur Village in the Yuan dynasty, rapidly changed into a multi-ethnic community and the process of its re-development. It demonstrated that some space occupied by people of different ethnic groups, their foodways and dietary patterns, and their tactics and performance are all the component parts of their identity. Therefore, the essence of the emergence of Xinjiang Road shows the social meanings that are attached to specific locations. We might not able to point out exactly the reason why Uygurs chose to come 'back' to Weigongcun as there is no evidence to show a constant community. However, the pulling force of its Uygur ethnic setting does show how other reinvented cuisines found their way to success on the Xinjiang Road in the 1990s.

The first group who moved into the Xinjiang Road were the Uygur restaurateurs. Over the past twenty years their cuisine has attracted many local residents, college teachers and students, and many other people who love Uygur cuisine. Some extracts from teacher and students investigation reports quoted above show that the Uygur 'significant history' and their cohesion have made them successful in business. As we can see, the bright and capable owner of the Dongxiang restaurant is a very good case in which the owner successfully used cultural resources to run her business. The Shambhala Restaurant also successfully played to the Beijingers' imagination of the Tibetan herdsmen's life and Tibetan cuisine. The customers came into a dining hall with Tibetan Buddhist decorations and with an atmosphere reminiscent of a Tibetan herdsman's home. Therefore she won a lot of repeat customers. Coincidentally, the owners of the Dongxiang and Shambhala restaurants both received a higher education in colleges for minority ethnic groups. Probably their anthropological knowledge helped them to do socio-cultural analysis and helped them attain success in business. The 'Mao Family Dishes' added a new element – political symbolism – to the reconstruction of the Xinjiang Road. However, the symbolism here is not for playing up political ideology, but is adopted as a modern marketing tactic. The development of the cuisine business in the Xinjiang Road and the process of the creation of the menus may reflect the history and the essence of the coexistence, co-ordination, adaptation, and conflicts of different social groups and cultures.

Acknowledgement

I must thank all the students who have helped to conduct the interviews with restaurant owners working at the Xinjiang Road. Without their help, this chapter could not have been completed.

References

北京大學歷史系。年。《北京通史》。北京出版社。History Department of Peking University (1990) *History of Beijing*. Beijing Press.

馮家升，程朔洛，穆廣文。年。《維吾爾族史料簡編》上冊，民族出版社。Feng Jiashen, Cheng Shuoluo, Mu Guanwen (1981) *History of Uygurs* (Part 1) Minzu Press.

朗杰。年。<從飲食結構的變化看今日西藏人>《中國西藏》第四期，第 頁。 Namgyal (1996) 'Understanding Tibetans from their changing dietary structure' 21 Tibet in China, 4:21.

王岡。年。《北京通史》，第五卷，第 頁。中國書店。Wang Gang (1996) 108 History of Beijing 5:108. Zhongguo shudian.

王惲。<秋澗先生大全文集>，卷八八。《烏臺筆補》。(Wang Yun) (n.d.) Essays of Mr. Qiu Jian Vol. 88. Wutai Bibu.

余舜德 。年。<空間、論述與樂趣 ： 夜市在台灣社會的定位> ， 載 黃應貴 《空間、力與社會》。中央研究院民族研究所。Yu Shunde (1995) 'Space, Discourse and Pleasure: The Constellation of Night Markets in Taiwanese Society', Space, Power and Society, Huang Ying-kuei ed., 391–462: Taiwan: The Instutute of Ethnology, Academia Sinica.

Gilbert, A. (1988) 'The New Regional Geography in English and French-Speaking Countries', *Progress in Human Geography*, 12(2):208–228.

Johnston, J. Ronald (1991) *A Question of Place: Exploring the Practice of Human Geography*. Oxford, Cambridge: Blackwell.

Najam, Suzanne (1990) 'Aye Tae the Fore: The Fife Miners in the 1984–85 Strike', in Stephen Kendrick, Pat Straw and David McCrone (eds) *Interpreting the Past, Understanding the Present*. London: MacMillan.

Zunz, Oliver (ed.) (1985) *Reliving the Past: The Worlds of Social History*. Chapel Hill: University of North Carolina Press.

■ CHAPTER FIVE ■

Cantonese Cuisine (*Yue-cai*) in Taiwan and Taiwanese Cuisine (*Tai-cai*) in Hong Kong

David Y. H. Wu

Changing tastes, diets, eating habits, cooking methods, and public eating places are closely associated with socio-economic development. They are also part of the globalization of the international culture of consumerism that affects food and cuisine. This is especially true in East Asia. While economists and political scientists have paid close attention to industrialization and economic transformation in the region, little has been done to document their consequences on food habits. Nor have there been adequate investigations into the impact the changes in food culture as a consequence of changing social, ethnic and national identities. Inspired by earlier theoretical work on food, cuisine, and history and consumption (Douglas and Sherwood 1996: Hobsbawn and Ranger 1986; Messer 1984; Mintz 1993), this chapter hopes to offer insightful interpretations on the chain reaction going on in the geo-political-economic spheres and made manifest in the local cuisines of China, Taiwan, and Hong Kong, by presenting a social history of the emergence of Cantonese cuisine (*yue-cai* 粵菜) in Taiwan and Taiwanese cuisine (*tai-cai* 台菜) in Hong Kong.

Earlier anthropological work on Chinese food attempted to explain issues relating to the origin of food items and consumption patterns, classifications of food, structural symbols, and taboos related to food, body, and health (Chang 1977; Wu 1979; Anderson 1980, 1988; Cooper 1986). Certain new approaches in anthropology have recently focused on the social history of certain food items such as fast food (Wu 1997), regional food and banquets (Goody 1982), or national food or cuisine (Appadurai 1986, 1988; Ohnuki-Tierney 1993). These studies on food reveal the meaning of local tradition, the process of culture change, and the formation of ethnic and national identities. These popular approaches were followed as fieldwork was conducted for the present investigation.

This chapter proposes a comparative study of the emergence of Cantonese and Taiwanese cuisines in Taiwan. It will show the socio-political meanings of this emergence, which parallel changes in ethnic and national identities. Both Cantonese cuisine (in Chinese, *yue-cai* or Guangdong *cai* 廣東菜) and Taiwanese cuisine (*tai-cai*) are served in restaurants in Taiwan today and are popular and considered prestigious. Also, new 'ethnic' restaurants have emerged in Hong Kong under the name of Taiwanese cuisine. These are recent phenomena. Prior to the 1980s, Taiwan had few restaurants serving these two types of cuisine. Even the generic terms 'Taiwanese cuisine' and 'Taiwanese restaurant' were not commonly known. In this chapter, I shall discuss the background and reasons behind these developments by examining the two types of popular cuisine, and how they relate to the social and political development in Taiwan and to global economic interactions and consumerism in East Asia.

The Social History of the Cantonese Cuisine in Taiwan

To study the social history of Cantonese cuisine, many chefs in leading Cantonese restaurants and a few popular media food columnists were interviewed in Taiwan from 1994 to early 1995. They all agreed that Cantonese cuisine only appeared in Taiwan after 1950, following the Nationalist government defeat on mainland China in 1949 by the Communists, and following their retreat to Taiwan together with a flood of refugees. Many ranking military officials, heads of government branches or local administrations, and wealthy merchants brought their family cooks to Taiwan from many parts of China. The cooks later opened their own restaurants. During the 1950s restaurants serving food from Hunan (湖南), Jiangsu (江蘇), and Zhejiang (浙江) (including the Shanghainese) were the most popular and numerous, as there were more high ranking Hunanese generals and Jian-Zhe (short for Jiangsu and Zhejiang) officials and merchants under the leadership of Chiang Kai-shek (or Jiang Zhongzheng 蔣中正, a native of Zhejiang and with a Shanghai power base).

During the two decades from 1950 to 1970, some Cantonese restaurants were opened by cooks who fled from the mainland. Because these cooks were native to Guangdong Province, their restaurants only served traditional style Cantonese food. In the 1960s, Taipei had only a few known Cantonese restaurants, and they were small and considered old fashioned or backward. However, when international standard hotels opened, including the Grand Hotel (owned by Madame Chiang Kai-shek) and the First Hotel, they were equipped with a Cantonese restaurant. At that time, the Grand Hotel was the place where heads of state stayed and where many important overseas Chinese guests, who were predominantly Cantonese, of the government were also received. These few Cantonese restaurants in the hotels served a 'foreign' clientele, not local customers. They served 'cold style' Cantonese dishes.

People who were interviewed remarked that not only was Cantonese cuisine not popular, it held a low status compared to other regional cuisines such as Jiang-Zhe and, at a later date, Hunan and Sichuan. Each of these other cuisines in turn dominated the style of food served in restaurants for quite a number of years. Again, some (young) informants, most of them in their thirties and forties, insisted that there was no Cantonese cuisine in Taiwan prior to the retreat of the Nationalist government in late 1949. Such statements reflect historical facts to a certain extent, but must be subject to further scrutiny. Because the domination by the Jiang-Zhe people in the 'central' government, government officials brought with them the style of cooking from Jiang-Zhe making it the high cuisine for Taiwan's power centre. It was natural that Jiang-Zhe cuisine was considered to be 'refined' or high-class in the food and banquet culture of those years. Even though Cantonese cuisine traditionally enjoyed a good reputation among all Chinese regional cuisines. During the 1950s, it did not represent or symbolize the centre or '*zhongyang*' of national political power. It basically could not please the palates of powerful people in high places and thus could not occupy such a position in the food culture hierarchy of Taiwan's élite society.

However, in their reports to me these informants did not recognize their lack of knowledge of the high Chinese cuisine that existed in Taiwan prior to the 1940s, nor did they mention the popularity of Japanese cuisine in Taiwan during the 1940s and 1950s. It was because food writers and other food experts prior to the late 1990s were China or centre oriented, they could not imagine a local style of Taiwanese or Japanese cuisine. For them it was inconceivable to consider the existence of peripheral local cuisine of any significance prior to the domination of the central government from China. If there was a Taiwanese cuisine, it was not considered to have the same rank as the latter day mainland cuisines in terms of status and popularity.

What I have discovered during fieldwork is that, contrary to either common perceptions or classifications by food experts or writers in Taiwan, during the Japanese occupation (1895 to 1945), Cantonese cuisine was served in a few leading restaurants in the capital city of Taipei. It came as a surprise to me to see that the Japanese menu of Peng-Lai-Ge (蓬萊閣) restaurant in Taipei, printed in Showa fifth year (1930), included an extensive menu of Cantonese (Guangdong cai 廣東菜) as part of three major Chinese cuisines served in the restaurant – Cantonese, Fujian (福建), and Sichuan (四川). It is even more amazing to compare that menu with one of any leading Cantonese restaurants in Hong Kong or Taipei today, as Peng-Lai-Ge served more varieties of expensive high status dishes that used as main ingredients shark fins, fish lips, abalone and bird nests. In other word, the high class cuisine during the Japanese period in Taiwan was on a par with that of mainland China before the Second World War. Of course,

Peng-Lai-Ge was one of the high class and most expensive restaurants in Taipei at that time. Today, however, in reconstructing the history of food and cuisine, food writers are so accustomed to ranking local, Taiwanese food traditions as low status in the culinary hierarchy, that they found it not worthy of mention. The period under the Japanese simply is left blank.

According to a food critic and managers of several Cantonese restaurants in Taipei and Gaoxiong in southern Taiwan, the rise in the status of new Cantonese cuisine began after 1970. During the 1970s, a new wave of Hong Kong popular *yum cha* (飲茶) restaurants arrived in Taipei and made Cantonese food fashionable. Yum cha means to drink tea in the Cantonese language (see also Chapter 8 for more detail). In old time Canton or Guangzhou Province, people of the leisure class went to restaurants for breakfast or a light lunch. Since these people had the time to spend long hours at the restaurants, they continued to drink tea while eating only small quantities of a snack called *dim sum* (點心). I myself remember that in the early 1960s the Central Hotel (later the Futuna) in Taipei had already begun serving *yum cha* breakfast on Sundays and well-to-do families with children watched cartoon films (this was before the TV era). Among the tourist hotels the Ambassador was the first to serve 'Cantonese style morning tea'. These few hotel restaurants, as mentioned earlier, were not known or accessible to ordinary citizens.

The introduction in the 1960s of *yum cha* as a new type of dining out experience is indicative of the transformation of the economic and political environment of Taiwan. When the so-called traditional Cantonese *yum cha* was introduced from Hong Kong to Taiwan, its status was elevated as a new style of food reserved for the élite and the wealthy. Originally in Taiwan it did not attain great popularity among people from all walks of life. It was only after the 1970s, when economic transformation in Taiwan brought prosperity to the entire society that *yum cha* became popular for even ordinary people. Shoppers dined at the emerging big department stores such as Ren-Ren and Jin-Ri where an entire floor was devoted to *yum cha* restaurants. During the late 1970s, Taiwan was still a closed society due to a security conscious authoritarian government. Officially it was impossible to promote outside cultures. Unofficially popular culture, and 'good' culture in particular, were tolerated, making it much easier for such Hong Kong imports to succeed.

By the 1970s, the better known *yum cha* restaurants or 'tea houses' or *chalou* (茶樓) in Taipei were the Red Diamond, the Dragon and the Phoenix, and the Ten Thousand Happiness. As business for these tea houses was so good, they all opened more branches and became chain restaurants. In the 1980s there was further development among these tea houses, and signs for 'Hong Kong style *yum cha*' began to appear on the name boards outside of the tea houses. This is a further clear indication of Hong Kong's influence on Cantonese food in Taiwan. The signs also demonstrate that Hong Kong style (*Kangshi* 港式) became the symbol of Western or cosmopolitan (*yang* 洋) values, and *yang* replaced the 'provincial' (*tu* 土), the 'mainland' (*dalu* 大陸), and the 'old' or 'backward' (*lao* 老) Cantonese style (*Guangshi* 廣式).

To support my point of the newly found popularity of 'Hong Kong style' in consumerism since the late 1970s, I would like to mention an interesting and parallel development of Hong Kong style beauty parlours in Taipei. Since Hong Kong was considered the centre of high fashion, by the 1980s, all beauty parlours and hair styling shops also advertised 'Hong Kong style'. Male hairstylists from Hong Kong, instead of local, female hairdressers, enjoyed a high status in beauty parlours. Hong Kong hairstylists became so popular that a parlour not only had to hire Hong Kong stylists, but also the Cantonese language became the *lingua franca* among the stylists in the beauty parlours. Eventually many Hong Kong stylist 'imposters' worked in the parlours (just like today's so-called Hong Kong chef in some Cantonese restaurants). The imposters are actually Taiwanese who have visited Hong Kong or who have worked as assistants to a Hong Kong hairstylist. Once I had my hair cut in a parlour and overheard the stylists (they are not called barbers any more) speaking Cantonese with another worker in the shop. I thought he was a native Cantonese speaker from Hong Kong so I started to chat with him in Cantonese. To my surprise he could not carry on a conversation and admitted that he was Taiwanese who could only speak a few professionally related Cantonese words about hairstyle. I questioned him about why they spoke in Cantonese? His reply was that they 'were used to speaking Cantonese in the shop'.

It was reported that a single Hong Kong investor opened the first 'Hong Kong style Cantonese restaurant' named Fong Lum (meaning Maple Woods). This investor was instrumental in introducing the new Hong Kong style Cantonese cuisine into the refined or high class food culture market in Taipei in the early 1970s. This period also marked the beginning of the tourist industry. Food and cuisine for entertaining foreign guests related to international trade, all centred in the Zhongshan district of north Taipei where tourist hotels were concentrated.

In any event, Hong Kong style *yum cha* became a popular form of eating out after the economic boom in Taiwan during the 1970s, and it continues today. After three decades, this type of eating has been transformed from an 'introduced' and 'foreign' style of eating into 'local' style Chinese eating. An experienced executive chef, chef A, of a Cantonese restaurant had this opinion: 'Yum cha will never be out-dated in Taiwan because it has never served authentic style of yum cha in Hong Kong'. The snack dishes served in Taiwanese tea houses are somewhat different from those served in Hong Kong. Japanese style salads, sashimi, and Shanghai steamed dumplings and the like were added to menus as an adaptation to the tastes of Taiwanese customers. In reality, they are no longer Cantonese food. However, customers continue to cherish and restaurant managers continue to emphasize authenticity or tradition in superficial ways, while maintaining they are enjoying authentic Cantonese cuisine. The question of authenticity is always an interesting subject for anthropological inquiry. If we follow anthropological examples concerning the maintenance of cultural traditions or cultural diffusion, then we understand that the dynamics are beyond popular comprehension. It takes complicated theoretical interpretations to explain this phenomenon, but here I shall make a few generalizations only.

I argue that authentic material culture, such as traditional dishes, exists only in the mind of ideas or ideals; even in Hong Kong it is doubtful whether one can find consensus for defining what is authentic Hong Kong Cantonese cuisine or Hong Kong style *yum cha*. As soon as *yum cha* was introduced in Taiwan, it was definitely changed and deliberately altered.

For example, the Fong Lum Restaurant cited above for introducing new Cantonese cuisine to Taipei was reported by informed food critics to be the initiator of authentic Hong Kong style Cantonese cuisine. However, the restaurant was created by a refugee Hakka family who fled communist China in the early 1950s. Before investing in Taiwan, they opened a Hakka restaurant in Shatin, Hong Kong, to support their extended Hakka family and to keep it intact (I happen to have known members of this restaurateur family since the early 1970s and have visited all their branch stores in Hong Kong and in the United States) (Please also see Chapter 6 for a discussion of the emergence and spread of Hakka cuisine in Hong Kong from the 1950s to the 1970s.).

By the 1980s and 1990s, the dishes served in Taiwanese *yum cha* restaurants best symbolize characteristics of Taiwanese ethnicity as represented by fried dumplings (*guotiei* in Mandarin or *yakigyoza* in Japanese) and fried pancakes (*cong you bing* 蔥油餅) that originated in north China, the long rice and tofu soup (油豆腐細粉) that originated in Shanghai, and the salads and *sashimi* that originated in Japan. The content of Taiwanese ethnicity, if represented by food items and eating habits, shows a mixture of elements from different parts of China and Japan. The indigenized 'Hong Kong *yum cha*' in Taiwan becomes a mix of mainland snacks, Jian-Zhe snacks, and Japanese *liaoli* (料理) – a hybrid 'Taiwanese' cuisine. This mixed ethnicity reflects a phase in the development of a Taiwanese cultural identity in Taiwan.

The above-cited chef A also commented on Taiwanese breakfast in the 1990s. His comments help to further understand ethnicity from the point of view of its cultural representation in food habits. He explained:

Taiwanese (*Taiwanren* 台灣人) eat *mantou* (饅頭 steamed bun), soy bean milk, hamburger, and noodles for breakfast. Their eating habits have indirectly affected the hours of service at *yum cha* restaurants. Because these food items are not served in *yum cha* restaurant, *yum cha* restaurants in Taiwan do not open for breakfast, only for lunch.

Taiwanese *yum cha* restaurants open for business about eleven in the morning to serve lunch, but in Hong Kong, they open at seven in the morning. Should we accept this chef's comments as an indication of Taiwanese food habits, then breakfast as eaten by the Taiwanese would include items introduced from many parts of mainland China and from the West, but it does not include 'authentic' Hong Kong *yum cha* items. For instance, *mantou* (meaning steamed buns) eaten with *doujiang* (meaning soy bean milk) were introduced from north China after 1949, and they became the standard breakfast served in Taiwanese military camps (for soldiers at that time were predominantly northerners).

The indigenization of *yum cha* in Taiwan can also be judged by the manner in which the food is served. The original 'push car' style of service has been replaced by 'order to make' service. Some managers explained that this change was due to space limitations in Taiwan. Crowded and smaller *yum cha* restaurants were unable to accommodate food carts. Whatever the explanation, in Taiwan in the early 1990s *yum cha* became so popular that this type of restaurant spread from Taipei to Taichung (the largest city in central Taiwan), and to southern Taiwan. It has become an important part of Taiwanese popular food culture.

The 1997 return of Hong Kong to China and the Exodus of Hong Kong Chefs

By the end of 1980s, a new advertising phrase, '*gang-chu-liao-li* (港廚料理) or Hong Kong chefs in charge of cooking', was added to the sign-boards of many restaurants in Taiwan. After the British government begin to negotiate in the early 1980s with the People's Republic of China on the return of Hong Kong to China, a population exodus began in Hong Kong, with professionals emigrating to North America, Australia, and Taiwan. Two types of cooks associated with Cantonese cuisine arrived in Taiwan in large numbers during the middle of 1980s.

The first wave of Hong Kong cooks to arrive in Taiwan were *shaola* (meaning barbecue, mainly pork) chefs. They came to Taipei to open small eating places that specialized in barbecue meat and Hong Kong style noodles. In the mid 1980s when the *yum cha* business reached its peak and began to go downhill, the introduction of many Cantonese barbecue eateries brought new excitement and appreciation of Cantonese cuisine. The majority of the barbecue cooks came to Taiwan as single men. They soon took Taiwanese girls as wives and planned to settle down. They obtained residence status and Taiwan identity cards. Due to the low status of barbecue meat in the hierarchy of Cantonese dishes and because most of the barbecue meat was sold in wet markets and street-side food stalls in Hong Kong, this new type of Cantonese food quickly fitted into a new niche in Taiwan. The barbecue restaurant became the new style fast food shops catering to a luncheon clientele. A Taipei restaurant known to serve fast and inexpensive lunches, the Phoenix City, soon introduced Hong Kong style porridges, noodles and barbecue meat lunch plates into the popular Taiwanese lunch-box or *'biandang* (便當)' culture. The 'Hong Kong style lunch' served at the Phoenix City included *'shaola biandang* (燒臘便當)', 's*anbaofan* (三寶飯) or three treasures plate lunch', 'beef tendons on rice', and 'Guangzhou fried noodles.' *Sanbaofan* is actually a popular lunch dish in Hong Kong called *'sanping* (三拼)' serving three kinds of barbecue items on rice (for instance, choice of two kinds of roast pork, including *chasiu* (叉燒), and *shoyu* chicken). In short, Cantonese style barbecue meat on rice or noodles replaced earlier types of simple dishes in small luncheon restaurants in Taipei.

The second wave of Hong Kong cooks to arrive in the late 1980s were known as *'chiuqi* (九七) or '1997'. Hong Kong began to invest capital in local restaurant businesses to create expensive 'high class' Cantonese dining, using 'Hong Kong Style Sea Food' or *gangshi haixian* (港式海鮮) as the new catch phrase for their advertising. According to a Hong Kong television report in 1995, there were six to seven hundred Hong Kong cooks working in Taiwan. Taiwan was able to support these immigrants and the new restaurants because of its economic growth and its political transformation. First, between 1988 and 1992, there was a non-stop bull market on Taiwan's stock market, creating a *nouveau riche* class who sought a lifestyle of conspicuous consumption. Easy money earned in both the stock market and in real estate led to the consumption of expensive and what is considered high class food. These people were not content with the conventional banquet dishes of chicken and duck, but sought more exotic and expensive dishes.

Second, when martial law was lifted in 1987, the government allowed Taiwanese tourists exit visas (previously Taiwanese who wanted to travel abroad had to fake overseas business engagements). Soon after the Taiwan government permitted its citizens to openly, rather than secretly, visit mainland China to meet with their relatives. Because Hong Kong was almost the exclusive port of transit for Taiwanese tourists visiting China, this opening up created a boom in Hong Kong of Taiwanese shoppers and restaurant customers. According to one Cantonese chef at a leading hotel in Taipei: 'Taiwanese tourists in Hong Kong tasted high class Cantonese dishes such as birds nest soup, shark fins, and other expensive dishes for the first time. Upon their return to Taiwan, they then desired to have the same kinds of dishes.' Hong Kong style seafood and Hong Kong chefs were therefore introduced to restaurants in Taiwan.

Meanwhile, in 1989, the June fourth incident in Beijing brought uncertainty to Hong Kong's business community, causing uncertainty in Hong Kong's capital market. A significant flow of capital was reinvested in Taiwan including in Hong Kong style restaurants in Taiwan. Many expensive and luxuriously decorated restaurants were opened to win Taiwanese customers who wanted to entertain and show off in order to gain 'face'. Because of increased competition and pressure locally owned restaurants had to adapt by either hiring cooks from Hong Kong or sending their cooks to Hong Kong to learn new tricks about 'high class cooking'.

Counting the number of Cantonese restaurants operated in the major cities in Taiwan is yet another indication of the popularity of Cantonese cuisine. In Taipei alone in 1995 there were at least fifteen Cantonese restaurants run by tourist hotels. In addition, there were more than thirty expensive, large scale Cantonese restaurants. In the city of Gaoxiong, seven tourist class hotels had Cantonese restaurants; another four large restaurants were identified as Cantonese. A small sampling of the Hong Kong cooks in the major Cantonese restaurants also indicates how many cooks worked in a good restaurants. For example, the Cantonese restaurant at the Grant Hyatt Hotel (the most luxurious hotel in Taipei) had six Hong Kong cooks; the Sheraton Lai Lai had seven (predominantly bachelors); the Liba Hotel had four; and the newly opened Sherwood Hotel had eight.

Cantonese Dishes: Hong Kong Style versus Taiwanese Style

Are there differences in the cooking abilities of local, Taiwanese chefs and Hong Kong chefs? And, are the chefs treated differently because of the difference? Yes, according to many informants interviewed. The differences can be explained from the point of view of social hierarchy and ethnicity. In the first place, customers usually believe in the authenticity of the Cantonese cooking when it is prepared by a Hong Kong cook. A restaurant manager at a leading hotel says: 'Fellow Chinese are biased in their belief that only Hong Kong people know how to cook Cantonese food'. Therefore, Hong Kong cooks are awarded a higher status than Taiwanese cooks. Because of this opinion in the culinary profession, Hong Kong cooks receive higher pay than Taiwan-trained cooks of Cantonese cuisine.

As a matter of fact, cooks of the same generation generally have a similar level of skill; the only difference between them is in the decoration of a dish, for which Hong Kong cooks are presumed to be more creative. As mentioned above, the older generation Cantonese cooks of the 1950s and 1960s in Taiwan came from the mainland themselves. They have actually maintained the flavour of traditional Cantonese dishes from the mainland province of Guangdong. By the 1990s, they have long retired and have been replaced by local-born ethnic Taiwanese cooks. However, no matter how the local cooks attempt to improve themselves, including by visiting Hong Kong for training, they are still not regarded as an equal to the Hong Kong cooks in terms of their ability to match 'flavour' and in their use of 'ingredients'.

In one informant's opinion, Hong Kong cooks dare to use expensive ingredients that are considered high class. They are more conservative about preserving 'Hong Kong flavour'. However, this flavour may not suit the palates of Taiwanese customers, yet because of the Taiwanese (conspicuous) consumers' desire for the expensive dishes offered by Hong Kong cooks there is a market for them. In Hong Kong, customers desire cooking skill and good taste. They are not impressed by the price or the expense of ingredients. Banquet dishes in Hong Kong include chicken and duck as long as they are cooked with special care and taste good. Taiwanese customers, on the other hand, desire high price dishes, such as shark's fin, bird nests, abalone, and Jinhua ham from southern Zhejiang Province in China. As a result of these differences in customer attitude, Hong Kong style restaurants are only affordable for the select few wealthy people in Taiwan, thus, the high class.

The Emergence of Taiwanese Restaurants in Taipei and Hong Kong

The emergence of restaurants claiming to serve Taiwanese cuisine is a recent occurrence. Today, indigenous Taiwanese are descendants of early emigrants from Fujian Province across the Taiwan Strait, and different from the aborigines of Malayo-Polynesian stock. So, local Taiwanese cuisine originates from Fujian (Hokkien) cuisine. Taiwanese home cooking used to display Fujian flavours. However, after 50 years of acculturation under the Japanese colonial administration (from 1895 to 1945), post-war local restaurants in cities served predominantly Japanese food. Only on the occasion of a religious festival did the Taiwanese (not mainlander immigrants) hold street-side banquets to celebrate by cooking special dishes of Fujian cuisine and serving them in public. During the 1960s, the Taiwanese version of Fujian food could be found at expensive 'wine houses' (*Jiuja* 酒家), where wealthy businessmen entertained clients or government officials, and where the emphasis was on beautiful girls keeping the guests company not on food. Before the 1970s, prior to Taiwan's economic boom and Japanese-centred tourism in Taipei, no known restaurants claimed to specialize in so-called 'Taiwanese cuisine or *tai-ai.*' The image of Taiwanese food as lower class also contributed to its lack of recognition, because for ordinary people, Taiwanese food was only served in public eating places specializing in snacks such as food stalls in night bazaars or sidewalk restaurants.

The emergence of Taiwanese restaurants also coincided with a boom in a tourist-oriented sex industry located in north Taipei, centred in the Zhongshan (or Dr Sun Yat-sen) District. A restaurant named Qingye (青葉)

or Green Leaf became famous for Taiwanese style dishes, popular among tourist escorts or bar girls and their clients searching for midnight snacks after heavy drinking. Known for serving light porridge and little dishes (*qinzhou xiaocai* 清粥小菜) but charging excessive prices, Qingye was a place to find something to 'cleanse drinkers' intestines', not for a real meal. I visited the restaurant in the mid-1970s and found that most of the dishes reminded me of old style home cooking from rural Taiwan, such as 'pickled reddish omelet', 'bitter melon with braised pork', and 'fried peanuts with tiny dried fish'. Instead of serving the usual bowl of rice to accompany the dishes, they served a rice soup with sweet potatoes, which was a common peasant food eaten during the hard times of the Second World War and before the 1950s. Later, another chain restaurant, named *Meizi* (梅子), or the Plum, started to serve 'Taiwanese dishes', including bazaar snack dishes, but added fresh fish and other fresh seafood kept in containers, cooked to order. However, Taiwanese restaurants in the 1980s were a novelty. They were few in number, not particularly popular, and never of a high class, compared to Shanghainese, Sichuan, or Cantonese restaurants.

The status of Taiwanese cuisine did not change until the 1990s, when the rising consciousness of a Taiwanese identity was openly asserted in public. By the early 1990s, ethnic Taiwanese held in governmental positions at the highest echelon of power, assuming their positions from ageing mainland politicians and bureaucrats, including the assumption of the presidency of the Republic of China by Mr Lee Teng-hui. Demand for Taiwanese independence was openly expressed at legislative meetings and public forums.

A craving for 'Taiwanese flavour' suddenly became fashionable as the new élite sought new tastes that openly expressed their preference for ethnic Taiwanese cuisine. Several government cabinet members were reported to frequent a newly opened Taiwanese restaurant, which served peasant style banquet dishes but charged high prices. Then another luxurious Taiwanese restaurant was opened to cater to the new Taiwanese élite and the nouveau riche. When it was reported that President Lee frequented this Taiwanese restaurant, it generated enough publicity to make this place a hot spot for the rich and powerful ethnic Taiwanese in Taipei. Interestingly enough, the architecture of this four-storey restaurant was fashioned after a mainland Chinese palace; while the interior imitated a garden pavilion of the Jiangsu region. Once I attended a dinner banquet there and discovered that most dishes were newly created; none had the old, 'authentic' Taiwanese or Fujian flavour. Most dishes were inventions combining the influence of Japanese, western, and mainland Chinese cooking.

In the late 1980s, changes in the geopolitics of the triangle formed by mainland China, Hong Kong and Taiwan certainly influenced the food scene in Hong Kong. Although Hong Kong's ethnic (or non-Cantonese) restaurants represented many regional cuisines of China, before 1990 there were no restaurants in Hong Kong that served so-called Taiwanese food. They appeared in the early 1990s and were closely related to the sudden influx of Taiwanese tourists, rich and conspicuous, in transit to mainland China. In 1993, one fancy Taiwanese restaurant opened in the Mongkok district of Kowloon. The business was good. Upon entering, guests were greeted by hostesses dressed in a sort of aboriginal costume of the Ami tribe of Taiwan. By the entrance of the second-floor dining room, a Taiwanese style noodle stall was recreated, copying the standard symbols and décor used in Taipei's tourist hotel restaurants. During the research, it was discovered that this restaurant was under the ownership and management of a Hong Kong enterprise. All the workers and kitchen staff were Hong Kong residents. In addition to the Taiwanese noodles, their dishes imitated others served in Taiwanese restaurants in Taipei, with apparent Hong Kong adaptations, along with the usual Hong Kong seafood dishes. The clientele of this restaurant were local Hong Kong people, attracted by the novelty of Taiwanese dishes. Another new restaurant to serve Taiwanese cuisine in the tourist area of Tsimshatsui was also part of a corporate enterprise. The manager, a Vietnamese Chinese, had sojourned in Taipei. He admitted that the restaurant did not have a Taiwanese chef; but under his supervision many dishes were created to represent Taiwanese 'flavour.' They therefore claimed to be more authentic than other so-called Taiwanese restaurants. This one, situated in a large shopping plaza, catered to both local customers and Taiwanese tourists.

In addition to formal restaurants serving Taiwanese cuisine, dessert and sweets parlours (equivalent to the ice cream parlours and soda fountains of the 1950s in the US) have made Taiwanese food popular in Hong Kong since the mid-1990s. Young people, especially females, were especially attracted to these small eateries serving milk-shake type 'Taiwanese' drinks or desserts that were invented in Taiwan in the 1980s. Some of the sweets and drinks were adaptations of pre-1960 rural Taiwanese desserts sold by pushcart street venders or in ice cream parlours.

Conclusion

The above social history shows the inter-connected effects caused by economic development, identity politics, and tourism on tastes, types of restaurants, and regional cuisines in Taiwan and Hong Kong. While we have shown Hong Kong's impact on the emergence of Cantonese cuisine in Taiwan, the internal dynamics of Taiwan's political economy is certainly a contributing force. One may still ask: why Cantonese? Why not another type of Chinese regional cuisine?

It is not exactly an historical accident. Several facts were conducive to the emergence of Cantonese cuisine in Taiwan. First was the political situation, with international politics sustaining the Nationalists' claim of Taiwan as the political centre of all China, including Hong Kong, obliging Taiwan to take in Cantonese migrants, including cooks, who considered themselves political refugees. Then secondly, for many years Hong Kong led Taiwan to look to Hong Kong for inspiration for up-to-date Chinese popular culture, including films, music and high fashion. Thirdly, the acceptance of Hong Kong style Cantonese cuisine reflected the admiration of the emerging middle class in Taiwan for Hong Kong's modern, fashionable, international and cosmopolitan way of life.

By the end of the 1980s, the eventual opening up of Taiwan's political system to democratization also gave rise to the expression of a Taiwanese identity in the seemingly unrelated domains of food and cuisine. Taiwanese restaurants and Taiwanese cuisine were eventually elevated from their humble rural origins to the top of the urban gastronomic echelon. Taiwanese cuisine has enjoyed the same fate as Taiwanese politicians and ethnic identity politics: from denial to recognition; from street vendors to expensive restaurants; from the night bazaar and temple to the palace style banquet house; and from low class to high class. In the eyes of Hong Kong people, Taiwan's influence by the 1990s evaporated and Taiwan was deemed insignificant. However, the changing political relationship between Taiwan and mainland China transferred status to Taiwan on the commercial streets of Hong Kong – with the Taiwanese now becoming ideal tourists, visiting Hong Kong to shop and dine. This eventually caused Taiwanese restaurants to become fashionable novelties in Hong Kong, thus giving rise to Taiwanese cuisine in Hong Kong.

Acknowledgement

This research is part of and benefited from the 'Food Culture in Taiwan' project, sponsored by the Chiang Ching-Kuo Foundation for International Scholarly Exchange (1995–1997). I am grateful to the Foundation for its generous support in research.

References

Anderson, N. Eugene (1980) '"Heating" and "Cooling" Foods in Hong Kong and Taiwan', *Social Science Information*, 19 (2):237–268.
—— (1988) *The Food of China*. New Haven: Yale University Press.
Appadurai, Arjun (1986) *The Social Life of Things: Commodities in Cultural Perspective*. Cambridge: Cambridge University Press.
—— (1988) 'How to Make a National Cuisine: Cookbooks in Contemporary India', *Comparative Study of Society and History*, 30 (1):3–24.
Chang, Kwang-chi (ed.) (1977) *Food in Chinese Culture: Anthropological and Historical Perspectives*. New Haven: Yale University Press.
Cooper, Eugene (1986) 'Chinese Table Manners: You are How You Eat', *Human Organization*, 45 (2):179–184.

Douglas, M. and B. I. Sherwood (1996) *Consumption Classes In their The World of Goods: Toward an Anthropology of Consumption.* New York: Basic Books.

Goody, Jack (1982) *Cooking, Cuisine and Class: A Study in Comparative Sociology.* Cambridge: Cambridge University Press.

Hobsbawn, J. Eric and Terence Ranger (eds) (1986) *The Invention of Tradition.* Cambridge: Cambridge University Press.

Messer, Ellen (1984) 'Anthropological Perspectives on Diet', *Annual Review of Anthropology*, 13:205–249.

Mintz, W. Sidney (1993) 'Sweetness and Power: The Place of Sugar in History', in John Brewer and Roy Porter (eds) *Consumption and the World of Goods.* London: Routledge.

Ohnuki-Tierney, Emiko (1993) *Rice as Self: Japanese Identities through Time.* Princeton: Princeton University Press.

Wu, Y. H. David (1979) *Traditional Chinese Concepts of Food and Medicine.* Singapore: Institute of Southeast Asian Studies #55.

—— (1997) 'McDonald's in Taipei', in James L. Watson (ed.) *Golden Arches East: McDonald's in East Asia*, pp. 110–135. Stanford: Stanford University Press.

CHAPTER SIX

Food and Cuisine in a Changing Society

Hong Kong

Sidney C. H. Cheung

Chinese food is known to people around the world and Chinese restaurants can be found in almost every city on the globe. Nevertheless, we also see great variation in Chinese food from different regions of China, including some that are more 'traditional' and some that are newly 'invented'. What, though, is Chinese food? Some people might argue that Chinese-style food prepared by non-Chinese chefs is not really Chinese food. The definition of Chinese food is fraught with controversy. The ethnic background of the one who cooks the food might show the persistence of cultural tradition. At the same time, the contents and meanings of Chinese food extensively and thoroughly reflect people's social lifestyles and expectations. By looking at different kinds of Chinese food in different periods within one society, we would like to question whether there are any similarities or commonalities to the patterns of change that cross the regionally distinct varieties of Chinese food and variation in social development.

In this chapter, I seek to examine the different kinds of food and cuisine available in Hong Kong (where over 95 per cent of the total population is Chinese, and the majority come from South China, particularly the Pearl Delta River area), in order to understand how Chinese food survives and what it means in a metropolis with western influences during the last century. The main focus of my investigation is to explain the social historical changes in the adoption and adaptation of western foodways and variations in the Chinese diet in Hong Kong. In other words, this chapter will describe changes, variations and innovations in the globalization of Chinese food in Hong Kong, with particular attention paid to phenomena related to changing lifestyles and social tastes. I hope to broaden our knowledge of Chinese food and eating culture in different parts of the world, and to advance anthropological inquiries by addressing recent theoretical issues concerning ethnic identity and boundary formation, consumerism and global food distribution, and the invention of local cuisine in a society with rapid social and economic growth.

The Meanings of Chinese Food

When one thinks about what makes Hong Kong different from other cities in the world, probably the colours of neon lights in the streets, crowds in every single restaurant and people's passion for eating and drinking with friends and families come to mind. People's high expectations to fully enjoy food in Hong Kong may best be expressed in the old saying: 'A Heaven of Eating and Drinking'. However, the great variety of food in Hong Kong not only means decisions must be made to choose the kind of Chinese food, Asian food and western food to be consumed, but also complicates relations with people's lifestyles and values. How do we determine the meanings of food embedded in Hong Kong society, and how do they differ from those found in other Asian cities such as Tokyo, Taipei, Seoul and Beijing, where a great variety of choices is also available? Apart from considering eating as the basis for acquiring nutrients as well as satisfying the human instinct for survival, as in many societies, Hong Kong people strongly consider food as one of the markers of their social status.

Nowadays, in Hong Kong, there are many different kinds of food ranging from cheap to expensive, ordinary to rare, and local to global. Apart from some popular food such as Cantonese seafood, American fast food, Japanese *sushi* bars and Korean barbecue, there are also various snacks sold as street food, luxurious high-class restaurant food, traditional festive food and exotic foreign cuisine. Such a recounting of the common types of food available in Hong Kong is not sufficient to even sketch the relations between food and culture in Hong Kong. Rather, it is necessary to understand what kinds of food are consumed by what kinds of people, and why? Even though it is obvious that the logic behind food choice is different for different people, because one person's food can be another's poison, it is important to examine the meanings behind different foods as they shape different people's choices. For example, we can see that some food items are well accepted by the majority of people. Regarding the re-invention of tradition in contemporary Hong Kong society, Cheng (1997:70–71) argued that the emergence of the 'modern' herbal tea shop, with its strong emphasis on a sense of nostalgia, should be understood as part of the 'process of construction, maintenance and negotiation of Hong Kong identity'. And, in a study of the meaning of Chiu Chow cuisine in Hong Kong, Lee (1997) suggests that popularity was achieved because of the success stories about the hardworking Chiu Chow people were well accepted by the Hong Kong public and they accepted an 'upgraded' Chiu Chow cuisine serving as a metaphor for upward social mobility. Their acceptance stems from the fact that the majority of Hong Kong residents have been searching for a true Hong Kong identity because of their migrant backgrounds.

Anthropological research in earlier studies on food and cuisine centred largely upon questions of taboo, totems, sacrifice and communion, shedding light on the approach of cultural symbolism and, moreover, with an emphasis on how food reflects our understanding of humans and their relations with the world. Previous structural anthropological research on edibility rules emphasizes not only why food is a symbol through which the 'deep structure' of humanity can be investigated, but also how corresponding concepts of the body and spatial territories can be discerned (Levi-Strauss 1965; Douglas 1966). More recently, scholars have broadened the studies on food as: (1) an indicator of social relations, as in gifts of food, marriage banquets and other special feasts (Watson 1975, 1987); (2) a symbol of caste, class and social hierarchy (Goody 1982; Mintz 1985); and as (3) a metaphor through which the mechanism of self-construction with regard to ethnicity and identity can be discerned (Tobin 1992; Ohnuki-Tierney 1993). Most importantly, among various ethnographies regarding ethnicity and identity in Asian countries, food is viewed as playing a dynamic role in the way people think of themselves and others (Watson 1987; Janelli and Yim 1993; Tam 1997). As an example, Janelli and Yim (1993:186) point out that dog-eating in Korea reflects not only traditional eating habits but also political relations between South Korea and the USA during the 1980s

> Similar comments surrounded the positive evaluations of certain foods identified as Korean, such as *posint'ang*, a stew made with dog meat. The meat was a good source of nutrition and easy to digest, several men told me. On the way back from a restaurant where a few older managers had taken me to try *posint'ang*, my companions told me that eating it had made me a Korean. The owning family was said to be especially fond of this dish. Posint'ang was a particularly potent symbol of identity because it has old-fashioned and folksy connotations, because all but a very few Americans disliked it, and because it had prompted foreign animal-rights activists to threaten a boycott of the 1988 Olympics?

Let us now take a look at how food is distinctive and unique for Hong Kong's Chinese majority, and the ways in which dietary change reflect the cultural construction of people's social lives. In classical studies of norms and traditions regarding how Chinese people choose food in various environments and circumstances, the most popular ideas are the hot/cold dualism and maintaining a balance in the body by regulating the intake of certain foods. This is related to seasonal concerns in choosing food such as 'hot' food for keeping the body warm in autumn and winter, and 'cold' food for keeping it cool in spring and summer. Also, there are traditional practices related to the consumption of seasonal food as it is harvested in nature; for example, people tend to eat fruits such as *laichee* and *long an* (also called dragon eyes) in July/August, crab in September/October, snake in early autumn and other wild animals in winter. In addition, the balance of hot/cold and wet/dry food in people's diet will tell us how eating habits are related to their conceptualization of the body. If the phrase 'we are what we eat' is true, then the next item on the agenda should be to examine how and what Hong Kong people actually eat. In this chapter on food culture in Hong Kong, I aim to pay more attention to the actual change in foodways during the post-war era and examine how traditional kinds of food have remained the same yet changed, and how new kinds of food have been introduced and localized in Hong Kong society.

Changing Eating Habits in Hong Kong Society

Over the past 40 years, Hong Kong has undergone drastic changes in urban development due to both economic growth and changing political relations with mainland China. With two large-scale immigration waves from 1945–1947 and 1949–1952, Hong Kong's population grew from 600,000 in 1945 to 2,340,000 in 1954. The migrants included both Hong Kong residents who had previously fled the Japanese occupation and mainland Chinese who left China after the Communist Revolution in 1949. In addition to increasing the labour force, the latter group brought capital, skills and an urban outlook, which providing an injection of human capital that met the needs of Hong Kong's economic system at that time. This led to enormous social development in the post-war era. Beginning in 1954, a long-term housing policy devised by the Hong Kong government raised the overall living standards of Hong Kong residents.

With the stability offered by new public housing for most working class people, a large low-cost labour force emerged and helped to develop Hong Kong's light industry. By the mid-1960s, Hong Kong had achieved great success in economic development; at the same time, the Cultural Revolution was occurring in China, beginning a period of great suffering and turmoil on the mainland. The Hong Kong Government began different local campaigns to create a sense of mutual belonging among people living in Hong Kong. Generally, most scholars agree that it was in the late 1960s that a 'Hong Kong identity' emerged, especially after the riots of 1967. This identity developed more fully in the 1970s – campaigns such as Clean Hong Kong, Against Corruption, and the Hong Kong Festival are just a few examples. One further indication of a more defined Hong Kong identity, beginning in the late 1960s was the popularity of using the Cantonese language in the mass media and in television channels, and the concomitant growth of a Cantonese-based popular culture. Before this time, English and Mandarin had been the dominant languages of the mass media in Hong Kong. The replacement of the languages had a profound impact as Cantonese movie production grew and even attracted world-wide attention in the 1970s.

Regarding the mentality of people living in Hong Kong, scholars suggest that the Hong Kong ethos represents a flexible mixture of traditional Chinese culture and modern traits (Lau and Kuan 1988). None the less, social scientists have recently paid more attention to aspects of Hong Kong's everyday social life such as food, comics, heritage tourism, computer networks and the mass media, etc. (Evans and Tam 1997; Cheung 1999, 2001; Cheung and Ma 1999). In the following sections, I seek to examine the varieties of foodways and their changing meanings in Hong Kong society during the last few decades; in particular the growth and decline of Hakka restaurants in Hong Kong is suggested as a witness to its social change and economic development.

Hakka Food and Nouvelle Cantonese Cuisine

In the study of Chinese food and cuisine, both Anderson (1988) and Simoons (1991) point out that Hakka food, compared to other regional food, is simple, straightforward, well prepared and without exotic or expensive ingredients involved. Hakka food, developed along the East River in Guangdong province, became popular in Hong Kong soon after the Second World War and developed as a representative cuisine during the 1950s to 1970s, and eventually survived with difficulty in the last two decades.

Regarding the origin of Hakka restaurants in Hong Kong, it seems that they started in Shek Kip Mei (石峽尾) during the late 1940s and early 1950s when many Hakka people moved to Hong Kong and took up residence in the Shek Kip Mei squatter settlement. During that period, the Shek Kip Mei squatter settlement consisted of four villages: Shek Kip Mei village (石峽尾村); Pak Tin village (白田村); Wor Tsai village (窩仔村) and Tai Po Road village (大埔路村), all of which started out as farming communities. With the influx of refugees from mainland China during the Liberation in 1949, there were about 60,000 people living and working in this area by the early 1950s. There were domestic huts and cottage factories making rubber footwear, toys, torches, soaps and other goods. Hakka restaurants in the area were opened by Hakkas who had migrated from Xingning (興寧) in Guangdong Province.

Wing Yuen Mu (永源茂) in Shek Kip Mei is one of the few remaining Hakka restaurants to have survived the changes. The kind of Hakka food that they made was mostly snacks including fried large intestine, bean curd, and beef balls, though all these are quite different from the Hakka cuisine that we now have. The Hakka restaurants were started in the late 1940s by Hakka people and they persisted up to the Shek Kip Mei Great Fire. In the following decades, the further spread of Hakka restaurants to different areas opened a new page for Hong Kong people's food culture. It is important to consider the corresponding changes in lifestyle in Hong Kong society after the great fire. The Shek Kip Mei fire catalyzed public housing projects in Hong Kong. On Christmas Eve 1953, a total of 53,000 people lost their homes in the Shek Kip Mei fire. The subsequent rehousing work which was carried out led to Hong Kong's permanent multi-storey public housing system. Twelve months after the great fire, the Shek Kip Mei public housing estate was built. It was Hong Kong's first public estate, with a total of eight seven-storey H-shaped housing blocks. In other words, rehousing and the housing policy which followed had a direct influence on family structures, living environments, job opportunities and lifestyles. It was mainly because of the great fire that Hakka restaurants spread out to different parts of Hong Kong.

I suggest that there are two reasons why Hakka food gained popularity in Hong Kong. First, because it is eaten with rice, which is the staple food in South China, Hakka food was easily accepted because of the sense of familiarity with Cantonese cuisine. Second, Hakka food is also quite different from domestic food in Cantonese families in terms of taste, ingredients and culinary skills. In its transformation from ordinary food to high cuisine (Goody 1982), key features of Hakka cuisine included the exotic flavourings (e.g. sandy ginger powder 沙姜, preserved vegetables 梅菜 and red wine 紅糟) with expensive ingredients (e.g. chicken, pork and beef balls). The use of a large amount of meat gave valuable animal protein to generate energy for the extensive demands required for working in the light industry which flourished in the late 1950s. Thus, I suggest that Hakka 'cuisine' became popular because of its rich salty taste and meat which were important for energy-demanding jobs, especially from the late 1950s to the 1970s. This also explains why chicken, pork and beef balls became such popular dishes in Hakka cuisine from the 1950s. Nevertheless, Hakka cuisine, as experienced in Hong Kong, should not just be considered in terms of authenticity or originality, but should also be understood as a cuisine chosen and selected within a particular social context. At that time, the typical family diet consisted primarily of fish and vegetables. Hakka restaurants were places to satisfy a need for meat as well as protein. Salty baked chicken (鹽焗雞), pork stewed with preserved vegetables (梅菜扣肉), bean curd with fish (釀豆腐), beef balls (牛肉圓) and fried large intestine (炸大腸) are still popular dishes in Hong Kong; however, not many people know that these originated in Hakka cuisine and are closely related to the history of Hong Kong's social development.

Starting in the 1970s, Hong Kong's living standards improved with the increase in its economic achievements, and people were able to spend more on travelling and eating. Increasing overseas tourism heightened the demand for choices and distinctive forms of lifestyles; also expectations for

105

more delicate, exotic and complicated food and cuisine were heightened. The demand for high quality lifestyles as well as the development of individuals' 'taste' can be seen through the emergence of *nouvelle* Cantonese cuisine which combines exotic taste, expensive ingredients and western catering. Goody (1982:105) emphasizes that high cuisine refers to its characteristics whereby 'the higher in hierarchy, the wider the contacts, the broader the view ingredients from outside', and he draws our attention to the disparity between cuisine in terms of ingredients and technique within a context of global exchange. Changes in taste, cuisine and eating habits are understood as social construction, closely associated with the commodification of cultural objects used to express individual and group identities. Similar approaches in the study of food emphasize the social history of certain items such as Indian curry, rice and hamburgers to understand the cultural meanings of local tradition, the process of cultural change, and the formation of ethnic and national identities (Appadurai 1988; Ohnuki-Tierney 1993; Watson 1997).

In Hong Kong, the emergence of *nouvelle* Cantonese cuisine served as an important indicator of the social construction of Hong Kong society. By the late 1970s, a visibly cosmopolitan Hong Kong with generations of western-educated citizens were firmly in place. Parallel to this post-war transformation, this modified Cantonese cuisine reflected how Hong Kong's social values were constructed. The transformation occurred in the form of *nouvelle*, or new, Cantonese cuisine from the late 1970s that combined exotic or expensive ingredients and western catering. The emergence of *nouvelle* Cantonese cuisine was first found in a host of tastefully decorated restaurants in Tsimshatsui East. Other restaurants opened in different areas such as Tsimshatsui, Causeway Bay and Central, etc. are developing their own *nouvelle* Cantonese styles. This style of cuisine was characterized by the use of exotic ingredients (peacock, crocodile and kangaroo, etc.), new recipes (stewed in western red wine), adventurous cooking techniques, excellent catering service (individual portions rather than family-style shared dishes and changing dishes for each course of the meal) and outstanding décor and ambience. *Nouvelle* Cantonese cuisine was a taste deliberately created for, and pursued by, the 'new rich'. This process of culinary invention may reflect broad social and cultural trends: Hong Kong's increasing wealth and new middle-class aspire to a lifestyle that is more glamorous and that stresses greater refinement.

Yum cha and Tea Cafés

In Hong Kong, food can be used as an important indicator for different ethnic groups too. By comparing the staple foods – rice and congee, the ethnic difference between the Cantonese and the Fujianese can be examined. Guldin (1979) points out that:

Older Fujianese women will often subsist on little more than spinach, peanuts and congee (rice gruel) and the other fare typical of the poorest in Fujian: sweet potatoes and salty melons. Older women will eat these foods on preference even in Hong Kong and even if the family can afford better. These older Fujianese firmly believe Fujianese food to be the best cuisine and rank Guangdongese only third in choice.... The traditional Fujianese custom of eating congee three times daily is yielding to the Guangdongese preference for rice, especially during lunch times on the job when congee is often unavailable' (Guldin 1979: 233–234).

Guldin (1979) points out that another difference between the Guangdongese/Cantonese and Fujianese is how often they go to *yum cha*. *Yum cha* literally means 'drinking tea,' and is a Cantonese-style breakfast meal taken outside the home with *dim sum*, or various kinds of snacks, as its principle feature. The origin of this eating style was from Guangzhou; customers were mostly merchants and traders and the main purpose was social rather than to simply satisfy hunger. *Yum cha* came to Hong Kong during the pre-war era and was not widely eaten. During the post-war era, especially in the 1950s and 1960s when Hong Kong experienced an influx of refugees from mainland China, *yum cha* was largely an activity of single males, who met over their breakfast tea to socialize or exchange tips about job-seeking and bird rearing. At that time, men brought birds with them in a small bamboo cages, to chat with other single male customers. This was the backdrop in Hong Kong tea houses (茶樓) and most were closed in the 1990s. Tea houses are different from the restaurants (酒樓, 大酒樓) where we now go for *yum cha*. First of all, restaurants are usually bigger in size and are located in crowded or busy areas. Some of them are even chain stores such as Maxims, Treasure Seafood Restaurant and Hon Po Restaurant; and some are able to provide wedding and birthday banquet feasts for up to one hundred tables. Some restaurants also provide entertainment and these are called 'restaurant and night club' (酒樓夜總會). *Yum cha* has changed from being a venue for men to socialize in the old days, to a gathering place for the entire family today. Since *yum cha* restaurants are flexible enough to accommodate different numbers of participants, spending varying amounts of time, *yum cha* serves to draw together family members who may now live and work in different parts of Hong Kong, and hence reinforces the institution of the family. The changed function of *yum cha* reflects the full indigenization of a whole generation of early immigrants in Hong Kong society.

Another point to observe is the change in the *yum cha* menu. Much of the food eaten at *yum cha*, was originally street food. It was made and eaten in the street rather than in restaurants. For example, fried rice rolls (煎腸粉),

fried bread in rice rolls (炸兩), fried peppers with fish meat (釀青椒), fish balls and pig skin (魚蛋豬皮), curried squid (咖哩魷魚), sweet sesame or red bean soup (豆沙糖水), bean curd flower (豆腐花), etc. all began as snacks sold in the street but have now been 'upgraded' to popular dishes served in *yum cha* restaurants. This reflects an interesting underlying structural change in Hong Kong society; that is, the large upward mobility of the lower working class to so-called middle class status within a few decades. Ironically, the food that people choose reveals the fact that even though people's 'taste' moves from street to restaurant, the content of the food may not differ at all.

In contrast to *yum cha*, another unique Hong Kong style eating establishment is the café, which is a typical example of Hong Kong's east-meets-west character. Tea cafés (茶餐廳) are small restaurants selling both western and Chinese food, that exist on every Hong Kong neighbourhood corner (see Wu 2001). They have a reputation for providing a wide range of food choices that are cheap and fast. Tea cafés are not only typical of Hong Kong as a melting pot for different cultures, they actually produce typically Hong Kong foodstuffs which reinforces a unique Hong Kong identity that belongs neither to the Chinese nor the English cultures. Drinks such as 'boiled coke with ginger juice (薑汁煲可樂)' and *yin yeung* (鴛鴦) (the former is a special combination with a reputation for curing cold and influenza and the latter is a mixture of coffee and tea with milk) both serve as good examples to represent Hong Kong's complicated mixture of western and Chinese characteristics. Instant noodles with egg and luncheon meat (公仔麵), congee and noodles (粥粉麵) and bakery goods (出爐麵包) form the unique combination of food being served in tea cafés. Most of the tea cafés are independent and small in size, but recently a tea café chain store has appeared. From both the drinks and food served in tea cafés, one can see a localization of both eastern and western cuisines that rejects the authentic food and drinks of both cultures in favour of a new, uniquely Hong Kong flavour.

Puhn choi and Buffet Meals

Another kind invented or reinvented cuisine is *puhn choi*. *Puhn choi* (盆菜) is a festive food commonly seen in ancestor worship rites and wedding banquets among the indigenous inhabitants living in Hong Kong's New Territories. Only one dish is served in this meal and all ingredients are contained in one basin, or *puhn*, which everyone at the table eats from together. In a village that I have been visiting, it is usually called *sihk puhn* (meaning 'eat the basin') and boasts a history longer than colonial Hong Kong in the New Territories. There are different stories about its origin; one common story told by villagers is that originally it was food for an army feast in the southern move during the Song dynasty. At that time, there were not enough food containers to hold food for everyone, so washing basins used by villagers became the containers for the army's feast.

However, apart from its historical origins, the basin food is now served as a banquet food in the single-surname villages marking corresponding ethnic boundaries. It is ceremonially used to signify one whole lineage joined by the way they eat together (Watson 1987). *Puhn choi* not only reinforces the *punti* (meaning local) single-surname lineage system, but also seems to exclude Hakka groups from *punti* Chinese groups within the New Territories' political context. In other words, *puhn choi* is metaphorically considered the real food of the New Territories, dating back to its very earliest inhabitants. Toward the end of British rule in Hong Kong in the 1990s, *puhn choi* suddenly became very popular, not only in the rural New Territories but also in the urban part of Hong Kong. I noticed that one downtown hotel even served *puhn choi* in its Chinese restaurant. This nostalgia for *puhn choi* is pregnant with political meaning and can be regarded as a metaphor for Hong Kong people's search for a sense of cultural belonging during a period of great political change.

With respect to festive food in Hong Kong, apart from some typical dishes with lucky names such as those used for Chinese festivals such as Lunar New Year's Eve, Lunar New Year, Mid Autumn, and Winter Solstice, etc., it is common to see people sharing buffet dinners for some western holidays such as Christmas, New Year and for various celebrations including graduations, birthdays, farewells, etc. In Chinese, buffet means a 'self-serve meal' with an emphasis on all you can eat. However, in some restaurants, a penalty is levied to those who leave too much food uneaten. Buffets gained popularity in Hong Kong in the late 1970s. Nowadays, we can find that most of the hotels offer a buffet lunch and dinner for these holidays. Apart from these 'formal' buffets, there are other various buffet-style meals offered by different ethnic restaurants such as Korean BBQ (apart the high-class type, most of them serve all-you-can-eat style), Japanese sushi bars (most advertise choices in addition to authentic Japanese food), steam bowl and even seafood buffets, etc. It may be the case that the 'free to choose' style seen in Hong Kong's food culture reflects people's expectations in their social lives.

Conclusion: Food as Metaphors

Today, the trend is for food items to be unusual, eye-catching and distinctive. This may indicate new ideas that lead to an 'anything can be mixed', and 'anything can be chosen' mentality, widely seen in the food business. The following example is another personal experience that can be used to demonstrate the plethora of food choices and combinations available to Hong Kong. In May 1998, I went to eat in a local chain restaurant which is supposed to be famous for Cantonese wonton. Based on their recent promotion, I chose a new noodle dish which was rather complicated: *tom-yum* soup (Thai-style), Cantonese wonton and special mushrooms (mostly cultivated in Fujian province) as toppings, Yunnan rice noodles and with a coke.

So, what do people get from mixing up different kinds of ethnic food? It might just be curiosity, or it could also be explained as a representation of Hong Kong identity which includes anything from the East and the West, traditional and modern, local and foreign for its own sake. Either one of these explanations may be correct; however, I would suggest that these kinds of food choices centre on the idea of 'freedom of choice', which can be understood in light of Hong Kong peoples' search for identity in their social lives, an improvised version of Hong Kong style. Individual taste is surely continuously being reformulated in the existing consumer society, and ways of mixing, combining, prioritizing and re-inventing become indicators of expected identity and status. Emergence of a style emphasizing 'freedom of choice' might be an approach to understand the changing 'taste' of Hong Kong people in the last few decades.

However, it may be the case that in addition to a discourse on 'freedom of choice' to understand Hong Kong's culture, it is far more complicated to examine the issue from social and historic perspectives. For example, is the idea of 'freedom of choice' a traditionally inherited, imported, newly invented, or a 'domestified' concept (Tobin 1992) as in Japan's culture of consumerism within the global context. For further discussion, I would like to highlight my speculation by comparing Hong Kong eating habits inside the home with those outside, which clearly show some indicative differences between the two. It was shown that when people dine out, they seek variety and a wide range of choices. Perhaps eating in McDonald's for breakfast, lunching at a Japanese restaurant, buying snacks at the Taiwan tea shop, and having Indian curry for dinner. They might be eager to try Korean barbecue after appetisers of raw oysters from France and Boston lobster from the United States. All these different kinds of food from all over the world can easily be found in Hong Kong nowadays – they are available to the majority of people not just the rich.

As we can observe from the changing material culture, when Hong Kong became economically advanced and culturally international, individuals sought to identify themselves with society by varying means. By looking at food and cuisine as a cultural marker of the identity and status of people, international cuisine in restaurants serves to identify a means for people to compete as equals in the international arena. However, food consumed inside the home is far more traditional and conservative, with concerns for safety, health, traditional hot/cold balance and ritual taboos. A boundary is maintained and well defined between eating at home and outside. Nevertheless, this negotiation between traditionalism and globalism in relation to domestic issues can be wholly observed in the case of Hong Kong society. Furthermore, the ingredients used are highly similar in most families, and cooking styles seldom vary from day to day. For example, boiled soup, steamed fish, fried seasonal green vegetables with small pieces of meat, and bean curd are all typical family dishes, and rice is almost always the staple food in Hong Kong homes. The difference between eating habits inside and outside the home is a telling one, and reflects the dichotomy of Hong Kong itself. Hong Kong is a cosmopolitan city boasting international sophistication on the one hand, while on the other it is an extension of Chinese culture with long-standing Cantonese traditions.

References

Anderson, N. Eugene (1988) *The Food of China*. New Haven: Yale University Press.

Appadurai, Arjun (1988) 'How to Make a National Cuisine: Cookbooks in Contemporary India', *Comparative Study of Society and History*, 30 (1):3–24.

Cheng, Sea Ling (1997) 'Back To The Future: Herbal Tea Shops in Hong Kong', in Grant Evans and Maria Siumi Tam (eds) *Hong Kong: The Anthropology of a Chinese Metropolis*, pp. 51–73. Surrey and Honolulu: Curzon and University of Hawaii Press.

Cheung, C. H. Sidney (1999) 'The Meanings of a Heritage Trail in Hong Kong', *Annals of Tourism Research*, 26(3):570–588.

—— (2001) 'Hakka Restaurants: A Study of the Consumption of Food in Post-war Hong Kong Society', in David Wu Y. H. and Tan Chee Beng (eds) *Changing Chinese Foodways in Asia*, pp. 81–95. Hong Kong: The Chinese University Press.

Cheung, C. H. Sidney and Eric K. W. Ma (1999) *Advertising Modernity: 'Home,' Space and Privacy*, HKIAPS Occasional Paper No. 93, Hong Kong: Hong Kong Institute of Asia-Pacific Studies, The Chinese University of Hong Kong.

Douglas, Mary (1966) *Purity and Danger: An Analysis of the Concepts of Pollution and Taboo*. London and New York: ARK.

Evans, Grant and Maria Siumi Tam (eds) (1997) *Hong Kong: The Anthropology of a Chinese Metropolis*. Surrey and Honolulu: Curzon Press and University of Hawaii Press.

Goody, Jack (1982) *Cooking, Cuisine and Class: A Study in Comparative Sociology*. Cambridge: Cambridge University Press.

Guldin, E. Gregory (1979) *'Overseas' at Home: The Fujianese of Hong Kong*. Ann Arbor, Mich.: University Microfilms International.

Janelli, Roger and Dawnhee Yim (1993) *Making Capitalism: The Social and Cultural Construction of a South Korean Conglomerate*. Stanford: Stanford University Press.

Lau, Siu-kai and Kuan Hsin-chi (1988) The Ethos of the Hong Kong Chinese. Hong Kong: The Chinese University Press.

Lee, Wai Yee (1997) Food and Ethnicity: A Study of Eating Habits among Chiu Chow People in Hong Kong (in Chinese), M.Phil. thesis (unpublished). Department of Anthropology, The Chinese University of Hong Kong.

Levi-Strauss, Claude (1965) 'The Culinary Triangle', *Partisan Review*, 33:586–595.

Mintz, W. Sidney (1985) *Sweetness and Power: The Place of Sugar in Modern History*. New York: Viking.

111

Ohnuki-Tierney, Emiko (1993) *Rice As Self: Japanese Identities Through Time.* Princeton: Princeton University Press.

Simoons, J. Frederick (1991) *Food in China: A Cultural and Historical Inquiry.* Boston: CRC Press.

Smart, Josephine (1989) *The Political Economy of Street Hawkers in Hong Kong.* Hong Kong: Center of Asian Studies, University of Hong Kong.

Tam, Siumi Maria (1997) 'Eating Metopolitaneity: Hong Kong Identity in *yumcha*', *The Australian Journal of Anthropology*, 8 (3):291–306.

Tobin, J. Joseph (ed.) (1992) *Re-made in Japan: Everyday Life and Consumer Taste in a Changing Society.* New Haven: Yale University Press.

Watson, L. James (1975) *Emigration and the Chinese Lineage: The Mans in Hong Kong and London.* Berkeley and London: University of California Press.

—— (1987) 'From the Common Pot: Feasting with Equals in Chinese Society', *Anthropos*, 82:389–401.

—— (ed.) (1997) *Golden Arches East: McDonald's in East Asia.* Stanford: Stanford University Press.

Wu, Y. H. David (2001) 'Chinese Café in Hong Kong', in David Wu Y. H. and Tan Chee Beng (eds) *Changing Chinese Foodways in Asia.* pp. 71–80. Hong Kong: The Chinese University Press.

CHAPTER SEVEN

Food Consumption, Food Perception and the Search for a Macanese Identity[1]

Louis Augustin-Jean

This chapter rests on two basic assumptions that can be complementary but can also be contradictory. The first is to accept that both food type and method of preparation are used by people within a given society to demarcate themselves from other groups within that society, and from other societies. Second, over time both food and methods of preparation are nevertheless frequently borrowed from other cultures and other cuisines, leading to a process of assimilation and reinterpretation.[2] These two preliminary observations are especially relevant in a place like Macau where at least two completely different cultures (and therefore two completely different culinary traditions) have been brought together and have coexisted for over 450 years. Thus, Macau is on the surface a Chinese-dominated society like Hong Kong, with over 95 per cent of its population Chinese, but it is also a place where Portuguese and other Asian influences (such as Malaysian and Indian) have coalesced to create a distinctive cuisine.

As a result of this Chinese predominance, with western influences and a colonial experience, reminiscent of Hong Kong, it seemed interesting to ask how the Chinese population of Macau differs from that of Hong Kong by means of the culinary traditions these two groups have borrowed from their adopted communities (Portuguese or English, respectively). In fact, the problem quickly revealed itself to be very complicated because of the above-mentioned Asian influences on one hand, and on the other, the fact that Hong Kong is often used as a model and referent to Macau, including its eating habits. Moreover, defining the differences between Hong Kong and Macau seemed insufficient to understand the reasons for these differences and then might prove to be useless.

Refining the question further was, therefore, necessary. We will consider the different ethnic groups which make up Macanese society and will show how food is used as an indicator to delineate identity from other groups, especially with regard to reunification with China in 1999 (also see Lam 1997; Berlie 1999). Regarding this, three points will be examined. First, the culinary landscape of Macau will be sketched. This will allow the identification of certain problems which will be addressed later in this chapter. Second, the survey method will be detailed, and finally the results from that survey will be presented. However, it is important to mention that because of the number of interviews carried out was small, these are preliminary research findings; therefore, the major results obtained in the present study should be considered with care, even though they seem significant and plausible.[3]

The Culinary Landscape of Macau and its Recent Evolution

Like Hong Kong, Macau has a first-class network of restaurants. A wide range of styles, prices and atmospheres can be found. Besides this diversity, Macau has experienced a rapid change in its culinary setting over the last few years. Like most cities in the world, the Macau Special Administrative Region (SAR) has experienced globalization and westernization, which have often led to standardized restaurants. Fast food restaurants have appeared and multiplied in Macau during the last few years. There are several McDonalds and Kentucky Fried Chickens, one Pizza Hut and so on. This wave of globalization can also seen by the presence of restaurants that claim to be western, but where, for want of carefully prepared food a lot of attention is given to decoration. This tendency toward globalization is further expanded by an added original Macanese element, its close relationship with Hong Kong, and is exporting its own fast food model. Thus, Hong Kong chains of fast food restaurants, such as Maxim's and Fairwood, have been successfully implanted in the Portuguese colony and offer simple Chinese dishes as well as more typical western fast food such as sandwiches and hot dogs. Likewise, Japanese *sushi* restaurants, where customers seated around a conveyor belt can choose rotating dishes, has been adopted from Japan by way of Hong Kong.

This new culture of fast food is extremely powerful in Macau and is made up of a mixture of standardization, westernization and for lack of a better term, what might be called 'Hongkongization', the latter corresponding to a factor of differentiation when compared with other cities. However, what makes Macau really original is the presence of the second tendency, westernization, which obviously shapes the culinary landscape of the territory. In fact, besides the dominant number of Chinese restaurants, the enclave is distinguished by the presence of either Portuguese Macanese or Portuguese and Macanese restaurants.[4] Several of these restaurants are mentioned in tourist guides, which has contributed to making culinary activity one of Macau's main tourist attractions, besides casinos. The popularity of these restaurants also explains why so many visitors from Hong Kong flock to Macau at weekends. This trend demonstrates that many popular western or hybrid western-Macanese restaurants constitute an element of originality in Macau compared to those existing in the ex-British colony.[5] This shows that the sociological interest represented by Portuguese and Macanese restaurants is coupled with a powerful economic interest.

Nevertheless, it is not the presence of these restaurants in itself that is both important and interesting. For example, the existence of Portuguese restaurants in a territory which has been under Portuguese sovereignty for more than 450 years does not seem surprising at the first glance. Rather, what is noteworthing is when most of these restaurants were established. This kind of restaurant appeared very recently compared to the long history of the Portuguese colony, most of them being created only in the late 1980s or early 1990s.[6] The first Portuguese bakery was opened only in 1993 (Doling 1995:107) while Riquexó, considered to be the most Macanese of the Macanese restaurants (and one of the older), appeared only in 1978 (ibid.:62). Other restaurants, such as Litoral (Portuguese-Macanese), were also established in the early 1990s (1994 for Litoral[7]).

To conclude this brief synopsis of Macau's culinary landscape, one finds that Macau has followed, and is still following the tendency of most other Asian and other world metropolises, in how readily it is accepting fast food. At the same time the influence of Hong Kong is clearly felt. It is also worth noting the presence of numerous Chinese restaurants, most of which have not yet been properly studied. Even though these restaurants more or less resemble similar ones in Hong Kong, with regard to the cuisine they offer as well as the habits of consumption they cater to, some differences exist. A more detailed study of the subject would probably show that a significant number of Macau's Chinese restaurants have received Portuguese influence, as shown by their menus offering codfish as well as a typically Portuguese soup accompanied by olive oil.[8]

However, besides these factors, what really distinguishes Macau is the presence of Portuguese and Macanese restaurants. Visually speaking, three types of restaurants (except for fast food restaurants) coexist in Macau: Chinese, Portuguese and Macanese. The recent appearance of the latter two categories poses an evident enigma, the answers to which will be given at the end of this chapter. Moreover, the use of the expression Macanese, as distinct from those of Chinese and Portuguese, suggests the presence of a specific category which needs to be defined and eventually associated with a specific group of the population and of its identity. The front of the restaurants clearly shows that the adjective Macanese cannot be uniformly applied to everything occurring in the enclave. Beyond a simple definition, it refers to the problem of Macanese identity in juxtaposition with Chinese and Portuguese identities. The study was, therefore, centred on the term Macanese and its definition in relation to the food subject.

115

Methodology of the Survey

The survey was aimed at delimiting the food habits of the Macanese and their perception of the various categories of cuisine found in the territory. As will be shown, the ethnic identity of the interviewees has not been presumed in the questionnaires because this would have biased the answer to the question of identity.

Four series of questionnaires were devised, each aiming to meet specific objectives. However, the low number of interviews carried out in each series only allows some tendencies to be brought out and does not permit definitive conclusions to be drawn. Thus, a future study is needed, especially because the fluidity of the subject and the rapid evolution of food habits warrant a need for such research to be conducted in the future. All the questionnaires were handed out between April and August 1997.

The first kind of questionnaire, an open one, targeted restaurant owners (or managers) and personnel working in the restaurants (cooks, waiters, etc.). It was the only questionnaire addressed directly to food professionals. Only seven questionnaires could be processed: four on Macau peninsula, and three on the outlying island (two on Taipa island and one on Coloane island). Five of the restaurants were Macanese, Portuguese or Portuguese-Macanese; the sixth (which was an exception) can be defined as Macanese-Chinese while the last was a small Chinese restaurant in the peninsula.

The questions focused mainly on these topics: the clientèle (local people or tourists, ethnic groups, etc.); the type of food offered by the restaurants; and on the elements of the definition of each food style found in Macau (Chinese, Portuguese and Macanese) as opposed to other styles. In other words, each interviewee was systematically asked the differences between Portuguese, Macanese and Chinese food and had to justify his/her answers based on specific examples of dishes and their methods of preparation. Finally, to clarify the concept of Macanese, the interviewees were also asked to explain in non-culinary terms if they considered themselves Macanese and, if so, why. The questionnaire was meant to compare the opinion of specialists with that of laymen, but their remarks did not reveal any major differences compared with those of knowledgeable people, at least not related to the themes of this survey.

The second and third series of questionnaires were directed to the 'average consumer', regardless of gender, ethnic origin, age or profession. The second series was conducted at places of consumption (i.e. in particular restaurants)[9] while the third was carried out on the street at various places. The open interviews were carried out in English and Chinese (Cantonese). Due to a shortage of funds, only about 50 questionnaires were distributed and analysed. This low number explains why no sampling was carried out. However, a preliminary condition set before the interviews required that all interviewees should have lived in Macau for at least one year. This, therefore, excluded both tourists (including Hongkongese) and people who had just arrived in the territory (such as recent immigrants from mainland China who had not yet adapted to the local context), but the survey included interviews with most Portuguese, even those who had arrived recently to work for the local government.

While composing and/or distributing the questionnaires, ethnic criteria were deliberately ignored, so as to avoid subjective judgements about respondents, in particular regarding the various connotations associated. On the other hand, more objective parameters providing information about respondents were introduced: place of birth (Macau, Portugal, China or other); date of arrival in Macau; nationality and the date of obtaining nationality (Portuguese or not, Portugal having bestowed nationality on most of Macau's residents); the standard of linguistic knowledge (mother tongue, spoken and written fluency in Cantonese and Portuguese). It was also asked what Macanese meant to them and whether they themselves felt Macanese (and why). In the survey, the questionnaires also questioned respondents' food habits as well as their perception and definition of Portuguese, Macanese and Chinese cuisines. The selection of the survey sites (which included Portuguese, Macanese and Chinese restaurants or in more neutral, public places) was initially considered to be a parameter affecting the answers given by interviewees (e.g. people who patronize restaurants and those who do not), but few differences were noted.

Finally, the last questionnaire was self-administered. For a period of a week, each person was in charge of recording, for every meal and in between meals the type of dishes (or snack[10]) and drinks, as well as the name of every dish, consumed. Every two days at most, a surveyor came to monitor the quality of the answers given and to ask for further details if needed. The same descriptive information as before was asked (age, sex, profession, nationality, level of linguistic knowledge, etc.). This questionnaire intended to compare people's actual practices with the conclusions drawn from the series of earlier questionnaires. Twelve people were interviewed in this way.

Food Habits and Representation in the Territory

The methodology, as presented, aimed at answering several types of questions. First, it served to show what the Macanese cuisine was and how it compared to Chinese and Portuguese cuisine.[11] This also implied defining the position occupied by this cuisine, in the consumption habits as well as in the symbolic and mental realm of the people interviewed. The question that should be considered then was whether a given group of people (as defined above) had distinctive perceptions about different cuisines compared to other groups, and, more specifically, whether there was any identification of a particularly Macanese cuisine by one of these groups. A positive answer to this double question might well facilitate a more precise definition of one or more population.

As it can now be clearly seen, in this chapter I employ the method of using eating habits to define a population group, which is contrary to what has been done by previous researchers in this field. For example, Ana Maria Amaro defines the Macanese community before analysing some of its social behaviours (marriage, religion, etc.):

> We suggested as an hypothesis a survey of two to three-thousands individuals, whose parents would either be both Euro-Asiatic, one Euro-Asiatic and one Chinese, one Euro-Asiatic and one Portuguese or one Portuguese and one Chinese. Such was the 'universe' of possibilities of our definition of Macanese, as someone born in Macau with original Portuguese culture and ascendants (Amaro 1994:218).[12]

Expenditure on food for the families in Macau

Using food to define a group of population might at first seem arbitrary. However, two reasons justify this choice. First, in Macau food is an obvious marker, as shown by the range of restaurant choice in the territory. Second, using food practices seemed meaningful in the sense that food constitutes the most significant position of an average resident family's budget.[13] According to estimates given by the Macanese government in 1993–1994, food expenses represented 31.2 per cent of a family's budget. However, this figure was lower than in 1987–1988 when 38.4 per cent of a household's expenses was allotted to food. Nevertheless, this decline does not seem to be meaningful because of increased expenses for housing in the intervening years. For example, the budget portion allotted to housing increased from 19.7 per cent (1987–1988) to 26.4 per cent (1993–1994) (Direcçao de Serviços de Estatistica e Censos 1994:14). In all, the fact that nearly one-third of the budget of the household is dedicated to food clearly shows that the way Macau people eat is an indication of the way they live. The significant portion of their budget that households spend on food, therefore, strengthens the relevance of this study.

Eating Chinese food – An everyday habit for most people of the territory

The questionnaire results show that, regardless of the meal (breakfast, lunch or dinner), people in Macau often eat out. This is particularly true for lunch, but many interviewees also have breakfast either in fast food restaurants, small Chinese restaurants which they refer to as 'canteens', or at their place of work (where they consume food that may have been prepared at home or bought outside). In Hong Kong, one survey clearly indicates that even for children attending primary school and kindergarten, a significant proportion of them (about 30 per cent) eat their breakfast outside their home (Guldan *et al.* 1994a:7; 1995b:10).[14] Dinner is more often taken at home or with the family, but exceptions are common. The Macau government's survey mentioned above confirms the tendency shown in the questionnaires, and indicates that for the period 1979–1980, more than 44 per cent of expenditure on food by families was due to food eaten outside the home (FAO 1994:51). Even though more recent figures are not available, it is likely that this tendency has not significantly changed.

Concerning the style of food eaten, most people in Macau, regardless of their origin, eat Chinese food. At lunch, for example, many patronize a Chinese restaurant near their place of work. Recently arrived Portuguese generally follow a similar tendency, as illustrated by Mrs Rodriguez's example.[15] Mrs Rodriguez's arrived from Lisbon in 1995 and works for the government of Macau; her husband is an engineer at the new international airport. Generally, she has lunch with a colleague in the restaurants near her workplace, declaring that the choice of restaurant depends mainly on the mood of the moment. Yet, on closer examination, it seems that the chosen restaurant is almost invariably Chinese. In other words, contrary to what she used to do in Lisbon, Mrs Rodriguez basically eats Chinese food for every lunch during weekdays. Although the reasons for this choice are not clear, it is possible to suggest the following possibilities.

One reasonable possibility is that Mrs Rodriguez's restaurant choice was imposed by a potentially Chinese colleague. Although this argument is not valid because this colleague is Macanese (that is, having a Portuguese father and Chinese mother, according to this interviewee) and, in particular, because this practice seems to be followed by all those interviewed in the Portuguese community, except for a man who lives near his work place and whose lunch was prepared by his maid. Another reason for Mrs Rodriguez's choice might be that Portuguese or Macanese food (the latter still being defined by the restaurants, without referring to the actual contents of the dishes) are considered too rich and excessive for lunch. A third reason, even though less elaborated, is economics, because Portuguese and Macanese restaurants are substantially more expensive than Chinese ones.

The survey demonstrates a clear consensus among groups in Macau for Chinese food at lunch time. Because of the limited range of this survey, however, it is difficult to be precise about the extent to which all groups eat the same type of Chinese food, go to the same type of restaurant or whether there are significant differences. The former of the three seems the most plausible.

Thus, the menu is set around a bowl of rice or a plate of noodles and generally includes a fish or seafood dish. Consumption of pork and chicken is also extremely frequent. The practice of eating *dim sum* (small dishes usually steamed and served in bamboo baskets[16]) for lunch was rarely mentioned by our interviewees and those completing the self-administrated questionnaires. However, the crowds that come to the restaurants seeking this type of food show that it is as common in Macau as it is in Hong Kong and Guangdong province. Moreover, the traditional practice of tearooms – where *dim sum* is served from early in the morning – reinforces the impression that different population groups in Macau (in particular the Chinese) regularly consume this type of food. Even though tearooms are presently on the brink of extinction in Macau, this is not related to an evolution in the taste of the people, because those tearooms which still remain are generally full.

The dinner: a greater diversification of food consumption

A difference in eating habits mainly appears at dinner. In fact, although people in Macau frequently eat out, dinner is more often taken at home. Among the Chinese, in Macau as well as in Hong Kong, the soup is an important part of the meal, even though it is not served everyday. As shown by the self-administrated questionnaire, nearly two out of three dinners have a soup and this practice is particularly common when there is a gathering of the whole family. This agrees with observations made by Cheng Sea-Ling (1996:Chapter 3) in Hong Kong. It is nevertheless important to note that the place of the soup in a Chinese dinner in Hong Kong or Macau has lost some of its importance, even though it remains a fundamental dinner component for most people.[17]

Among non-Chinese groups, eating habits vary much more. The Portuguese, for example, tend to eat more Portuguese food at home, generally prepared by a maid. Because the eating habits of the 'Macanese' are so distinctive, Macanese food and the way it is both consumed and perceived by Macau's residents will be given special treatment in the rest of this chapter.

Macanese food as seen by the people in Macau and the question of identity

The data from the questionnaires show that all the people interviewed were able, if not to define Chinese food with precision, at least to cite a number of Chinese dishes that can be found in Macau: steamed fish, *dim sum*, etc. Similarly, Portuguese cuisine is relatively well identified, even if it appears to be less easily definable by the Chinese population who sometimes have difficulties in naming the dishes. On the other hand, familiarity with Macanese cuisine has elicited varied comments that need to be clarified. It will be shown how the level of knowledge or acknowledgment of this cuisine is related to the question of identity. This will then permit a clearer understanding of the words Chinese, Portuguese and Macanese, which so far have too often been used without any precise definition, and were based either on what was written on a restaurant's street sign or on people's anecdotal comments.

The first observation is that many people neither know nor acknowledge Macanese cuisine. To the question, 'what is Macanese food to you',[18] they answered in one of two converging directions. Many denied the very existence of a Macanese cuisine. Others suggested that Macanese cuisine was assimilated with all types of cuisine found on the territory without any particular distinction. Answers were, therefore, as follows: 'in Macau, one can eat different types of food: Chinese, Portuguese, Indian, Malay, Japanese, etc. Macanese cuisine is the whole of what can be found in the territory'. Whatever the answer given, it is clear that the very existence of Macanese cuisine is not acknowledged by these people, who generally are native Cantonese speakers, bear a Chinese patronymic and do not speak Portuguese. Even though most of them have Portuguese citizenship, these people can, without doubt, be classified as Chinese. This, of course, does not mean that all Chinese cannot define Macanese food, and the presence of many Chinese in such restaurants clearly demonstrates this. However, it implies that the proportion of the people who are not aware of this style of food is much more significant among the Chinese than among other groups in the population. The answers given are rather surprising because so many Macanese restaurants thrive throughout the territory and are therefore extremely visible. However, it is true that the phrase 'Macanese restaurants' is seldom translated into Chinese characters in the restaurants' advertisements. This observation is still more surprising when one considers that the longer these Chinese have spent in Macau does not significantly increase their familiarity with Macanese cuisine.[19] Therefore, among the Chinese, it is possible that many might be willing, consciously or otherwise, to identify with the territory while simultaneously denying the existence of an identity different from their own. Thus, these people legitimately feel Macanese because they live in the territory and/or were born there.

Among other population groups, the familiarity with Macanese food is more significant. Before giving details about their degree of familiarity with Macanese cuisine, it should be said that if the survey does not allow for a precise definition of the Macanese community, it does none the less provide elements for defining the contours of that community. As will be shown, there remain important uncertainties on the margins.

Thus, it is possible to determine different degrees of familiarity with Macanese cuisine. The first degree corresponds to a general, but relatively shallow knowledge; some people have difficulties with details and/or specific names of the dishes. Whenever possible, they generally name the dishes that can be found in restaurants (for example, African chicken – Galinha Africana), but often are unable to give the ingredients or the ways of preparation.[20] Similarly, the question about the difference between Portuguese and Macanese cuisines remains relatively blurred. There is, however, a significant insistence on the fact that Macanese cuisine is richer and heavier than Portuguese cuisine.

At the other end of the scale, some people can provide names of dishes, ways of preparation, ingredients and even the time of the year when a particular dish should be consumed. For example, Mr Lopez gave the recipe for *Diabo* (literally meaning the devil), prepared after a celebration (especially after Christmas), when all the meat left over from the celebration is combined and then fried with mustard. Generally, people like Mr Lopez identify themselves with this cuisine which forms part of their tradition, and they remember the dishes prepared by their mother or grandmother. Nowadays, this cuisine is no longer prepared at home, because the dishes take so long to prepare, yet it has been completely integrated to the local tradition. Thus, reinforcing its specific and identifying character, a myth has been created around this cuisine. To the question 'what is Macanese cuisine to you', one of the answers was:

> The first Portuguese to arrive in Macau were mainly men, who often married Asian women, Malay, then Chinese. At first, they would show their wives how to prepare Portuguese food. On the first day, they themselves cooked and showed the ingredients, the cooking, etc. to their wives. Then, when the wives tried to prepare the particular dish, but as it was difficult to find certain ingredients, they often improvised and adapted it to what they could prepare, since it was difficult to find certain ingredients. Thus, the Macanese cuisine was born.

Regardless of the validity of this story, it is significant how this group of the population perceives itself, being proud of its mixed Portuguese and diverse Asian origins. This group's sense of unity is reinforced by people's sharing a Portuguese patronymic. Many were born in Macau, speak Portuguese and are Portuguese nationals. Often they also speak Cantonese but are unable to write Chinese; the learning of the language generally occurred via daily contacts with the local Chinese population ('I learnt Chinese on the street', several of them said). Finally, it should be noted that they often have a strong feeling of being Macanese, even if they have some difficulty in defining the term precisely. As one young Macanese student studying in Portugal affirmed, one should first of all have the sense of belonging to this restricted community.

These people can be classified as Macanese. Therefore, by virtue of their shared sense of cuisine, it is possible to identify the existence of a particular group within the population, although it might not be possible to set the limits of that group with precision. This is because there are many borderline cases which are difficult to categorize. For example, many people possessing the characteristics defined above do not define themselves – at least not openly – as Macanese, but rather as Portuguese; while a few years ago, the same people would say without any hesitation that they were Macanese.[21] This does not necessarily mean that their perception of their identity has changed, but it instead implies that at least the image they want to convey to others has changed.[22] Another borderline case is that of people born in Macau of Portuguese parents, speaking Chinese and knowing perfectly the Macanese cultural practices, including the culinary ones. The questionnaires show that some of them consider themselves Macanese, while others claim a Portuguese identity. The fact is that it is difficult to classify them and the extensive knowledge they have – in this case, from within the Macanese group. One should not consider them to be Macanese solely because they derive from the Macanese culture. However, because some claim this Macanese identity with so much conviction, one hesitates to deny them this claim that they feel so heartily.

As we can see, the answers to these questions are not devoid of ambiguity and it is beyond the scope of this chapter to definitely resolve them. However, it has been shown that food is used as a cultural referent and proves the existence of a community which is specifically Macanese, at the interface of the Chinese and Portuguese communities. Hence, the adjective Macanese, whether used to qualify a cuisine or a population, cannot be applied without distinguishing it from the whole range of food and people found in the Portuguese colony. Characteristically, only the Chinese attribute the term Macanese to everything found in the territory. Although they are often unable to identify Macanese food, they still call themselves Macanese and justify it by the fact that they live in the territory. Consequently, it is probable that the associations of the following terms are made by the Chinese population: Macanese food = food of Macau (regardless of origin)/Macanese population = inhabitants of Macau.

Conclusion: Macanese Restaurants and the Visibility of the Macanese Identity

With the above analysis as background, is it possible to explain the recent appearance of Macanese and Portuguese restaurants in the peninsula? It should be remembered that this question was asked at the beginning of this chapter, but no answer was then given. Now that a proper context for it has been provided, the following answer can be proposed.

Since its origins, the Macanese community has always been placed between the Chinese and the Portuguese. In recent years, the economic power has been mainly controlled by the Chinese, while the Portuguese still held political power. The Macanese community could defend its interests by making use of its buffer position. However, regarding the 1999 issues, political power has returned once and for all to China. On the other hand, the Chinese majority logically considers itself as Macanese, but refuses to acknowledge the existence of the indigenous Macanese population. The fact that it does not know the Macanese food, visually significant and easily identifiable, suggests that this is the case. It is, therefore, possible that the Macanese felt threatened as a specific group and might have perceived a risk of being absorbed. The recent creation of many Macanese restaurants would, therefore, suggest to outsiders the existence and the identity of this community (estimated at about 10,000 people in the enclave and perhaps 60,000 people throughout the world). Similarly, the creation of Portuguese-Macanese restaurants would show the attachment of this community to its Portuguese origin. With regard to the Portuguese restaurants, it is also possible – although this is highly conjectural – that some Portuguese are willing to show that they want to remain in Macau after the return of the enclave to the motherland and continue to play an important role there.

Finally, the fact that economic success has followed the creation of these restaurants – and notably the government of Macau is using the territory's distinctive cuisine as one means of promoting tourism – shows that the bet could well be won by the Macanese and that the community, by becoming visible, finally becomes undeniable, although it can no longer rely on the arrival of more Portuguese to ensure its partial renewal. By using food as a barometer of culture, it is therefore possible to show how a community asserts its identity and, above all, what is at stake regarding food and culture in the aftermath of the 1999 handover.

Notes

1 A preliminary version of this paper was presented at 'Cuisine et politique', International Conference organized by the French Association of Political Studies, Bordeaux, 22–24 January 1998 and published in French in *Lusotopie 1998*, Paris, Karthala, December 1998, under the title 'Cuisine et identité macanaise'.

2 It is interesting to note that a number of dishes considered to be national, while serving as cultural landmarks with regard to other nations, owe much to eating habits borrowed from other nations. For example, pizza, an Italian dish, owes its existence to the adoption of the tomato, of American origin, in Italy.

3 I would here like to thank several persons who helped administer this survey. James Lee (thanks to his profound knowledge of Macau and his interest in culinary matters) introduced me to several restaurant owners and helped me better understand the culinary world of the territory. Discussion with members of the Instituto Cultural de Macau – mainly with Mrs Teresa Sena – allowed me to benefit from the results of a prodigious amount of research already conducted on Macau's cultural history. Finally, the questionnaires would not have been

realised without the help of three persons: Miss Anthea Cheung, who assured the translation of all the questionnaires into Cantonese and conducted the interviews in that language; and Jean Berlie and Isabel Morais, who distributed the self-administrated questionnaires and guaranteed the quality of information obtained in these questionnaires.

4 The meaning of the adjective Macanese will be clarified further in this chapter. However, the fact that the word is written on the main sign board or on the front of these restaurants as a qualifier of the restaurant allows me to use it now without providing prior definition.

5 For more details on these restaurants, see Doling (1995).

6 Interview, Instituto Cultural de Macau; Doling (1995).

7 Interview with the staff of the restaurant.

8 I am thankful to Isabelle Morais for bringing this point to my attention.

9 It should be noted that in 1981–1982, more than 44 per cent of food expenses was due to meals taken outside the home (FAO 1993:88). Also, see *infra*.

10 The difference between 'snack' and a proper meal lies in the fact that the meal consists of a set of dishes taken at particular moments while a snack is eaten without any order or at any particular moment (Raulin 1988; Louis Augustin-Jean 1992:17).

11 The open form of the questionnaire allowed other cuisines to be taken into consideration (for example, Japanese, western or Southeast Asian), but being only very rarely mentioned by our interviewees, they were largely neglected in the following analyses.

12 It should be noted that this definition is relatively inaccurate, in so far as an 'Euro-Asiatic', even in Macau, is not necessarily of Portuguese origin.

Other definitions also include as Macanese totally Portuguese people born in Macau. Jao de Pina Cabral, for example, quotes the following from an interview: 'Fundamentally, being Macanese is to be a native of Macau, but in order to interpret this community, the word includes everyone who is born in Macau and has a Portuguese culture.... What is certain is that, to find a clear definition, we know that someone is Macanese or not through certain signs, certain ways being, a way of speaking, of thinking which fully identify him as a Macanese.... (Cabral 1994:232).

13 Of course, many other criteria and numerous other cultural practices besides those that are food-related can be used to define population group, and I do not imply here that the analysis of food practices is exclusive of other research conducted on this question.

14 It should be noted that for breakfast the Chinese populations might regularly eat for breakfast bread together with a bowl of noodles or rice. This clearly indicates a western influence in the eating habits of the Chinese populations of Macau. This finding is also compatible with the survey of Guldan *et al.* (1994b:14) in Hong Kong, which indicates that if 35 per cent of the adults eat porridge and noodles and 17 per cent *dim sum* for breakfast, 34 per cent eat eggs, sausage and bread, 25 per cent biscuits and buns, 20 per cent sandwich and 7 per cent breakfast cereal.

15 Names given are fictitious.

16 There are other types of *dim sum*, including small fried dishes and many others. Therefore a precise définition and/or translation of this style of food is impossible to provide.

17 Interviews; Bartlett and Lai (1998:57–58).

18 The term Macanese is ambiguous in so far as it cannot be replaced by the expression 'of Macau', but this ambiguity introduces another dimension (which

is the subject of this chapter) that makes it difficult to translate the term Macanese into Chinese. Thus, 'Macanese cuisine' in Chinese has been translated as 'cuisine of Macau' and/or 'Macanese style cuisine'. The manner in which the open questions were set allowed the simultaneous use of both expressions as well as the use of the English term 'Macanese'. None of the three employed expressions showed any differences in the survey's answers.

19 This conclusion which emerges from our interviews is probably biased by virtue of the low number of completed questionnaires, especially in so far as the number of Chinese recently arrived in Macau are more numerous than those who have been there longer. It is possible that the Chinese born in the colony might have more opportunities to mix with the other groups of population in the territory and therefore become acquainted with other types of cuisine. This is only a conjecture and there is no evidence to support this hypothesis. Another hypothesis would be to relate the level of acquaintance with the Macanese cuisine with one's standard of education or social position. Cheng Sea-ling, in her study on Hong Kong, supports such a hypothesis and notes that embracing other types of cuisines significantly increases with the standard of education or with the frequency of contact with non-Chinese population (Cheng Sea-ling 1996:chapter 6). The link between the education level and the style of food eaten has also be noticed by Guldan *et al.* (1995b:15) who note that the more educated people are, the more they tend to eat western food for breakfast.

20 Annabel Doling (1995:118) gives the recipe for the African chicken. The ingredients comprise onion, garlic, pepper, white wine and paprika among others.

21 I am thankful to Jean Berlie for bringing this point to my attention.

22 The survey did not suggest the reasons for this behaviour.

References

Amaro, Ana Maria (1994) 'The Macanese: A Changing Society (preliminary result of an inquiry)', *Review of Culture English Edition*, 20 (2nd series):213–228.

Augustin-Jean, Louis (1992) *L'alimentation de rue pour la population asiatique de Paris*. Paris: Centre International de l'enfance.

Bartlett, Frances and Ivan Lai (1998) *Hong Kong on a Plate: A Culinary Journey with Recipes from Some of the World's Best Restaurants*. Hong Kong: Roundhouse Publications (Asia).

Berlie, Jean A. (ed.) (1999) *Macao 2000*. Hong Kong: Oxford University Press.

Cabral, Jao de Pina (1994) 'The "Ethnic" Composition of Macau', *Review of Culture English Edition*. 20 (2nd series):229–239.

Cheng, Sea-ling (1996) *Food and Distinction in Hong Kong Families*. Hong Kong: The University of Hong Kong (M.Phil. dissertation).

Direcçao de Serviços de Estatisca e Censos (1994) *Inquérito às despesas familares 93/94, Volume II, Resultados*. Macao.

Doling, Annabel (1995) *Macau on a Plate: A Culinary Journey*. Hong Kong: Roundhouse Publication (Asia).

Food and Agricultural Organisation (FAO) (1993) 'Compendium of Food Consumption Statistics from Household Survey in Developing Country, Volume 1 Asia', in *F.A.O. Economic and Social Development Papers* 116 (1).

Guldan, S. Georgia, Wendy Tao, Isabella Fung and Filomena Leung. (1994a) *Breakfast Eating Habits of Children in Hong Kong*. Hong Kong: Hong Kong Council of Early Childhood Education and Services.

Guldan, S. Georgia, Wendy Tao, Isabella Fung, Filomena Leung and Sophie Leung (1994b) *Eating Habits of Children in Hong Kong.* Hong Kong: Hong Kong Council of Early Childhood Education and Services.

Lam, Lai Sing (1997) *Generational Changes in the Cultural Attitudes and Activities of the People of Macau.* Macau: Instituto Cultural de Macau.

Raulin, Anne (1988) *Commerce, Consommation Ethnique et Relations Intercommunautaires.* Paris: Ministère de la Communication.

PART III

Globalization

Cuisine, Lifeways and Social Tastes

■ CHAPTER EIGHT ■

Heunggongyan Forever

Immigrant Life and Hong Kong Style
Yumcha in Australia

Siumi Maria Tam

Yumcha as a form of food consumption is popular in Sydney, Australia, among both Chinese and other ethnic groups. In particular Hong Kong Chinese immigrants who arrived in the last ten years are seen to be ardent supporters of the practice. They believe that authentic *yumcha* originated in Hong Kong, and are adamant that Hong Kong style *yumcha* is the best. Through patronage of restaurants that provide Hong Kong style *yumcha*, Hong Kong immigrants take part in the configuration of a Hong Kong outside Hong Kong and the construction of a *heunggongyan* (P: *xiang gang ren*, literally meaning 'Hong Kong people') identity. As *yumcha* epitomizes the Hong Kong lifestyle, *heunggongyan*'s participation in the activity helps to create and maintain a linkage with their place of origin. In the process a sense of a diasporic Hong Kong community in Sydney is constructed and reconfirmed, and a *heunggongyan* identity put into everyday praxis. As a result, *heunggongyan* as a local identity spreads from Hong Kong to Sydney, just as it has spread to other parts of the world where Hong Kong people immigrate. Such globalization of local identity centres around Hong Kong the parent culture which is characterized as inclusive, open to change, inventive, and sophisticated – in other words, a metropolitan culture that prizes diversity, syncretism and adaptability. Ironically, in the process of globalization, the metropolitan Hong Kong identity transforms into an exclusive and enduring tradition to be preserved and guarded by an immigrant community that seeks to dispel a sense of insecurity, alienation and displacement.

In this chapter I examine the practice known as *yumcha*, as well as its various offshoots, against the backdrop of immigrant life for Hong Kong families in Sydney. The study is based on ethnographic fieldwork conducted between July 1996 and July 1997.[1] Observations were done in Chinese restaurants mainly in metropolitan Sydney. I also interviewed Hong Kong immigrants, most of whom arrived after 1990, and took part in their family activities. Cantonese dotted with English as the lingua franca of Hong Kong immigrants was used throughout interviews. As such I felt that transliterations of Chinese terms would be more appropriately based on Cantonese than pinyin. Transliterations are indicated as Cantonese by (C) using Yale Romanization, and followed by a pinyin transliteration in parenthesis when a special term first appears in the text, which is indicated by (P). Certain terminologies however will follow the conventional usage in order not to confuse the reader. These include place names such as 'Hong Kong' instead of Heunggong (C) or Xianggang (P), and accepted forms of usage such as *'yumcha'* instead of *yam chah* (C) or *yin cha* (P), and *'heunggongyan'* instead of *heung gong yahn* (C) or *xiang gang ren* (P).

Yumcha and Hong Kong people in Sydney

Sydney is a multiethnic city in multi-cultural Australia. Albeit criticized as superficial and hypocritical, there is a general attitude that the existence of foreign (read: non-English) cuisines is a manifestation of a successful state policy encouraging multiculturalism. Consuming foreign foods is seen to be an act of inclusivity, liberal-mindedness and acceptance of these cultures themselves into Australian life (see for example Australian Women's Weekly n.d.). As a foreign cuisine, Chinese food has been popular and the Chinese people have been accepted as part of the ethnoscape in Sydney. Among the many types of Chinese food available in Sydney, *yumcha* is considered a representative form of Chinese cuisine. Indeed the difference between regional cuisines from China is seldom articulated among non-Chinese people. So while there are restaurants that specialize in regional cuisines such as Shanghainese and Pekingnese, to non-Chinese people they are all Chinese restaurants. As a matter of fact, these 'specialized' restaurants themselves contribute to the confusion because they emphasize their Hong Kong style *yumcha* service in addition to their own regional menu, even though they do not provide Cantonese dishes *per se* as main courses. This shows that Hong Kong style *yumcha* is the most popular and well-known form of Chinese food consumption among Chinese and non-Chinese alike.

A brief explanation of *yumcha* is in order here. *Yumcha* literally means 'drink tea'. The kinds of tea being consumed are categorically Chinese. Although many Hong Kong people drink 'red tea' (or 'Ceylon tea', such as English breakfast tea) and perfumed teas such as Earl Grey during tea breaks, *yumcha* typically never involves 'foreign' teas. The practice of *yumcha*, in addition, is not limited to just appreciating tea. *Yumcha*, as understood and practised by *heunggongyan*, involves food as a necessary component. The mainstay of Hong Kong style *yumcha* interestingly is not the tea that is drunk, but the food that is eaten. The food involves a wide variety of snack-size food items called *dimsum* (C: *dim sam*, P: *dian xin*).

Restaurateurs believe that there are over two hundred varieties of common *dimsum*. The types of tea consumed in *yumcha*, however, are very limited. Very often *yumcha* goers order one of the two most popular teas: *pou leih* (P: *pu er*) or *sauh meih* (P: *shou mei*). Since the focus of *yumcha* is to eat *dimsum*, the justification for drinking tea during *yumcha* is mainly to achieve a physical balance: because *dimsum* is usually fatty, drinking tea with it helps to neutralize the grease. In addition, the standard of *yumcha* at any restaurant is not judged by the quality of tea that is served, but the quality and variety of *dimsum*. Thus *yumcha* is a misnomer. It is not 'drink tea' *per se* that is practised, but 'eat *dimsum*'.

Although the emphasis on delicate *dimsum* is directly descended from its prototype Canton style *yumcha* (C: *gwong sik yum cha*, P: *guang shi yin cha*), Hong Kong style *yumcha* (C: *gong sik yum cha*, P: *gang shi yin cha*) has developed a distinct identity among southern Chinese cuisines (Chang 1977, Dak 1989, Hu n.d.). This identity today specifically incorporates a metropolitaneity that embraces a synthesis of 'Chinese tradition' vaguely defined, an international flavour characterized by syncretism, and a spirit to constantly invent new varieties of *dimsum*. This is expressed in popular discourse as a combination of the Chinese and the West: *jung sai gaau lauh* (in Cantonese; and P: *zhong xi jiao liu*, literally 'Chinese-western inter-flow') or *jung sai hahp bik* (P: *zhong xi he bi*, literally 'Chinese-western combined jade', implying a perfect fit of the two traditions). But, more importantly, consuming Hong Kong style *yumcha* is in line with a sense of superiority that arises from being *heunggongyan*. When asked what '*heunggongyan*' meant, most interviewees found it hard to verbalize a definition. But overwhelmingly the essence of Hong Kong's success boils down to the common folk's ability to integrate and make the best of what comes available, an ability that goes far beyond just a superficial mixture of Chinese and western traditions. Thus Hong Kong style adaptability is the hallmark of the *heunggongyan* identity, and the perseverance to put this into practice amidst unfavourable situations is what Hong Kong people proudly call the Hong Kong spirit (C: *heung gong jing sahn*, P: *xiang gang jing shen*). The *heunggongyan* identity is therefore a tapestry interwoven with Chinese and western components, but at the same time going beyond them to being truly international. The vibrancy of the *yumcha* setting, together with the inventive, transnational menu of *dimsum*, epitomizes its consciousness of metropolitaneity and its sense of cultural identity that recognizes, but strives to mature from, its Chinese roots (Tam 1997).

Hong Kong style *yumcha* is a relatively new phenomenon in Sydney. Informants who had been living in this city for more than a few years attested to the fact that *yumcha* had become readily available only in the previous two or three years. Rachel Lee[2] explained this to me while pointing to a row of Chinese restaurants in Castle Hill, a suburb where many Hong Kong immigrants reside. She was a Hong Kong woman who went to Sydney to study for her bachelor's degree in the late 1970s and had stayed on to start her family.

> These restaurants never offered *yumcha* a couple of years ago. You see the influence of *heunggongyan* [who came en masse in the early 1990s]. The new immigrants are wealthy. [Chinese] people who have been here for a long time are thriftier. They have to. They don't have any money to save. Their wages are so little, and tax is so heavy.

In other words, the pervasiveness of Hong Kong practices and customs has gathered significant momentum mainly after the most recent wave of Hong Kong diaspora as a result of the 1989 Tiananmen incident in Beijing. Typical of this wave of immigrants are middle-aged professionals and their children, who are relatively well off and well educated, and are often reluctant emigrants who have to make a lot of economic sacrifices for an Australian passport. They have brought with them a heavy demand for Hong Kong based popular culture including TV melodrama videotapes, weekly tabloids and women's fashion. Indeed every family member in the study had their favourite imports from Hong Kong. The children wanted Cass Pheng and Andy Lau CDs, pirated computer games and VCDs, and most recently electronic pets called tamagotchi. Adults frequented the suburb council libraries to read Hong Kong publications such as the *Eastern Daily*, *The Next Magazine* and Jin Rong's sword epic novels. They would have their hair done by Hong Kong hair-stylists and facial treatments by Hong Kong beauticians. Groceries, fish and meat came from shops with Hong Kong owners, and the family cars were serviced by mechanics from Hong Kong. Whether consciously or unconsciously, the consumption of Hong Kong popular culture and enactment of a Hong Kong lifestyle in a foreign country, combined to maintain a membership in a Hong Kong community. As individuals *heunggongyan* consumed these and many other products of a Hong Kong lifestyle for their everyday needs, and as a group they put their *heunggongyan* identity into practice in the regular ritual of Hong Kong style *yumcha*.

Continuity in discontinuity

A lot of Hong Kong immigrants found in *yumcha* the safe haven that provided the comfort of continuity in a social-cultural milieu of discontinuity in diaspora. Uncle Cheung, an elderly man who reluctantly emigrated with his son's family, remembered the days when he lamented the lack of *yumcha* restaurants (C: *chah lauh*,[3] P: *cha lou*):

> I didn't know where to go. I had nothing to do. After the young ones left for work or school, I was alone in the house. Yes, I could

take care of the garden and things like that, but what else could I do after that? I'd read the day's newspaper over and over again. Now it's better. I can go to *chah lauh*, have a cup of tea and chat, like I used to do in Hong Kong.

Obviously among the Chinese in Sydney, especially recent Hong Kong immigrants, *yumcha* had gone beyond simply being a form of public eating. It provided a familiar situation wherein one could find a sense of meaning in an isolated, alienated, and 'foreign' environment.[4] In Hong Kong, *yumcha* is also widely used as an opportunity to reinforce and renew social relations (Tam 1996). But among Hong Kong immigrants, the reinforcement and renewal of relationships among family, friends, ex-colleagues and ex-schoolmates assumed particular importance. This need arose from feelings of insecurity, alienation and displacement which were very much part of the process of migration.

The sense of insecurity manifested itself in various aspects of immigrant life. Recent Hong Kong immigrants who were mostly from middle class backgrounds were used to living in close proximity and high population density. For them, living in free-standing houses with their own backyards was a novelty as well as a sign of upward mobility. However, after the initial curiosity and sense of achievement were over, everyday life posed serious security problems. Smoke detectors, motion-sensing electronic alarm systems, front gates and garden fences were all new to *heunggongyan*. Especially for the so-called astronaut[5] families in which adult males continued to work in Hong Kong leaving the female-headed households living in Sydney, it was felt that safety was a most important issue. A large house that was impossible to secure entirely, and worry for the physical safety of women and children due to an absentee husband-father were two main sources of anxiety. A major means to tackle the problem of physical danger was to form a network of close friends who lived nearby. Indeed, knowing someone who spoke your language and understood your problems was essential to counteracting the sense of insecurity.

Hong Kong immigrants suffered from a sense of alienation that arose from a physical immobility and a lack of social interaction. A different sense of space and space organization created a sense of isolation for Hong Kong immigrants. The relative abundance of land in Sydney and the spread of residences over a large area caused the necessity to drive a car to go anywhere. Many informants talked of the driving test as a major hurdle to overcome in the initial stages of immigration. Coupled with an entirely different code of traffic conduct including English-only road signs and an inconvenient public transportation system, it was impossible to not go out of the house, but it was impossible to go out freely. *Heunggongyan* seemed to be caught in a double bind in mobility. Often the result was to avoid mobility to different degrees. Everyday mobility was limited to taking children to school, or, if possible, walking to the supermarket. Aside from physical isolation, social isolation was a serious problem in everyday life. Although most of the *heunggongyan* who were given residence status were screened for English ability, the typical *heunggongyan* did not feel comfortable communicating in English. Living among English-speaking neighbours and an English mass media all contributed to a tendency among immigrants to withdraw from mainstream Australian life. Many would listen only to Cantonese radio programmes run by Hong Kong immigrant based radio stations, and would only watch videotapes of Hong Kong movies and TV melodrama series. Often they lamented that if their English standards were higher they would be more active in Australian life. It was thus inevitable to feel physically isolated and threatened, socially aloof and lost, as *heunggongyan* were disconnected from social support networks and cultural symbols that they had grown up with.

In addition, a sense of displacement was keenly felt. Most immigrant families had sold their apartments in Hong Kong prior to departure for Australia. With the loss of this major personal property came a sense of exile because it had become impossible to return to Hong Kong if there was no guarantee of residence where real estate was a very expensive commodity. They also felt a cultural severance with Hong Kong when their children had become unwilling and/or unable to use the Chinese language. Returning to Hong Kong had become a more remote choice since the children would not be able to adapt to the Hong Kong education system. The idea of being culturally uprooted in one or two generations was most disturbing to first generation immigrants. Paul Wong, a middle-aged former high school teacher, said of his situation:

> My children won't go back to Hong Kong. They're studying here... If they go back they'll have to study at an international school. They can't go back to regular schools... I agree with what my neighbour (an elderly Caucasian woman) said. My generation finds it difficult to integrate, but in my sons' generation [assimilation] is already half-and-half. My grandchildren's generation? They'll be totally assimilated...
>
> When I first got here, it was very sad. I had no friends or relatives here. My wife had a former colleague who taught in the same school. He took us in, let us live in his house until we bought our own house. Through him we got to know Kevin, Mei-sheung, her brother-in-law, and his sister ... so it's all through friends' introductions, and the [Hong Kong University] alumni association...
>
> The older chambers of commerce, no, you can't get in. They have been here for decades. They have their own language and they keep to themselves.

The importance of networks of recent immigrants from Hong Kong could not be more strongly emphasized. First and foremost they acted as agents of adaptation. Polly Chan, a lawyer's wife whose husband kept his practice in Hong Kong, said of a similar experience, 'It was really the "brothers and sisters" [of my church group] who helped me survive in the first stage. They all immigrated here in the past five years or so. They helped me find a house, took me to church, and even bought groceries for me'. Interestingly, a major venue for meeting these agents of adaptation was overwhelmingly the Chinese restaurant. Many informants talked of bumping into high school friends, former colleagues, even relatives, when they went to *yumcha* on Sunday. Very often they did not even know that these people had immigrated to Australia, that is, their social ties had been remote in Hong Kong and were not defined as necessary. Once these connections were re-activated at *yumcha* restaurants in Sydney, many saw the need to maintain these ties now that they were in a foreign environment. And more often than not, these relationships were maintained through regular *yumcha* gatherings. In many ways *yumcha* offered a means of recapturing a communal feeling and a sense that one belonged to a community that welcomed one's membership. It was a convenient means too. Just by going to a *yumcha* restaurant they could re-immerse in a setting that was familiar, safe and secure, where they would surely run into someone they knew.

Culturally, *yumcha* was constructed in popular discourse as a legitimate manifestation of Hongkongness. The reasons were twofold. First, even before their emigration *yumcha* had been an activity that for Hong Kong Chinese was loaded with localized social symbols and was regularly practised. The resumption of a familiar practice in a foreign country helped to recover a life disjointed by emigration. Thus when gatherings for friends and relatives were organized, the most frequent suggestion was to meet at a Chinese restaurant for *yumcha*. Second, as the larger society had accepted Hong Kong style *yumcha* as the representative of Chinese food, it became easy for Hong Kong Chinese to ascribe *yumcha* with an elevated status in the immigrant-host relationship in which they acted as cultural agents. When a Chinese meal was suggested for lunch, Hong Kong immigrants often invited colleagues to *yumcha*, which helped to explain the numerous tables of mixed ethnic groups in *yumcha* restaurants downtown. *Yumcha* had obviously become an integral part of the Hong Kong immigrants' attempt to identify themselves with their Hong Kong home, and an effective means to rekindle the candle of rootedness which was gradually going out both for themselves and for their children. Thus for many Hong Kong immigrants especially those who emigrated after 1990, Hong Kong style *yumcha* had become the archetypal institution that re-created for them a Hong Kong outside of Hong Kong. As such it helped to globalize the local identity of *heunggongyan* as the Hong Kong diaspora spread to this part of the world.

137

I must hasten to add that the immigration experience is certainly a much more complex process, and the unintended consequences are many and varied. Indeed for most of my informants, the decision to emigrate was a complicated one, and the process of adapting to the host country was doubly difficult. Many of them recalled moments of regret, especially when they came into contact with complicated bureaucratic procedures in government offices and 'strange habits and customs of the Australians' in their daily life. Familiar things were undoubtedly sources of comfort amidst a socio-cultural environment perceived as unfriendly at best and racist at worst.[6] This need, coupled with the relative economic affluence of the new immigrants, gradually created a market over the years in which Hong Kong style commodities of all kinds were imported or locally produced, and popularly consumed. This market had so developed that as a newcomer to Sydney in 1996, my real culture shock came from the proliferation of Hong Kong things in this city down-under. Chinese grocery stores and video rental shops not only numerously and prominently occupied Chinatown and its periphery, but also conspicuously permeated suburbs where Hong Kong immigrants congregated. There were local public schools in which Hong Kong children were numerous and Cantonese had become the *de facto* second language. There were churches that provided Cantonese services attended solely by Hong Kong immigrants and weekend Chinese schools that used Cantonese as the medium of teaching, not to mention the real estate advertisements in newspapers presented in typical Hong Kong Chinese usage, the Toyota commercials in Cantonese played daily on TV, and a proliferation of Chinese weekly magazines available in suburban news agencies. These and many other exhibitions of continuity of the Hong Kong lifestyle and values had become part of the cultural landscape, albeit heavily concentrated in pockets of metropolitan Sydney. It was on the basis of these that Hong Kong Chinese immigrants constructed a sense of familiarity, tradition and a pride that they associated with *heunggongyan* identity.

'Everyday *yumcha*' and Hongkongness

Given the importance of *yumcha* as a Hong Kong Chinese group activity, it came as no surprise to find *yumcha* being the most frequently used index for Cantonese restaurants listed in the Chinese Gold Pages Sydney (Tu 1997), a bilingual yellow page business guide that had a distribution of over 30,000. KY Restaurant was one of the 381 restaurants listed in the guide. It was a small restaurant located in Epping, one of the North Shore suburbs that could be characterized as quiet, white-collar, middle class and young-to-middle aged. I arrived at the restaurant looking for 'Chinese-Malaysian cuisine' as that was how it described itself on the business card, only to find four big Chinese characters posted on its front door – *tin tin chah sih*, meaning 'everyday tea market' (P: *tian tian cha shi*). Each fifteen inches tall and written in black ink with a Chinese calligraphy brush, the characters commanded immediate attention from passers-by. Obviously the restaurant wanted attention from those who could read Chinese, in particular from their potential customers – the Chinese from Hong Kong. 'Every day tea market' is a Hong Kong usage that does not mean the tea trade but rather 'every day *yumcha* service.' It did not take long to find out that Hong Kong immigrants had congregated in this and surrounding suburbs and they needed a *yumcha* restaurant. The owner of the restaurant had shifted his marketing strategy from one offering only noodles and rice porridge during lunch to that of *yumcha*, while the Malaysian part of the menu had dwindled to a few vermicelli dishes. As mentioned in the above section, *yumcha* had as its main clientele the relatively well off recent Hong Kong immigrants, and observations of *yumcha* patrons in KY Restaurant pointed out that it was in fact the case. Many of the customers came as couples or couples with children, bringing with them Chinese newspapers and magazines to read at the table. The presence of men of working age eating as part of a family on a weekday was conspicuous, and my hunch was these were either 'astronaut husbands' coming to visit, or were immigrants who were unable to find a job in the sluggish Australian economy.

Much of what could be observed in this restaurant was very common not only among restaurants in Sydney, but also in other cities such as Brisbane and Melbourne where Chinese immigrants had chosen to settle. From the arrangement of space and the variety of food, to the dress code of waiters and their way of service, all reminded the customers that it was an imitation of the Hong Kong style. In terms of the menu, the *dimsum* available were many and varied, but none the less expected: from *ha gaau* (shrimp dumplings), *siu maaih* (pork balls), *laahp cheuhng gyun* (sausage roll), to *cha siu baau* (roast pork buns). Trays of familiar kinds of *dimsum* served on small plates or bamboo baskets were brought out steaming hot from the kitchen. As in Hong Kong, tables were so closely placed that one could not get up from the table without the back of the chair hitting someone else's at the next table. I would have thought that space was not a concern in Australia and that rent was relatively cheap. The popularity of *yumcha* would partly explain this over-utilization of space, but perhaps more importantly it reflected a consciousness of how space ought to be organized for *yumcha* – if tables were placed too far apart, it was not the *yumcha* way. Then there was the din made up of spoons hitting rice bowls and people trying to out-yell the others that provided the background for the aptly named 'everyday tea market'. Female waiters dressed in white shirts and black skirts were ever busy yelling out names of the *dimsum* they carried. They were also busy convincing customers that the *dimsum* was delicious, and then putting a coloured stamp on the food record sheets for every dish they sold. Male waiters in white shirts and black trousers squeezed between tables, adding boiling water to teapots at each table and taking orders in Chinese. It was the physical overcrowding and the ultra-hectic organization of social space that was the proper setting for authentic *yumcha*.

With a greater intensity the *yumcha* brunch on Sunday resembled even more closely its prototype in Hong Kong. As in Hong Kong, one needed to be at the restaurant at least an hour before in order to get a table, that is, *to wan waih* (literally to 'find a seat'). So as soon as one entered a restaurant, rows of chairs with customers waiting impatiently were the usual sight, making a most busy, bustling Australian scene, just as in Hong Kong. Even class relations and ethnic divisions on the shopfloor seemed to have been transplanted. In Hong Kong, many of the minor staff were recent immigrants from mainland China. Similarly, in Sydney, those who carried *dimsum* trays were mainland Chinese. Thus whether in space, form and structure, *yumcha* here unmistakably resembled the Hong Kong genre.

The difference between Hong Kong and Sydney could be observed in the availability and use of *yumcha*. *Yumcha* in Sydney started every day at around 11 a.m. and finished at around 3 p.m. There was no 'morning market' (C: *jou sih*, P: *zhao shi*) nor 'evening market' (C: *yeh sih*, P: *ye shi*) for *yumcha*. In other words, *yumcha* was only offered during lunch time. In Hong Kong *yumcha* was available in different time slots – morning, noon, afternoon and night. One could therefore *yum* morning *cha*, *yum* afternoon *cha*, or *yum* night *cha* as well as *yumcha* for lunch. While morning tea and afternoon tea implied a relaxed and leisurely enjoyment, with the intention to chat, take a break or meet up with friends, the practice of *yumcha* for lunch as a meal pointed to a hurriedness for time and the purposefulness of filling the stomach. But, in Sydney, as restaurateurs observed, older folks from Hong Kong seldom knew how to drive, so their mobility was severely limited. Unlike their counterparts in Hong Kong who almost monopolized the morning 'tea market', for the elderly here *yum joh cha* ('drink morning tea') remained wishful thinking. For similar reasons, *yum hah ngh cha* ('drink afternoon tea') was not popular. To *heunggongyan*, then, whether in Sydney or Hong Kong, *yumcha* during weekdays was treated as a form of meal, as a lighter alternative to a full meal with rice (C: *faahn*, P: *fan*) and meat/vegetable dishes (C: *sung*, P: *cai*), and a preferred option to a *gwai lou*[7] diet of hamburgers, chips and sandwiches. Thus in Sydney where *yumcha* was available to the entire family only on Saturday and Sunday, or 'family days', *yumcha* had become almost synonymous with family gathering.

Perhaps *yumcha* as a specifically Hong Kong practice with a distinct Hong Kong definition could best be understood when contrasted to 'not *yumcha*'. On the periphery of Chinatown, an old, small two-storeyed house at a busy street corner proudly displayed the sign *joai yam chah* (C) in Chinese characters, written in coloured chalk on a piece of slate on the sidewalk. *Jaai yam chah* (P: *zhai yin cha*) literally means 'vegetarian *yumcha*' because in Cantonese, *jaai* means vegetarian. But it could be extended to mean 'just', 'only' or 'nothing else'. Thus one could call plain noodles *jaai mihn* and plain rice congee *jaai juk*. The word *jaai* here was obviously a pun. On the one hand it stressed the fact that the restaurant was a *jaai* 'vegetarian' restaurant, and at the same time it served *jaai* 'only' *yumcha* and no à la carte menu. On the other hand it implied that *jaai* 'pure' *yumcha* was served, with no artificial additions and preservatives, etc. and was therefore healthy.

The fact that a chalk-and-slate board was used to announce its cuisine gave away the 'unauthenticness' of the restaurant, because as a practice coloured chalk on slate was used by western restaurants in Sydney, while plastic signs were popular with Chinese restaurants. Indeed as I arrived on the second floor of this restaurant I doubted if I really was in a *yumcha* restaurant. I found myself in a hall with no golden dragon motifs on red wallpaper, no red lanterns and no crimson carpet. The furniture consisted of plain black wooden tables and pine folding chairs. Green paint and hemp lampshades dominated the walls, and the wooden floor was a hard, cold black colour. Wooden stems of birds of paradise occupied bamboo vases, while wooden busts of the Buddha smiled kindly on the customers. The dining hall thus created a sense of tranquility, which was a sharp contrast to the joviality expected of Chinese *yumcha*. Imitations of elements of *yumcha* were obvious, such as food record sheets and bamboo *dimsum* baskets, but at the same time adaptations to Sydney customs abounded. Carrying *dimsum* trays around the restaurant were young female staff. But instead of more formal shirt and suit uniform, they were wearing white T-shirts, black jeans, black aprons and black sneakers. If the entire atmosphere was to conjure up a new-age image, then observation pointed to a clientele consistent with this intention as most of the twenty plus customers could be categorized as yuppie business people or young hippie families. Customers and staff alike spoke in a whisper; and there was no banging of spoons against bowls and teacups, no yelling out *dimsum* names. If anything resembled *yumcha*, it was the existence of a variety of *dimsum*. A casual tabulation showed at least 28 vegetarian varieties, including vegetarian versions of *ha gaau*, *siu maaih*, *cha siu baau* and *ngauk yuhk cheuhng fan* (beef wrapped in steamed rice sheets) and so on, as well as miniature vegetarian dishes like cabbage rolls with black moss and mushrooms. Though the restaurant called itself *yumcha*, it was anything but *yumcha*. In terms of food, setting, staff and customer behaviour, it was the diametrical opposite of Hong Kong style *yumcha*. Not surprisingly, I seemed to be the only *heunggongyan* customer there on that day. While all other *yumcha* restaurants in Chinatown were full to the

141

brim, this restaurant remained unattractive to *heunggongyàn* who would find it difficult to define '*jaai yam chah*' as authentic *yumcha* or to identify themselves with it.

Immigrant life and Hong Kong identity

Certainly to different people the term *heunggongyan* means different things and it should be more appropriate to say that there are many *heunggongyan* identities rather than one *heunggongyan* identity (Evans and Tam 1997). But among my interviewees it was clear that being *heunggongyan* was 'forever' and the identity was something that, as one informant described it, 'could not be washed off' no matter where one emigrated or for how long. The two most frequently mentioned 'characteristics' of *heunggongyan* were adaptability and metropolitaneity. Although interviewees seldom emphasized it, they did allude to the fact that most Hong Kong people are immigrants from the mainland or are their descendants who have been affected by the political upheavals in contemporary Chinese history. This common experience in first adverse conditions, and then in the social and economic development in the 1960s and 1970s, contributed much to the high value placed on the ability to adapt. The economic success in the 1980s and 1990s that Hong Kong as a society has enjoyed greatly enhanced the popular belief that, because of the very hardworking and versatile population of Hong Kong, the city has matured as a metropolis not only in the Asian region but also in the world. Such sense of pride and identity as part of this socio-economic miracle has acquired a mythical aura in the Hong Kong ethos. In effect, then, the identity of *heunggongyan* as a separate group of Chinese was built up in the past 50 years, congealed around the mythical Hong Kong spirit. To the diasporic community in Sydney, a *heunggongyan* community marked by adaptability and metropolitaneity certainly existed. It may be partly imagined but it was real to its members, yet simultaneously it was contingent and ready to be negotiated. This was evidenced by the fact that among the numerous Chinese associations in Sydney, there was no Hong Kong Association. In contrast to associations such as the Chinese Australian Services Society which aimed to help Chinese immigrants from mainland China, and the New South Wales Indo-China Chinese Association that served those from Vietnam, Cambodia and Laos, there was no 'Hong Kong Chinese Association' that aimed to service Hong Kong immigrants. The non-existence of such a Hong Kong association attested to the fact that the geographical boundary of the place of origin as a basis for communitas was not considered important. Leslie Ho, an immigrant of five years, once worked as a volunteer in a free information service for immigrants run by the local council. He said,

> We were a multi-ethnic team [in the service]. There was a Greek guy who provided service to the Greeks, a Lebanese who helped to answer Lebanese immigrants' questions, and so on. And I was responsible for Hong Kong people. But I was bored to death! I played chess all day at the Centre. No one came to ask me anything. [It's because] Hong Kong people knew everything already. They're too smart, or they just ask their friends, who are often able to help. And they're rich. They don't want to use this kind of service [which makes them look like they're pitiable].

The non-participation of Hong Kong immigrants in these immigrant-oriented activities, however, did not mean that they did not need social networks beyond friends and relatives. Membership in traditionally important associations such as *tuhng heung wui* ('fellow hometowners associations', P: *tong xiang hui*) and *seung wui* ('chambers of commerce', P: *shang hui*) were perceived as inappropriate by recent immigrants. While the former had provided for the financial, material, educational and emotional needs of Chinese overseas for many generations and fulfilled a largely welfare role, *heunggongyan* did not regard themselves as the needy that these *tuhng heung wui* should assist. For the newly immigrated business people, the chambers of commerce had become a closed network monopolized by the *suk fuh* (P: *shu fu*) or 'elders' who had been in Sydney for well over twenty years or even generations. They found that as newcomers they were unable to break into these established systems, and therefore proceeded to form their own connections. To fulfil their networking needs *heunggongyan* decided to organize new associations based on former elite memberships that were Hong Kong specific. These included university alumni associations such as the Chinese University of Hong Kong Alumni Association and the Hong Kong University Alumni Association, and secondary school associations such as the Hong Kong Wah Yan College Alumni Association and Queen Elizabeth Secondary School Alumni Association. These new, exclusive networks based on a common social background have clearly replaced the *tuhng heung wui* whose membership is based on place of origin and is inclusive of people from various class backgrounds. One of the main aims of these associations of Hong Kong people was to organize social activities such as fishing trips and annual dinners for their members, thereby maintaining contact and a sense of belonging. In addition, instead of providing welfare services to their own members, these groups volunteered service to others whom they considered less fortunate, such as the aged and mentally challenged. And interestingly when *heunggongyan* were involved in region-based associations such as *tuhng heung wui*, they were typically the service providers, often acting as Executive Committee members, professional social workers, counsellors or volunteers. So while on the one hand Hong Kong immigrants adapted to

143

the new socio-cultural environment of the host society by building their own networks, on the other hand they promoted a metropolitan hierarchy of community memberships which fitted well with their sense of superiority.

Contrary to this superiority complex, a sense of loss constituted an important part of the adaptability and metropolitaneity of Hong Kong immigrants. Patrick Lam settled in Sydney under the skilled migrant category and had been working in the local government. He was active in the Australian Chinese Community Association for a while as an executive committee member. Disgruntled as a result of lack of job satisfaction, coupled with being rejected to 'join the club' of old timers, Patrick was contemplating returning to Hong Kong after five years of immigrant life. Although a former colleague in a Hong Kong firm had offered him a two-year contract, he was worried about re-adapting to the workplace in Hong Kong. He rationalized his situation in the following way:

> Peter (Patrick's eldest son) will not be able to go to a regular school [in Hong Kong]. He's too slow. Kids here are so slow! They think and write slower than Hong Kong kids. Especially mathematics. Math is so backward here, but it is an important subject. Kids from Hong Kong are good in math, and so they succeed in school here. I think Peter should go to Hong Kong so he gets used to the speed and competition. It will help him in his future. Here in Australia people have no future. The economy has no future because there is no sense of competition. In the workplace, everybody just wastes away their time. In Hong Kong [with this attitude] you won't be able to *wan sihk* (literally 'get food', meaning to make a living).

Patrick did not speak directly of his worry for himself. His concern for his sons really reflected his anxiety and uncertainty because he had been away from the job market in Hong Kong for so long. He was conscious that he might have lost some of the competitiveness that could make him successful. This sense of competitiveness was valued by most parents from Hong Kong even if they were not returning to Hong Kong. In fact Patrick's son Peter was attending a highly competitive primary school. The school was reputed for its heavy load of homework and projects, frequent dictation and tests, high incidence of private tuition, and parental anxiety. Judging by the Asian faces in class photos, it could be safely estimated that about two-thirds of the school's students were of Asian origin, and Hong Kong students were a highly salient group among them. From talking to parents from Hong Kong, I found that the children were sent to the school precisely because of its high level of competition. An incident at the Parents and Citizens Association meeting illustrated this mentality well. The new principal opined that it was unhealthy as well as unnecessary for teachers to be still working in their office at 6 p.m. when school was over at 3 p.m. He proposed to decrease the amount of schoolwork so that both children and teachers could be more relaxed. This met with overwhelming opposition from the parents. Rachel, whose children were also going to this school, commented on the incident:

> The parents send their children there because of the schoolwork and the hope that this will lead to entry to a selective high school. Of course we disagree with the proposal. Some people do not like the competition. They are mainly *gwai lou*. I know a *gwai lou* who transferred his son to another school because he didn't like the competition in our school. We [Hong Kong] parents are very anxious. We even think the work they give at school is not enough. We give our children extra exercises, and take them to private tuition and mental training classes. Sometimes I think it's the parents and not the children who are tense and who are really doing the work.

In fact the main reason Rachel and her husband moved to this suburb was because they wanted their children to study in this school. Together with the other 'anxious' parents, they voted down the principal's proposals to change. Perhaps the sense of competition that formed such an important part of the Hong Kong ethos had a part to play in how this primary school in Sydney was run.

I joined Rachel's family for a *yumcha* lunch one Sunday. It was a very crowded restaurant in Castle Hill. The '*tin tin chah sih*' (every day *yumcha*) characters were prominently displayed on the glass panel at the shop front. We were greeted at the entrance by a female staff member dressed in red and gold *cheuhng saam* ('traditional' Chinese dress, P: *chi pao*). After squeezing ourselves through the maze of tables and toddlers running around them, we settled into a large table which Rachel's husband had *ba waih* (literally 'occupy seat') for 45 minutes. At the table were Rachel's husband's sister Jackie and her two children. Jackie was introduced as an 'astronaut' whose husband remained in Hong Kong in order to keep his well-paid job as a physician. There were also Anita, Jackie's husband's sister, and her only son with whom she lived as an 'astronaut household'. We were joined by Anita's husband Ronald who had come for a six-week stay. He was a secondary school teacher in Hong Kong, and was able to stay longer this time because it was summer vacation in Hong Kong. The *yumcha* gathering was in fact a farewell party for Ronald as he was due to return to Hong Kong in a few days' time. There was a lot of polite talk at the table and ordering *dimsum* in between, all yelled above the din in the restaurant. When lunch was over and the men were scrambling for the bill, Rachel casually asked Jackie if her husband could bring a set of mathematics textbooks from Hong Kong when he visited Sydney the following week. Rachel explained her request: 'the children must do more

145

math exercises. There's not enough from the school'. Jackie promptly agreed. Rachel then added, 'When your husband comes, I must take him to *yumcha*.'

Hongkongness: Keep Frozen

Yumcha has played an important part in preserving Hong Kong identity for immigrants. But though Sydney has reputedly the best and the most *yumcha* restaurants in Australia, *yumcha* has obviously spread to other parts of Australia. My first encounter with *yumcha* was in Tasmania. I was part of a local tour group. The tour bus pulled over at a cafeteria style eatery some two kilometres from the historic site of Port Arthur, where we were told to buy our own lunch. Everybody decided to try some of the famous crayfish, but my eyes caught sight of something in a metal serving tray, which suspiciously resembled *siu maaih*. *Siu maaih* is of course one of the core *dimsum* in Hong Kong style *yumcha*, and a good one should have a thin egg and flour wrapping filled with tender minced pork, steamed until just cooked. The more upmarket versions may have dried mushrooms, scallops or crab roe in them. I looked up at the plastic illuminated menu board: 'Dimsims $1'. I looked at the 'dimsim' again: they were deep-fried and four times the size of regular *siu maaih*. They were not served as four pieces together in a steaming hot basket, but rather served as a single piece, and looked as cold and hard as food models of tempura vegetables outside Japanese restaurants. It was intriguing that a common Hong Kong *dimsum* could turn up in Tasmania in this corrupted form. I ventured to ask the Caucasian staff who looked quite Aussie-style friendly: 'So what is inside dimsims?' I remember being given a rather surprised look, and after a few seconds the woman said with a shrug, 'Well, you never know what's in a dimsim'. I was holding up the line of diners and the conversation conveniently stopped. I did not find out what was inside the dimsim.

On another occasion, I was having lunch at the Union Cafeteria at the Macquarie University in Sydney. The venue was designed like a shopping mall food court which had an international theme with various sections serving different cuisines. I was following the line at the section called 'Mac Wok' that sold Chinese fast food. There they were again, 'dimsims' and cost A$1.20 a piece. This time the student-cum-partime-worker told me the filling was pork and chicken, and they 'should be pretty good'. Won over by ethnographic curiosity, I bought a dimsim and began to examine it sitting squarely on my plate. I had one bite. I still did not know what was inside a dimsim. Later I discovered that dimsim was in fact a common snack in Sydney. It was readily available as an instant food in supermarkets' frozen foods section, and could be ready in a few minutes by deep-frying. Boxes of dimsim were conspicuously displayed in chain supermarkets such as Franklins, Woolworths and Coles. It was a good example of the localization of Chinese *dimsum* in Australia where steaming was not a common practice in everyday cooking but deep-frying was. Since portions of food were generally bigger in Australian cuisine compared to Chinese, the size of the dimsim was much bigger, and served singly. I asked my interviewees if they knew what dimsim was, and answers ranged from 'no idea at all' to 'a *gwai lou siu maaih*.' Obviously dimsim was not part of Hong Kong immigrants' regular menu, and it certainly did not exist in Hong Kong style *yumcha* restaurants.

While giving a seminar[8] at the University of Queensland I brought up this question of what dimsim was. Professor Cheung Chiu Yee pointed out that dimsim might actually be *dimsum* pronounced in the Sei Yap dialect (P: *Ci yi*, an area in Guangdong Province which historically exported many labourers to Australia). He proposed that since there were many Sei Yap males among the first waves of immigrant labourers who took part in the gold rush, *dimsum* may have been brought to Australia at that time. It then dawned on me that I was sampling something brought over from Guangdong in the nineteenth century. I recalled images of early Chinese immigrants in Australia among whom old customs, practices, dialects and tastes of food and aesthetics were faithfully frozen.[9] I wondered if the *siu maaih* then was bigger in order to cater for the labourers' caloric needs, or whether it was the other way round – that rather *siu maaih* was delicatized in the twentieth century?[10] Globalization of Chinese food certainly started well before the Hong Kong diaspora, and the transformation of *siu maaih* in Australia would attest to it. However, the fact that dimsim was not considered *dimsum* and not consumed at all in *yumcha* by Hong Kong immigrants today, showed at least that *yumcha* as defined and practised by *heunggongyan* in Sydney did not accept a 'foreignized' dimsim to be authentic *yumcha* food. What *heunggongyan* in Sydney looked for in *dimsum* was familiarity in form and taste, and not inventiveness and exoticism. Indeed, *heunggongyan* were trying to keep *yumcha* frozen in the particular form and structure, acquired at a time that they considered the golden era of their life – in Hong Kong.

And literally *yumcha* was, in frozen form, ready for purchase in grocery stores. The variety of frozen *dimsum* closely resembled what was available in *yumcha* restaurants, and they occupied a sizable portion of the freezers in grocery stores owned by Chinese and non-Chinese alike. The range of choices was impressive. A casual survey at a Chinese grocery in Eastwood (a suburb where many Chinese and Koreans reside) showed that except for the conspicuous exclusion of dimsim, there were more than 20 different kinds of frozen *dimsum*. These included such core varieties as *siu maaih, ha gaau, fuhng jaau* (P: *feng juo*, literally 'phoenix claw', which are chicken feet), *saan juk ngauh yuhk* (P: *shan ju niu rou*, minced beef with beancurd sheets) and *cheun gyun* (P: *chuen juan*, commonly translated as spring roll, which are shredded pork and mixed vegetables in rice wrapping). There was also an array of steamed buns with different fillings: *cha siu bau* (P: *cha shao bao*, roast pork filling), *naaih wohng baau* (P: *nai huang baau*, duck eggs and custard filling), *mah yuhng baau* (P: *ma rong bao*, sesame paste filling) and *lihn yuhng baau* (P: *lian rong bao*, lotus seed paste filling). To further the list, there were *loh baahk gou* (P: *luo buo gao*, white turnip cake with mixed preserved meats), *jan jyu gai* (P: *zhen zhu ji*, literally 'pearl chicken', a mini-sized dumpling with chicken and rice wrapped in lotus leaves), and *noh maih gai* (P: *nuo mi ji*, glutinous rice stuffed with chunks of chicken, salted egg yolks and dried mushrooms, wrapped in a large sheet of lotus leaf). Sweet frozen *dimsum* included *tong yun* (P: *tang yuan*, glutinous rice balls with fillings such as peanuts, black sesame or lotus seed paste) and *mah laai gou* (P: *ma la gao*, literally 'Malay cake', a steamed raised cake). Frozen deep-fried *dimsum* included *ha do sih* (P: *xia duo shi*, literally 'shrimp toast', shrimp paste on toast sprinkled with sesame seeds), *ga lei gok* (P: *jia li jiao*, curry puffs with beef and onion filling), *siu hau jou* (P: *xiao kou ju*, literally 'laughing date', a crispy cookie that breaks open during frying).

The above list obviously was rather short compared to the number of *dimsum* available in *yumcha* restaurants, but surely most of what could be frozen and conveniently heated up in the microwave was there. Like their counterparts in restaurants, the size, filling, as well as presentation of frozen *dimsum* closely imitated their prototypes in Hong Kong. Undoubtedly these 'oven ready appetisers' tried their best to conjure up the authenticity of Hong Kong style *yumcha* with its red packaging and a decidedly Cantonese brand called Ho Mai, or 'good taste'. Their authenticity was further reinforced by Chinese characters prominently displayed on all six sides of the box. It seemed Hong Kong style *yumcha* had been frozen and transplanted here lock, stock and barrel. The only difference was, as the boldface words on the packet: KEEP FROZEN indicated, the *heunggongyan* who consumed this *dimsum* would be relating themselves to a culture that they were fiercely proud of yet reluctantly severed from, in a form that they remembered and kept frozen in time. Frozen *dimsum* allowed *heunggongyan* in Sydney to freeze, retrieve and consume their Hongkongness at their convenience; though the atmosphere at home is far removed from that in a *yumcha* restaurant and is not preferred.

The complexity of a diasporic psychology was salient in a metropolis such as Sydney, with the Australian government's official multiculturalism policy an everyday euphemism. Even in the frozen foods section of Sydney's chain supermarkets, the multicultural analogy was obvious: bright-red packets of ready-to-eat *dimsum* sat comfortably next to red, white and green boxes of Papa Giuseppi's pizza. Beside them were Sara Lee's carrot cake, Big Ben's Mexican mild lamb and curried rice dinner, Nanna's apple pie, Maggi's satay chicken, Sargent's meat pie and Lean Cuisine's French seafood dinner, and so on. Such a vivid display of multicultural culinary harmony projected a mixed milieu in which ethnic identities must be constantly characterized, essentialized and authenticated to prevent themselves from being eroded and assimilated. To preserve their *heunggongyan* identity, immigrants from Hong Kong would need to preserve the important identity marker of *yumcha* together with all its characteristic components of form, space and structure. In so doing, the inventiveness, inclusiveness and willingness to change that were indices of a global, metropolitan *heunggongyan* identity were suppressed to give way to a constructed tradition.

Conclusion

In this chapter I have briefly traced the kinds of eating practices related to *yumcha* that could be observed in Sydney. It was particularly intriguing to find that *yumcha* as an identification with Hong Kong culture had its nature almost reversed. Metropolitaneity was obvious in Hong Kong's *yumcha* genre, manifested particularly in the form and content of *dimsum*. In a different paper (Tam 1996) I cited the example of a restaurant in Ma On Shan, Hong Kong, and illustrated with its 60 item *dimsum* order sheet the inclusiveness and inventiveness that came to characterize the Hong Kong spirit. It was the willingness to change and adapt that were emphasized. In Sydney's scenario, it was the traditional and the familiar that were stressed. The authenticity of Hong Kong culture as lived through the consumption of *dimsum*, whether frozen or steaming hot, seemed to provide the emotional stability and the networks that were craved in immigrant life – as a balance against uncertainty, alienation and displacement – in short, a reassurance that one was still rooted in the great metropolis of Hong Kong.

Notes

1 Materials on *yumcha* in Hong Kong are based on findings from the project 'Cooking up Hong Kong Identity: A Study of Food Culture, Changing Tastes and Identity in Popular Discourse' funded by an RGC Earmarked Grant.

2 All names of informants are pseudonyms to ensure privacy.

3 *Chah lauh* (P: *cha lou*, literally 'tea house'), has been one of the major kinds of Chinese eateries where tea and food are served. It is distinguished from *chah sat* (P: *cha shi*, 'tea room') and *chah geui* (P: *cha ju*, 'tea home') which are smaller in scale and emphasize the quality of tea rather than that of food, and they generally do not serve meals. *Chah lauh* is also different from *jau lauh* (P: *jiu luo*, wine house) which caters for banquets and serves alcohol (C: *jau*, P: *jiu*). Today, many *chah lauh*, *chah sat* and *chah geui* have been demolished and substituted with the more general-purpose *jau lauh*. However, *chah lauh* has been so closely related to *yumcha* that whenever *yumcha* is intended, people say 'let's go to *chah lauh*' no matter which kind of Chinese eatery they are really going to.

4 Most of my informants considered all non-Chinese as 'foreign' people and Australia a 'foreign' country, even though they were officially permanent

residents and citizens of Australia. Thus it was an ethnic boundary built on cultural differences rather than nationality. For discusssions of symbolisms and national identities in food consumption see Douglas (1972), Appadurai (1988), Watson (1997), Mintz (1996), and Counihan and Esterik (1997).

5 Husbands who travel to the host country where their wives and children are staying as immigrants are dubbed 'astronauts'. The word astronaut in Cantonese is *tai hung yahn* (P: *tai kung ren*), or space person, which aptly describes the husbands' life of shuttling to and from Hong Kong several times a year. The three Chinese characters understood separately have another meaning, which is 'wife empty person', as their wives are absent from the original household in Hong Kong. Their families in the host country, now headed by the wife, are called astronaut families. Increasingly, however, the wives have come to be called astronauts, partly as a short form for astronaut families, partly for want of a comparable term for the astronaut husbands, and also partly because the three Chinese characters can be given a third meaning – 'too empty person', which sums up the loneliness of the astronaut wife.

6 The racism issue was widely discussed by politicians and non-politicians alike since September 1996, after the inaugural speech of Pauline Hanson, an independent member of parliament, in which she promoted an anti-immigration and anti-Asian stand. Subsequent media frenzy, government responses and international concern all served to sustain a public interest in the so-called racism debate. Surveys done by the local media and by government bodies such as the Tourism Board pointed to Australia being perceived as 'a racist society' by its Asian neighbours, and a survey by the Chinese newspaper Sing Tao revealed an increase in racist abuse experienced by Chinese in Australia. For a discussion of the historical changes in the social life of Chinese in Sydney see Fitzgerald (1997).

7 *Gwai lou*, literally ghost men, is a Cantonese term for westerners. Although it has been claimed that the pervasive use of the term itself has diffused the derogatory connotation and even westerners themselves have started to call themselves *gwai lou*, I am of the opinion that *gwai lou* is still very much a term that conjures up a hierarchical ethnic division in which Chinese call themselves *yahn* (human) as opposed to *gwai* (ghosts), thereby asserting their cultural superiority.

8 'Yumcha in Hong Kong: Constructed and Contested Identities', seminar given at University of Queensland, jointly organized by the Department of History, and Department of Sociology and Anthropology, October 1996.

9 Diana Giese (1997) reported in her book her Chinese informants' vivid description and photographs of such customs as the dragon dance, parades, and family gatherings practised in Chinese communities in Australia since their arrival in the nineteenth century.

10 In another paper 'Yumcha in Hong Kong' presented at the International Conference on Changing Diet and Foodways in Chinese Culture', June 1996, at the Chinese University of Hong Kong, I proposed that *dimsum* has been delicatized as part of the trend of internal involution in the practice of *yumcha* as a social institution.

References

Appadurai, Arjun (1988) 'How to Make a National Cuisine: Cookbooks in Contemporary India', *Comparative Study of Society and History*. 30 (1):3–24.

Australian Women's Weekly (n.d.) *Oriental Dinner Party Cookbook*. Sydney: Australian Consolidated Press.

Chang, Kwang-chi (ed.) (1977) *Food in Chinese Culture: Anthropological and Historical Perspectives*. New Haven: Yale University Press.

Counihan, Carole, and Penny Van Esterik (eds) (1997) *Food and Culture: A Reader*. New York and London: Routledge.

Dak, K.G.D. (1989) *The Roots of Cantonese Cuisine* (in Chinese). Hong Kong: Yam Sik Tin Deih.

Douglas, Mary (1972) 'Deciphering a Meal', *Daedalus*, 101:61–82.

Evans, Grant, and Maria Tam Siu-Mi (1997) 'Introduction: the anthropology of contemporary Hong Kong', in G. Evans and S. M. Tam (eds) *Hong Kong: The Anthropology of a Chinese Metropolis*, pp. 1–21. London: Curzon Press and Honolulu: University of Hawaii Press.

Fitzgerald, Shirley (1997) *Red Tape, Gold Scissors: the Story of Sydney's Chinese*. Sydney: State Library of New South Wales Press.

Giese, Diana (1997) *Astronauts, Lost Souls and Dragons*. Brisbane: University of Queensland Press.

Hu, T. L. (n.d.) *Irresistible Temptation: Gourmet Food from Hong Kong – yumcha* (in Chinese). New Women. Taipei.

Mintz, W. Sidney (1996) *Tasting Food, Tasting Freedom: Excursions into Eating, Culture and the Past*. Boston: Beacon Press.

Tam, Siumi Maria (1996) '*Yumcha* in Hong Kong', paper presented at the international Food Conference on Changing Diet and Foodways in Chinese Culture, The Chinese University of Hong Kong.

—— (1997) 'Eating Metropolitaneity: Hong Kong Identity in yumcha', in *The Australian Journal of Anthropology*, 8 (3):291–306.

Tu, Ben (ed.) (1997) *Chinese Gold Pages Sydney*. Sydney: Good Year Advertising & Promotion Pty Ltd.

Watson, L. James (ed.) (1997) *Golden Arches East: McDonald's in East Asia*. Stanford: Stanford University Press.

CHAPTER NINE

Chinese Dietary Culture in Indonesian Urban Society

Mely G. Tan

A discussion of Chinese dietary culture in Indonesian society requires an exposé of the ethnic Chinese people themselves, who were and still are the bearers of this culture. The history of the ethnic Chinese in Indonesia, and especially in Jakarta, dates back to the period prior to the colonization by the Dutch, which ended with the Proclamation of Independence of Indonesia on 17 August 1945. According to western and Chinese historical documents Chinese settlements already existed prior to the establishment of Jayakarta (in 1527), the local name of Jakarta before the Dutch (who arrived at the end of the sixteenth century and moved their base to this port city in 1618) changed it to Batavia, and the reference for the start of its recorded history. It is not intended in this chapter to go into the history of the ethnic Chinese in Indonesia. Suffice it to note that the Chinese have had a long and at times turbulent history in Indonesia and in Jakarta in particular (Mackie 1976; Coppel 1983; Suryadinata 1985; Blusse 1988; Williams 1996).

It is known through a wealth of literature that the Chinese have played, and continue to play, a crucial and decisive role in the economy of Indonesia (Robison 1986; Tan 1987; Yoshihara 1988; Schwarz 1994). Until recently about 70 per cent of the private sector economy was in the hands of ethnic Chinese entrepreneurs; they include some of the big businessmen referred to as *konglomerat* (conglomerates) by the Indonesian media. Some of them have become public figures, often featuring as 'cover men', decorating the slick economic and general affairs magazines published in Jakarta. To name those often in the news: Liem Sioe Liong (Lin Shaoliang) or Sudono Salim of the Salim Group of companies, reputed to be one of the wealthiest men in Asia; Eka Tjipta Widjaya (Oei Ek Tjhong or Huang Yicong) of the Sinar Group; Muhamad (Bob) Hassan (The Kian Seng or Zheng Jiansheng) of the Nusamba Group, and known for his control of the timber industry; Prajogo Pangestu (Phang Djun Phen or Peng Yunpeng) of the Barito Group; Mochtar Riady (Lee Mo Tie or Li Wenzheng) and son James Riady (Li Bai) of the Lippo Group (Suryadinata 1995). The latter in particular have been very much in the news internationally, especially in the United States, because of the alleged involvement of the Riady family in the fundraising efforts related to the election campaign of President Clinton.[1]

This media coverage of ethnic Chinese big businessmen has reinforced the still-existent stereotype of this group of people as extraordinarily wealthy, characterizing them as 'economic animals' only out to make a fast buck. As a matter of fact, the phenomenon of ethnic Chinese big businessmen became firmly established under President Suharto, whose government came to be known as the New Order government. This is related to the end of the government of President Sukarno, the first president of Indonesia, that started with the abortive coup of 30 September 1965. At the time of this serious political upheaval threatening the very existence of the nation, the economy was in a shambles with an inflation rate of 650 per cent. To remedy the situation one of the first acts of President Suharto, when he was installed as head of state to replace President Sukarno, was to open up the country for foreign investment (in 1967). A key stipulation was that these investments should be in the form of joint ventures with local business people, and those ready and equipped with the capital, know-how, experience and marketing networks to become a partner of the foreign investor were the ethnic Chinese entrepreneurs (Tan 1991). Thus, one might say, it is by default that these entrepreneurs acquired a head start over their ethnic Indonesian counterparts.

Strong ethnic Indonesian businessmen only began to appear in the late 1970s, some of whom continued the businesses founded by their fathers, for example, Bakrie and Brothers, the Sutowo's property development fame (which include the Hilton Hotel in Jakarta). Among them we can also count the sons (second son Bambang Trihatmodjo of the Bimantara Group and youngest son Hutomo Mandala Putra of the Humpuss Group) and daughters (the best known: eldest daughter Siti Hardianti Rukmana) of President Suharto. The discrepancy in the number and strength of the ethnic Chinese entrepreneurs as compared to the ethnic Indonesian ones has created feelings of resentment among the latter, who perceive this situation to be the consequence of unfair competition and unequal access to resources, both financial and otherwise (Schwarz 1994).

The contemporary literature on the ethnic Chinese has largely concentrated on the remarkable and pervasive role the ethnic Chinese have played in shaping the Indonesian economy, to the exclusion of their role in social and cultural areas. However, this has been remedied through some outstanding studies of the contribution by Chinese-Indonesians to the history and development of Indonesian literature, their participation in the formation of the pre-Second World War press, their role in giving a particular colour to the Indonesian language, in particular the Jakarta vernacular that abounds with loanwords originating from the Hokkien, Hakka and Cantonese languages, their share in the early attempts at filmmaking, in architecture (including some beautiful Chinese temples and utilitarian shop houses), and last but not least their role in adding variety to the Indonesian cuisine by bringing with them Chinese culinary culture wherever they settled (Salmon 1981, 1997; Suryadinata 1989).

In this chapter, I will focus on the situation in Jakarta, as this is the prime city of Indonesia. With about eight million inhabitants it is the most populous of all the urban areas in Indonesia, with the next largest, Surabaya in East Java, having a population of only about half that of Jakarta. This urban conglomeration, variously referred to as the Jakarta megapolitan or Jakarta metropolis, is the centre of all national activities: political, economic, social, cultural, educational, health, communication, media, defence/military. In terms of its population, it is a conglomeration of people representing virtually all of the 400 or so ethnic groups that make up Indonesian society. In addition, there are the people of foreign origin, the descendants of Chinese, Arabs, Indians, Dutch, and the foreign population (among them about 28,000 Chinese nationals), including the more recent expatriates. Another reason for focusing on Jakarta is the fact that, especially since the upheaval in 1965, the urban character of the ethnic Chinese in Indonesia has been firmly established.

Politically, Jakarta, the capital city of Indonesia is the seat of the central government, with all the ministries, the parliament and other government institutions clustered in certain areas of the city. Economically, the well-known names of virtually all multinational companies, including banks and other financial institutions, decorate the front or are splashed across the top of multi-storey office blocks, while big name international department stores are located in the many mega malls and superblocks that have sprouted along the main thoroughfares in the last ten years or so. Forests of multi-storey buildings jut into the sky, making the skyline of Jakarta similar to that of other mega cities in the world. For a city of this size, Jakarta can be considered a cultural wasteland. It lacks appropriate facilities for cultural performances of an international calibre; there is only one inadequate cultural centre.

However, entertainment centres abound, providing state-of-the-art electronic games for young and old, along with the ubiquitous karaoke bars. There are also a sufficient number of well-appointed movie houses showing mostly American films, but also Mandarin (mostly from Hong Kong) and Indian films, besides the Indonesian ones. Then there are the numerous restaurants, cafés and other eating places, representing cuisine from the best-known culinary cultures of the world, from the East and the West. Of the Chinese food recognized to be Chinese origin, there is an enormous range from the plush Shang Palace at the Shangrila Hotel, the

Xin Hwa at the Mandarin Hotel, serving such pricey delicacies as shark's fin, bird's nest, abalone and sea urchins, to porridge/congee and noodle parlours, to the curbside fried rice and seafood stalls, to the itinerant food vendors selling noodle soup with meat balls and not least to the rather obscure eating places selling snake (cobra and python), monkey and bat meat. There are also the many eating places serving local ethnic food, representing the various indigenous ethnic groups of Indonesia.[2]

Interestingly, the influence of Chinese culture is also seen in the building of the superblocks, megamalls and apartment buildings, many of which are owned and/or operated by ethnic Chinese property developers. This is shown in the emergence of an interest in *feng shui,* the art of geomancy originating from ancient Chinese culture. Today a demand for *feng shui* masters, who can give advice on the correct location of a building, the direction of the entrance and main door, the placing of furniture in the offices, especially that of the CEO. In other words, *feng shui* is the harmonious relationship between human beings and their physical environment, and today a very trendy philosophy (Tan 1996).

Another clear indication of the influence of Chinese culture is the evidence of 'loanwords' in the Indonesian vocabulary, especially in the so-called Jakarta dialect. One of the very few studies on this topic is a publication written by Philip Leo, a Jakarta-born Chinese-Indonesian, who compiled a list of 168 words used in the vernacular vocabulary of the people of Jakarta, of which 73 have become part of the national language, the Bahasa Indonesia. Then there are 95 words used by a more restricted group of China-born and Indonesia-born Chinese, who live in the northern part of the city, where many of them are concentrated, and a part of which is recognized as the 'Chinatown' of Jakarta. Another 86 words are spoken by ethnic Chinese who do not speak Chinese as their mother tongue. The fourth group consists of 31 archaic words used in literary Indonesian. The fifth and last group comprises 36 Chinese place and street names.

A further scrutiny of these loanwords reveals that originally most of the ethnic Chinese in Jakarta, and in fact on the island of Java in general, come from Fujian province, while the influx of Hakka and Cantonese people occurred at a later date. Of the 168 loanwords that have entered the Indonesian language, and especially the Jakarta vernacular, 84 per cent are from Hokkien (sample: *gua,* I; *lu,* you; *bakpao,* meat bun; *lumpia,* spring roll; *kucai,* leek; *pecai,* Chinese white cabbage; *toge,* bean sprout; *anglo,* charcoal stove; *angpau,* money gift in a red packet), 8 per cent are from Hakka, 5 per cent from Mandarin and 2 per cent from Cantonese. Of the 36 place and street names of Chinese origin, 89 per cent are from Hokkien, while only 2 are from Hakka, and one from Mandarin.

For the purpose of this chapter, it is important to note that a significant number of these loanwords refer to food (all words starting with *bak* signify meat, and words ending with *cai* signify vegetables), cooking utensils and cutlery, indicating the extent of the penetration of Chinese food and foodstuffs into the Indonesian diet. It is also a reflection of the importance of food in Chinese culture. In *Food in Chinese Culture*, which is perhaps one of the most comprehensive books on this topic, Chang (1977:11) aptly observed that:

> ... perhaps the most important aspect of the Chinese food culture is the importance of food itself in Chinese culture. That Chinese cuisine is the greatest in the world is highly debatable and is essentially irrelevant. But few can take exception to the statement that few other cultures are as food oriented as the Chinese. And this orientation appears to be as ancient as Chinese culture itself.

There is today both in the East and in the West an almost obsessive interest in the relationship between food intake and health. To quote Chang (1977:9) again:

> The overriding idea about food in China – in all likelihood an idea with solid, but as yet unrevealed, scientific backing – is that the kind and amount of food one takes is intimately relevant to one's health. Food not only affects health as a matter of general principle, the selection of the right food at any particular time must also be dependant upon one's health condition at that time. Food, therefore, is also medicine.

One of the proponents of this topic in Indonesia is a man known as Hembing H. M. Wijayakusuma, who is of Chinese origin, a Muslim, a practitioner of Chinese healing methods and a well-known herbalist. He has written various books on the topic and a highly popular (especially among ethnic Indonesians) Chinese cookbook in Indonesian, titled *Masakan untuk Pengobatan dan Kesehatan* (*Food for Healing and Health*), a sleek, beautifully illustrated book of recipes, first published in 1992 and in 1994 was already in its third printing. All of the 133 recipes are based on Chinese cooking, and each one has a description of what illness it is to cure or how it will keep one healthy, youthful and beautiful. However, there is no mention of pork in any of the recipes, a recognition of Indonesian society being 87 per cent Muslim, for whom eating pork is strictly taboo. Hembing also has a weekly (Saturday morning) programme, usually accompanied by a celebrity, on one of the private TV channels on the use of locally available materials, herbs, vegetables, and fruit, that are related to healing and health.

Undoubtedly, food and health are topics that easily cross borders, geographic, cultural, age, gender and even socio-economic status. Along with the weather, these two topics are handy conversation pieces. They can break the ice among people who are, for whatever reason, put together in one room or place, for example, when on a long trip, sitting in the waiting room of an airport or bus station, or on a plane or train.

After this brief description of the political, economic, social and cultural context of the Jakarta situation, and the place of the ethnic Chinese, we will now examine the extent of the penetration of Chinese dietary culture on food consumption patterns in Jakarta. I will start with food at home, followed by the various types of food available outside the home, continue with some of the speciality food that exists in Jakarta, and conclude with some remarks on the future prospect of Chinese dietary culture in Indonesia.

Food at Home

I will start with the question of which people were influenced by or were originally the bearers of Chinese dietary culture in Jakarta. First, there were the ethnic Chinese people themselves. This seems like a clear and straightforward answer, but actually it is not. The ethnic Chinese in Indonesia are a varied lot, comprising those who are part of the foreign population, people from the PRC, Hong Kong, Taiwan, Singapore, and ethnic Chinese from other parts of Asia, who live or have lived in Indonesia for business, or as members of a diplomatic or international mission. Then there is the local ethnic Chinese population that culturally forms a continuum with at one end those who are Indonesian citizens, but who are still very much influenced by Chinese culture, speaking Chinese at home, to those who do not know Chinese at all, except perhaps to write their name in Chinese characters, but who still recognize their Chinese origin. The people in these two groups are usually referred to, in English, as ethnic Chinese or Chinese-Indonesians or Sino-Indonesians. At the other end are those who identify completely as Indonesians and prefer not to be considered anything else. Nevertheless, this group too is often referred to as ethnic Chinese or Chinese-Indonesians.

Second, there are the ethnic Indonesians, especially the Javanese, who form the largest ethnic group in Indonesia, many of whom are fans of Chinese food, frequenting Chinese restaurants and considering egg and rice noodles, bean sprouts, Chinese cabbage, *taocho* or soya bean paste, and tofu, as part of their daily diet. The other Indonesian ethnic groups, especially those who are strict Muslim, are somewhat leery about going into a Chinese restaurant or eating Chinese food because of the association with pork. Nevertheless, the same ingredients mentioned above are also part of their daily diet.

If we look at the food at home in an ethnic Chinese family, be they still strongly Chinese oriented or already acculturated to the local situation, pork is still the preferred meat, next to beef, chicken, fish, or goat meat. Still, generally, pork consumption seems to have decreased, as can be seen at the supermarkets, where the counter for pork is separated from and smaller than the other meat counters. Besides the fact that there is now a more militant stance on the part of Muslim, towards the display of pork meat, the use of pork meat and the existence of pig farms, in line with the global resurgence of Muslim militancy, there is a recognition that pork meat can be a health hazard leading to high cholesterol levels and eventually to heart disease.

A meal in the home of a typical ethnic Chinese family, in terms of Chinese food, consists of pork made into a stew with garlic, ginger, soya sauce and spiced with the Chinese 'five flavours', known by the Hokkien name *ngo hiong*. Another meat dish is fried fish or fried chicken. Vegetables are stir-fried Chinese cabbage and/or stir-fried beansprouts mixed with tofu or with *tempe* (fungus-fermented soyabean cake, a popular Javanese home product, which is the major source of protein and a staple food for most Javanese) (Anderson and Anderson 1977:340). Then there is usually some kind of fresh red-hot chillies (mashed or pounded into a paste or eaten fresh and whole) and some of the many varieties of fried fish or prawn chips. For a snack between meals there may be *bacang* – a Chinese snack made of rice or glutinous rice preferably stuffed with pork meat, or sometimes other kinds of meat, and wrapped in bamboo leaves shaped into a kind of triangle. This is the kind of snack that is traditionally eaten during the dragon boat festival, but is now available and consumed year around.

To have a better picture of the influence of Chinese ingredients and food, we will examine the loanwords originating from the Chinese, mostly Hokkien, used in the Indonesian language and/or in the Jakarta vernacular, mentioned in the Introduction. From the listing by categories, we note that there are 55 loanwords referring to food, vegetables, fruit, drinks, meats, seafood, and 9 referring to health. Among them are words referring to food that have become part of the Indonesian vocabulary, such as *bahu*, dried crushed or shredded meat usually eaten with rice; *bakmi*, egg noodles made into a soup with meatballs or fried mixed with any kind of meat; *kuetiao*, rice noodles; *bihun*, Chinese vermicelli; *bakso*, meat balls; *juhi*, cuttle fish; *cumi*, small cuttlefish; *lobak*, radish or turnip; *lokio*, chives; *pecai*, white cabbage; *tim*, to steam, as in *nasi tim Hainan*, the local name for Hainan chicken rice; *capcai*, the local name for 'chop suey'; *pangsit*, Chinese ravioli or 'wonton'; *kuachi*, melon seed (Leo 1975:3–8).

These names of foodstuffs have become so much part of the Indonesian language that ethnic Indonesians, and even many ethnic Chinese, may not know that they are of Hokkien origin. These are also the food and ingredients that are part of the daily diet of Indonesians of Chinese origin as well as the indigenous Indonesians. They are made into side dishes to accompany rice, the staple food of people in Jakarta and most of Indonesia.

For special occasions celebrated at home the same basic foodstuff is used, but with more meat dishes and garnished with better quality, and therefore more expensive, ingredients. A must at a party is a pork dish, often crisply barbecued pork, that can be bought at food stores specializing in this delicacy, or even a whole barbecued piglet, also available at speciality stores. Another must, especially for birthdays, is a noodle dish, usually fried and mixed with a variety of meats. According to Chinese tradition, handed down from one generation to the next, noodles symbolize long life, associated with the long strings (the longer the better) of the noodles. Interestingly, at parties in the homes of ethnic Indonesians, fried noodles are also almost always on the menu, not so much because of the symbolic meaning, but simply because everybody likes them.

Actually, meals in ethnic Chinese homes, especially those that have acculturated to the local culture, are a combination of local food (characterized by the use of a lot of coconut milk and indigenous spices such as turmeric, and usually made into curries), and food recognized to be of Chinese origin, but with a local flavour. This kind of food is sometimes referred to as *peranakan* food which refers to food of the ethnic Chinese of mixed Chinese and Indonesian descent; *peranakan* literally meaning 'child of the soil' or local-born), which is also found is Singapore and the equivalent of the *nonya* food in Malaysia (Anderson and Anderson 1977:353).

There is a tendency, however, to have more 'pure' Chinese dishes for festive occasions, using more pork meat, chicken and fish, imported (usually from the PRC, Hong Kong or Singapore) Chinese mushrooms, spices, sauces, canned bamboo shoot, water chestnut, lotus root and lotus seed, sesame oil and Chinese cooking wine. These can be bought in the market in the Chinatown area of North Jakarta. More recently, however, some of the big supermarkets, with outlets all over the city, have added counters with Chinese imported speciality food (often near to the counter of Japanese imported food). The special ingredients needed for the recipes that are claimed to have the power of healing and health maintenance, collected in the cookbook by Hembing Wijayakusuma can, as indicated in the book, be bought in traditional Chinese medicine and health stores. They are usually also imported from the PRC. These 109 ingredients including dried medicinal herbs, roots, seeds, mushrooms, and pieces of tree bark, are displayed in colourful illustrations in the book.

Nonetheless, we will note that there has been a distinct change in food preparation and meal patterns due to the change in the role of women, in particular their move from the confines of the home into the workplace. With more and more women engaged in work outside the home, there is a tendency to get ready-to-eat or prepared food that can be bought on the way home and only needs to be cooked. This kind of food can be found at supermarkets, and eating places in shopping centres that serve for take-out only or a combination of restaurant and take-out. Alternatively, one can collect the whole family and simply eat out. This brings us to the next section of the chapter: food outside the home.

Food Outside the Home

As indicated in the Introduction, Chinese dietary culture has penetrated peacefully but pervasively into Indonesian food consumption patterns, among ethnic Chinese as well as among ethnic Indonesians. This is clearly seen in the pattern of eating out and the tremendous variety of eating places in terms of the food available as well as the ambience. Similar to the situation in mega cities all over the world, the choices range from the most sophisticated restaurants, usually called 'palace', such as the Shang Palace located at the five-star Shangrila, the well-known Summer Palace in the centre of the city, to the modest hawker food stalls perched on the kerb.

In *The Jakarta Post Life Style 1997* mentioned earlier, the listing of restaurants comprises about ten pages. These are undoubtedly the better quality restaurants, as this guide book is geared towards the readers of *The Jakarta Post,* today perhaps the best English language daily (at least in terms of the quality of the language), catering to expatriates and the upper level educated Indonesians, who can confidently be considered part of the middle class. This is still but a small layer of the population of Jakarta, however the number of people patronizing these eating places clearly forms a sufficient market to make them profitable.

If we focus on Chinese eating places only, we can count at least 80 from this ten-page list. This is probably an undercount, as all of the big hotels have at least one or two Chinese restaurants, while their coffee shops usually have Chinese dishes on the menu. Moreover, all the big shopping centres have two or more Chinese restaurants. This is especially the case in the shopping centres in the northern and western parts of Jakarta where ethnic Chinese are concentrated. The stalls in the food courts in these shopping areas usually serve food from various parts of Asia and Indonesia, but there are always at least two or three specifically Chinese. Many of them serve some variation of Cantonese food, while others indicate that they serve Sichuan food, or Chiu Chau food. Another popular item on the Chinese restaurant menu is *dim sum*. In fact it is so popular for breakfast and lunch that there are restaurants specially serving *dim sum* in buffet-style, charging a certain amount per person to 'eat as much as you can.'

There is a particular shopping centre that has a food court including a Chinese restaurant, named Ta Wan (Big Bowl), specializing in all kinds of rice porridge or congee. The menu lists about 40 kinds of porridge one can choose from, using a variety of meats, seafood and eggs, including the 'thousand-year egg', and combinations of them. There is something unique about this restaurant. The individual placemats on the table are made of paper on which the story of porridge is written in Indonesian and English. It says:

> The story of porridge. The oldest written material about porridge goes back more than a thousand years. Historically, porridge has been used as everything from a ceremonial food, to a nutritious sustenance given to homeless people. Throughout Chinese history, to all people, from the royal family to the common people, porridge has been served not only as food, but as a tonic as well. It has the ability to strengthen as well as prolong life. From the modern medical point of view, porridge – a semiliquid diet is adequate to regulate and enhance appetite. It is also beneficial to healthy digestion and absorption of nutrition. The benefits of eating porridge are indubitable. There is no other food that has such magnificent power.

We will return to this topic of speciality food and health in the next section of the chapter.

Other places to look for good quality Chinese food, usually with a Chinese style decor, are the restaurants located in the big multi-storey office buildings lining the main business districts. For example, there is the Hong Kong Unicorn Restaurant, located on the eleventh floor of the Total Building; the Golden Island Bird's Nest (Chiu Chau) Restaurant, located on the premises of the BRI (a government bank) Building, which advertises (in English) that: 'It brings experience of serving food and has applied the culinary traditions of Chiu Chau food in Hong Kong. All dishes are freshly presented by its skilled Hong Kong master chefs. Serving a variety of live seafood and delicious *dim sum*'; the Dragon City Seafood Restaurant, located on the ground floor of the Lippo Plaza and Mashill Tower: 'Sichuan and Seafood Cuisine at its best'; the Summer Palace Restaurant, located in the Tedja Buana Building: 'The Best of Sichuan and Cantonese Cuisine'; the chain of Tunglok Restaurants located in various office buildings: 'The Good Food People'; the Hong Bin Lou, located in the Bapindo (a government bank) Centre, which claims to be the first Chinese Moslem restaurant in Jakarta and serving among others: 'Hygienic Mutton Hot Pot' and 'Cold Dishes and other Most Delicious Chinese Moslem Food' (data from *The Jakarta Business: Shopping Phone Book*. Section on Restaurants). To convince potential patrons of the authenticity of the food and the cooking, these advertisements usually add that they have chefs imported from Hong Kong or Beijing.

These restaurants cater to the office crowd, and often during lunch hour one may have to stand in line to be seated. However, this means that after and outside office hours, in the evening and over the weekend, they may have few customers. University campuses are also a place to look for food, although they do not usually serve Chinese dishes except for the local version of noodle soup with meatballs or fried noodles.

Another highly popular type of food are all kinds of noodles. There are special noodle places that can be found in shopping areas, malls and in the business districts. One that is extremely popular is called Bakmi Gajah Mada. It started in the early 1960s as a hole-in-the-wall food stall with the customers sitting on stools at long communal tables, located in the busy downtown business area on a street called Gajah Mada. At the original location there is now a proper restaurant building, still run by the descendants of the ethnic Chinese family who started it. Over the years they have expanded and today they are in four more locations, two in premises with their logo prominently displayed on top of the building, while the other two are located in big shopping malls. Their advertisement in the Jakarta shopping/business phone book, runs the following slogan: 'The right place for the special noodle' (in English).

This noodle restaurant is indisputably the most popular in town. Although they serve other Chinese dishes, most customers come for the various noodle dishes, particularly the chicken noodle soup, and the dish they originally specialized in. Although at the beginning they must have used pork meat, today they are known as a 'pork-free' place, so, at their two outlets in the southern part of Jakarta, where there are fewer ethnic Chinese compared to the northern and western part, many of the customers are ethnic Indonesians. The popularity of this noodle place can be seen by the fact that there are always people waiting to be seated, even outside lunch and dinner times. In addition, there are the people waiting for takeout service. This place is a real family restaurant; whole families with grandparents and grandchildren, including the nurses carrying babies, descend on the outlets, especially on Sundays and during school vacation time. It is also much frequented by the foreign population, especially the young. What has made this place so popular are the noodles themselves, which have a special texture and taste and are made on the premises. Although there is fierce competition from other noodle places, which also have a number of outlets across the city, there is no doubt that the Bakmi Gajah Mada still reigns supreme.

That noodles have become part of the Indonesian diet, often constituting the regular breakfast meal or even substituting for a quick lunch, can be gauged from the many brands of processed instant noodle soup that are available at supermarkets and roadside stalls selling miscellaneous food items. The first brand of this kind of processed noodle soup was called Supermie, but today there are many more brands, including imported ones from Japan, and a great variety of flavours from beef, chicken (no pork), to vegetable (tomato). They come in individual plastic-wrapped packages or in various types of containers made of styrofoam in the shape of a glass or bowl (often with a plastic fork inside), from which the noodles can be eaten after being soaked in boiling water.

Another type of 'food outside the home' is the food sold by semi-permanent hawkers stationed on the kerb or in outdoor areas specially reserved for them. These hawkers often operate at night-time only, when the kerb or parking lots are free from vehicles. These places also serve a variety of Chinese food, such as fried noodle and noodle soup, all kinds of rice porridge, beef kailan, *cap cai* or chop suey, and seafood. Some aficionadoes claim that hawker food is much tastier than restaurant food. These are the people who care for the food only, and do not mind the surroundings. For instance, in the Chinatown area there is a porridge stall located on the kerb that is frequented by people driving expensive cars, and the place is crowded especially in the morning hours. Anderson and Anderson (1977:363) observed a similar situation in the New Territories of Hong Kong. This was a wonton and noodle shop, located in an ordinary working-class neighbourhood, which consisted of a small bare room with a few tables and chairs. Yet 'everyone yearned to eat there', and people from all walks of life flocked to it. Their conclusion: 'Western gourmets tend to require an elegant ambience as part of a meal. The Chinese are concerned with the food'.

Then there are the street vendors or mobile food vendors, who carry the ingredients, often including the cooking equipment, on a pole, on a push cart, or on a bicycle, going around the residential areas. In other words, they provide food delivery services. This phenomenon of street vendors can be observed in virtually all Asian countries. Some of the vendors use a bell or other instrument to attract attention or they may have a particular way of calling out what they sell that is known by the people in the neighbourhood. It should be noted that the vendors seen most frequently in Jakarta selling food who are recognized to be of Chinese origin (there are many others selling indigenous Indonesian food) are not ethnic Chinese, but almost all ethnic Indonesians. They are selling *bubur ayam*, chicken rice porridge for breakfast; noodle soup with meatballs called *mi bakso*; *siomay*, a kind of *dim sum*, which includes stuffed potato, tofu, cabbage, bitter melon, with a peanut butter sauce.

Health Food and Vegetarian Food

I will examine what is observed as an obsessive interest in the relationship between food and health. This is a phenomenon not only among the Chinese, but one that has probably become a global preoccupation or perhaps, for some people, more correctly, a pastime. One indicator of this is the choice of preferred food (usually vegetarian, specified into Indian, Chinese or western, or low-sodium or non-cholesterol) one can order ahead on long flights on all major airlines. Another indicator is the proliferation of alternative medicine and traditional healing methods. In Indonesia today indigenous traditional healing methods are popular, and a growing number of adherents Chinese medicine and healing methods are also popular. For instance, in Jakarta, acupuncture has become part of the mainstream healing methods and is available at the general hospital. Acupuncturists, acupressurists and reflexologists abound; on some Sundays in one of the Catholic churches in Jakarta, church-goers can come for reflexology treatment provided in the parish hall. Still another indicator is the popularity of fitness centres and the great numbers of people who go for morning walks or jogging around the block and health clubs have sprouted up in neighbourhoods. On Sunday mornings one of the big parks in the centre of Jakarta is filled with people, men and women, young and old, from all walks of life, who do exercises, including well-known Chinese types of exercises seen in the parks of Beijing.

This preoccupation with health and fitness is accompanied by a growing realization that there is a direct relationship between health and the kind and amount of food we eat, especially on a daily basis. Anderson and Anderson (1977), mentioned earlier on food and culture in South China, also provide comprehensive coverage of all aspects of foodways, which shows the similarities among the foodways of the people who have settled in the Nanyang, including in Indonesia, where most of the earlier ethnic Chinese settlers originated from South China.

A good indicator of the realization of the importance of food for health is the popularity of cookbooks, especially those that give recipes that have an effect on health. One such cookbook, already mentioned earlier in this chapter, is that by Hembing Wijayakusuma. The recipes are organized by categories according to the illness they may cure or prevent, that can keep one in good health, young and beautiful, that can enhance men's virility, and that can make women attractive and sexy. Hembing claims that the 133 recipes he has collected in this book produce dishes that have a beneficial effect on people with a heart condition; liver, kidney, stomach and lung problems; who suffer from rheumatism, high cholesterol levels, high blood pressure and cancer. For men, there are recipes to prevent impotence and raise their virility, while for women there are recipes to keep them young and beautiful, to avoid frigidity and 'women's diseases.' He made sure to emphasize, however, that these recipes are not so much to cure illness, but more to maintain and enhance health.

A further examination of this colourfully illustrated cookbook, yields more information (from the detailed Table of Contents). The greatest demand is represented by 15 recipes for food that makes one beautiful. Next come recipes that 'keep one trim by eating good and tasty food' (14 recipes), suggesting that one does not have to go on a diet and deprive oneself of enjoying good food, to look trim and attractive. There are also a number of recipes (10) to increase one's energy or stamina. These are obviously dishes geared towards increasing male virility, a constant concern of males who have reached a certain age.

The largest number of recipes is in the general category of food to prevent and cure illness by eating tasty enjoyable food. There are nine recipes concerned with diabetes, eight with respiratory problems, seven with high blood pressure and cholesterol levels, four each with problems of the kidney, back pain and menopause, rheumatism, cancer and tumours, and internal fever. Then there are three each concerned with heart conditions, problems of the liver, stomach, nerves, problems due to stressful conditions, ageing and menopause, miscellaneous problems, followed by two each concerned with problems of the eyesight, headache/ migraine and vertigo, feelings of fatigue and weakness, flu and fever, and increasing the growth of a child. Finally there is one recipe each concerned with low blood pressure, stomach problems, insomnia, dysentery, 'women's problems', and bleeding gums.

These recipes, and the health promoting properties they claim to contain, show that people are very concerned about their health, especially when they have reached mid-life, that is, about 40 years old. They know that there is a relationship between health and what they eat but they are not prepared to go the whole way and deprive themselves of good food. So, they look for a middle way, to keep healthy and trim and yet still enjoy good food. This concern seems to be shown more by women. An indicator of this is the programme of Hembing, where the guests are mostly women, often celebrities in the entertainment business. This is in contrast to many other popular cooking programmes, where the chef is a man, but the guests, who function as 'assistants', are more evenly distributed between women and men.

The popularity of rice porridge or congee and the healthful properties attributed to them have been described earlier. We find that among the ethnic Chinese in Jakarta, there is no clear knowledge of cold or *yin* food and hot or *yang* food. There is only the knowledge transferred from one generation to the next, concerning foods to avoid and foods to eat when one is ill. In regard to rice porridge, there is the custom, among ethnic Chinese as well as ethnic Indonesians, to shift from regular rice to porridge when one is sick because it is considered easily digestible, and not 'heavy' in the stomach. It is also a baby food, given to infants as part of the weaning process.

Then there is a whole category of foodstuffs that are considered to have real curing properties. This category contains animals that are not commonly eaten, for example, snake meat (cobra and python), monkey meat, meat of the big fruit bat, meat of a *biawak* – a type of big lizard – the gall of a snake that is freshly killed, rabbit brains and monkey brains. A well-known restaurant with the name Istana King Cobra (in English, King Cobra Palace) has the usual picture of a cobra with the head up painted on the entrance door. This type of logo is known to indicate this kind of speciality restaurant. The place we visited was actually very modestly set up, run by a young husband-and-wife team (the husband was the cook and the wife was the cashier and assisted in giving the cures to the customers). There were also two girls functioning as waitresses. King Cobra Palace has three outlets across the city. The one-page, foliosize flyer that can be obtained in the restaurant lists all the food that is available, with a description of what it is to cure and the price. It also claims (in Indonesian): 'We have twenty-six years' experience. Our restaurant serves food that is really safe and effective.'

One of the cures listed is 'blood and gall of a poisonous snake'. The gall of a freshly-killed snake appears to be one of the most popular cures. When we arrived at the restaurant one evening there was a group consisting of two young families with small children under ten years old. All the small children were getting the snake gall cure. The removal of the snake's gall can be seen from the corridor through a glass window at the back of the room where people sit to eat. At the back wall of this room are iron cages filled with live snakes. At a table facing the glass window a man skins the snake, pulls out the small round bag the size of a thumbnail containing the gall, then throws the skinned snake into a big barrel that is already full of skinned snakes still squirming around. It is then brought on a little plate to the woman cashier. She pierces the bag with a needle, catching the black liquid in a tablespoon, puts some honey (according to the flyer it should be rice wine) on it and gives it to one of the kids, who proceeds to swallow the contents with hardly a protest. All the kids take turns swallowing the gall and honey cure. When asked, one of the mothers explained that she is doing this because her children are prone to skin diseases. The price is about US$8 per cure.

As listed in the flyer this concoction is to cure diabetes, liver ailments, rheumatism, asthma, uric acid, skin diseases, back pain, allergy, stomach ailments, bad eyesight, wet and dry eczema, weak heart, weak uterus, high cholesterol levels, regulate blood pressure, muscle pain, and the onset of flu.

Other cures are snake blood and gall mixed with a certain rice wine to enhance libido in males. Then there is cobra meat, fried or made into a soup, that is to cure skin diseases, increase appetite, and cure allergies; python meat, also fried or made into a *sate* (pieces of meat on a skewer and barbecued) or soup, which is to cure itching and allergies; *biawak* lizard meat, also fried, made into *sate* or soup, to cure itching, wet or dry eczema; monkey meat, also fried, made into *sate* or soup, to cure skin diseases, wet and dry eczema; fruit bat meat, also fried made into *sate*, to cure asthma, problems in breathing, and allergy. All these foods cost between US$1.25 to US$4 per portion. They are also available in cured, dried, or shredded form and cost about US$8 for a small bag.

Still more cures on the list are the meat of these animals mixed into flour or oil. For example, snake oil is to cure burns, bruises from a fall, insect bites, wounds that will not heal, boils, itching skin and skin diseases. Oil of the *biawak* lizard is for pimples, skin diseases, itching, and wet and dry eczema. Then there is scorpion oil to tone the hair black, and to increase thickness and to prevent hair from falling out.

We note that, at least in this type of restaurant, with a few exceptions, such as diabetes, cholesterol levels, weak heart, weak uterus, almost all the curing properties that are claimed are more of a cosmetic nature, to enhance libido, or to get rid of skin diseases, in short, not for serious illnesses.

The final part of this section addresses vegetarian food. In Jakarta, this kind of food is associated with Buddhism. According to one knowledgeable person in the field, who is himself a Buddhist, but claiming no affiliation with any of the existing associations, there are different types of vegetarians. The best known, having developed vegetarian food into an art, are known as Maitreya Buddhists. They make an 'imitation meat' that is sold in restaurants associated with them. One of these restaurants is called Mudita and located in the centre of the city. The menu has coloured pictures of the dishes one can choose from and a description of the ingredients. The 'imitation meat' substitutes for beef, chicken, seafood and especially crab meat. It is made of flour, soyabean and other kinds of beans and is supposed to taste like the meat they substitute for. A sampling of the dishes revealed that the actual meals did not look like the pictures, and that the portions were very tiny in relation to the price, especially considering the materials used. Our informant explained that the use of 'imitation meat' is a controversial issue among the various Buddhist sects. There are those who condemn this, considering it against the spirit of vegetarianism, the basis of which is that one should not kill any living creature, and therefore not participate in eating them. To make food that resembles meat is a manifestation of hypocrisy and not taking their religion seriously. Others favour this practice and contend that there is nothing wrong with it; the point is that it is not meat. They claim that this is only a way to make people get used to vegetarian food, a kind of transition process, to wean people away from eating meat. From the increase in the number of vegetarian restaurants serving this type of 'imitation meat', it appears that the 'purists' are losing the battle. According to our informant, this kind of meat is being produced and put on the market in Japan and in the United States. These products have also found their way to Jakarta; the imitation crab meat in the restaurant we visited, for instance, comes from Japan. This exposé of the interest in speciality food and health indicates that there is a flourishing market for Chinese ingredients and foodstuffs that are claimed to have healing properties. There is a positive demand for authentic ingredients, especially imported from China, Hong Kong or Taiwan, health food recipes and for healers using alternative medicine.

Conclusion

My investigation of the influence of Chinese dietary culture in Jakarta, though limited in scope, shows conclusively that this culture has penetrated and is part of the food consumption patterns of the ethnic Chinese as well as the ethnic Indonesians in this capital city of Indonesia. This is shown in the loanwords, primarily of Hokkien origin and mostly related to food, in the Indonesian language and especially in the Jakarta vernacular. These words have become so much part of the language that many of those who use them, be they ethnic Indonesians or even ethnic Chinese, may not know that they are of Chinese origin.

Chinese eating places abound and are flourishing, ranging from plush establishments to noodle and porridge parlours, to hawker stalls, to mobile vendors who go around residential areas. The dishes available in these places reflect the variety according to the area of origin in China, and the patrons and customers are very knowledgeable and particular about this. Foods with healing properties are very much sought after, and cookbooks with recipes of this nature are very popular. Alternative medicine and healing methods of the Chinese variety, and also of the Indonesian variety, are in high demand. Traditional Chinese pharmacies are still to be found in the Chinatown area, where the owner is also a traditional Chinese healer making up cures from ingredients taken from drawers lining the wall of the shop.

Concoctions and food made of meat or parts of animals not commonly eaten such as snake, monkey, fruit bat and *biawak* meat, that are believed to have curing properties, are available in speciality restaurants though the demand for them is still limited. Then there is the vegetarian food, usually associated with Buddhist sects, whose adherents are mostly ethnic Chinese. Some of these sects are associated with restaurants selling vegetarian food of the Chinese variety that usually includes 'imitation meat', some of which is imported from the PRC, Hong Kong or Taiwan.

These manifestations of the influence of Chinese dietary culture are very evident and have become part of the Indonesian culinary scene. Because of its adaptability to the local demand, for instance, leaving out the use of meat unacceptable to potential customers whose religion prohibits meat consumption, indications are that it will continue to flourish, thereby enriching the total cultural setup of Indonesian society.

Notes

1 *Newsweek* magazine is one of the many magazines that picked up the story. One of the early stories was is in *Newsweek* of 28 October, 1996, where James Riady appeared on the cover together with Clinton in an inset with the caption 'Clinton's Asia Connection'.

2 This is taken from *The Jakarta Post Lifestyle 1997* a glossy magazine, put out by the English language daily *The Jakarta Post*. This special issue purports to be a comprehensive guide to the variety of the lifestyle in Jakarta.

References

Anderson, N. Eugene and Marja L. Anderson (1977) 'Modern China: The South', in Chang, Kwang-chi (ed.) *Food in Chinese Culture: Anthropological and Historical Perspectives*. New Haven: Yale University Press.

Blusse, Leonard (1988) *Strange Company, Chinese settlers, Mestizo Women and the Dutch VOC in Batavia*. Dordrecht-Holland: Foris Publications.

Chang, Kwang-chi (ed.) (1977) 'Introduction', in *Food in Chinese Culture: Anthropological and Historical Perspectives*. New Haven: Yale University Press.

Coppel, A. Charles (1983) *Indonesian Chinese in Crisis*. Kuala Lumpur: Oxford University Press.

Hembing, H. M. Wijayakusuma (1994) *Masakan untuk Pengobatan dan Kesehatan: Food for Healing and Health*. Jakarta: Kartini Press.

Leo, Philip (1975) *Chinese Loanwords Spoken by the Inhabitants of the City of Jakarta*. Jakarta: Lembaga Research Kebudayaan National.

Mackie, J. A. C. (ed.) (1976) *The Chinese in Indonesia. Five Essays*. Sydney: Thomas Nelson (Australia) Ltd.

Robison, Richard (1986) *Indonesia: The Rise of Capital*. Sydney: Allen and Unwin.

Salmon, Claudine (1981) *Literature in Malas by the Chinese of Indonesia: A Provisional Annotated Bibliography*. Paris: Editions de la Maison des Sciences de l'homme.

—— (1997) [1980] *Les Chinois de Jakarta: temples et vie collective*. Paris: Editions de la Maison des Sciences de l'homme.

Schwarz, Adam (1994) *A Nation in Waiting. Indonesia in the 1990s*. Sydney: Allen and Unwin.

Suryadinata, Leo (1985) *China and the Asean States: The Ethnic Chinese Dimension*. Singapore: Singapore University Press.

—— (1989) *The Ethnic Chinese in the ASEAN States. Bibliographical Essays*. Singapore: Institute of Southeast Asian Studies.

—— (1995) *Prominent Indonesian Chinese Biographical Sketches*. Singapore: Institute of Southeast Asian Studies.

Tan, G. Mely (1987) 'The Role of the Ethnic Chinese Minority in Development: The Indonesian Case', *Southeast Asian Studies*, 25(3):63–83.

—— (1991) 'The Social and Cultural Dimensions of the Role of Ethnic Chinese in Indonesian Society', in *The Proceedings of the Symposium on The Role of the Indonesian Chinese in Shaping Modern Indonesian*, conference held at Cornell University, July 13–15, 1990.

—— (1996) 'Feng Shui and the Road to Success: The Persistence of a Traditional Belief System in the Face of Market Expansion', paper presented at The Third Seminar on The Social and Cultural Dimensions of Market Expansion, organized by the Goethe Institute in cooperation with the University of Bielefeld, Germany and Gadjah Mada University, Yogyakarta, held in Yogyakarta 26–27 August.

Williams, E. Lea (1996) *The Future of Overseas Chinese in Southeast Asia*. New York: McGraw-Hill Book Company.

Yoshihara, Kunio (1988) *The Rise of Ersatz Capitalism in South-east Asia*. Singapore: Oxford University Press.

CHAPTER TEN

The Invention of Delicacy

Cantonese Food in Yokohama Chinatown

Sidney C. H. Cheung

When we discuss the process of globalization, we pay more attention to the large-scale world-wide flow of people, commodities and information from a transnational perspective, and less attention to the local adaptation and resistance related to socio-political backgrounds. Taking food and cuisine as an example of the practice of globalization reinforces the idea that one should never neglect different countries' social contexts regarding the way particular kinds of food are introduced, maintained, localized and even reinvented. As we can observe in some countries nowadays, Chinese food is preferred and popular merely because of its cheapness, convenience and familiarity, rather than because of any social status that can be achieved through its consumption. But there are also some exceptions. For example, Japanese people have had various reasons for choosing Chinese food in different periods over the last few decades, beyond those mentioned above. In this chapter, I will focus on the emergence of 'real' and authentic Cantonese food in Yokohama Chinatown, in order to shed light on the changing foodways as well as understanding relevant individual choice and 'taste' among Japanese during the last few decades. Here, what I mean by 'taste' does not refer to the bio-chemical reaction induced by consuming food, but the way people choose food as a reflection of their social and cultural identities, that is, the relevant social values that affect one's choices.

In considering the development of Chinese restaurants and the corresponding social meanings of eating Chinese food among the Japanese in the last few decades, I will distinguish between four phases after the Second World War. The first phase began right after Japan's defeat and ended with the Tokyo Olympics (1964). This was a period of enormous social change which Karatani (1993) refers to the 'post-war (in Japanese, *sengo*)' period; at that time, Chinese cuisine was high society oriented, while at the same time, Yokohama's Chinatown was just a market place for inexpensive food. I define the second phase as the decade between the mid-1960s and 1970s, the period in which Japan experienced rapid economic development. With a rise in living standards and the emergence of the 'new middle class' (Vogel 1971), there was a great demand for 'family restaurants' generally characterized by spaciousness, western style, easy highway access, attractive menu design with colourful pictures, and special children's meal sets. Most importantly, these restaurants were marketed and advertised as being suitable for families. At the same time, a similar change in Chinese cuisine was observed. This was reflected by the increasing popularity of the modified *chuka-ryori* (meaning Chinese cuisine in Japanese) combining different regional cuisines, further, when upscale Chinese restaurants in hotels were established to meet demand brought about by the Tokyo Olympics, the standard of Chinese cuisine for average consumers was upgraded.

In the third phase during the 1980s, with the tremendous increase in the numbers of Japanese working and travelling abroad for business and tourism came the idea of internationalization which infiltrated into individual lifestyles as well as foodways. Being able to appreciate foreign cuisine gave a person the reputation of being an international citizen. Nevertheless, the popularization of the distinctive and exotic Cantonese *dim sum*, starting from Yokohama Chinatown, serves as a good example of changing tastes and social values in the search for delicacies. And, finally during the 1990s to the present, as we have seen in the mass media, Chinese dishes have become something not only good to eat, but also good to know.

Yokohama Chinatown

Studies of overseas Chinese communities as well as Chinatowns have focused on extended social networks in terms of surname group, kinship and clan associations, and other cultural activities organized by volunteer associations; furthermore the linkage between a Chinatown and a person's original hometown should never be overlooked (Watson 1975; Chen 1992). However, apart from the above observations, Yokohama Chinatown is unique because it can also tell us a story about changing Japanese society.

Yokohama Chinatown, located in Kanagawa province at the western side of Tokyo, was established in 1859 and the Chinese population in its early period was about 1,000. In 1875, it was recorded that there were 1,300 Chinese and 1,100 European/Americans living there; by 1883, there were 2,700 Chinese and 1,300 European/Americans. After Yokohama city was founded, the number of non-Japanese residents increase rapidly. The following figures show the Chinese population for various years: 2,750 (1897); 3,000 (1899); 5,000 (1903); 6,000 (1908); 4,000 (1911); and

4,000 (1923) before the Kanto Great Earthquake (Yokohama Archives of History 1994). Regarding the occupations of these overseas Chinese living in Yokohama, Japanese people used to mention the 'three knives' (including tailor, barber and chef) as the three corresponding careers of Chinese migrants. Sometimes Chinese people also share this opinion. But, actually, from 1859 to 1923, there were more than 100 careers for Chinese in Yokohama Chinatown (Yokohama Archives of History 1994).

Similar to the situation in other Chinatowns around the world, the Yokohama Chinatown began as an ethnic community of residents who spoke regional or dialectic combinations of the Chinese language. Most residents were emigrants from Guangdong province (Canton). Contrasting with earlier observations concerning the residential aspects of other Chinatowns, the most remarkable quality of Yokohama Chinatown is its commercial character. Drawing from historical documents and conversations with Chinese overseas who have been living there for a few decades, it is not difficult to recognize that drastic changes have occurred within its bounded territory.

Yokohama Chinatown began as a residential community, only becoming more popular as a Japanese tourist destination with foreign rather than Japanese characteristics in the past few decades. It is important for us to understand how Yokohama Chinatown maintains relations with the dominant Japanese society, as it is the biggest foreign neighbourhoods and one of the major well-established ethnic communities in Japan, along with the Nanking Machi Chinatown in Kobe and the Tsurohashi Koreantown in Osaka (also see Tsu 1999 for the discussion of the emergence of a 'gourmet republic' in Kobe Chinatown).

Nowadays, anyone who walks inside Yokohama Chinatown will soon recognize that the whole neighbourhood is merely a concentration of Chinese restaurants and shops selling food and souvenirs, rather than its residential community that was first established. In other words, Yokohama Chinatown serves mostly as a tourist destination for visitors seeking good food and cuisine; and this idea has generally been supported by a large influx of local Japanese visitors. These local tourists are searching for 'real and authentic' Chinese delicacies, as opposed to the ordinary Chinese cuisine, *chuka-ryori*, already popular for several decades in Japan. Thus, apart from the reasons such as rapid economic development (*kodo seicho*) that have enabled families to afford eating out and have supported a general upgrade in the quality of the restaurant business, it is also important for us to understand how the search for delicacies reflects changing shared values, status, and 'taste' from the Japanese socio-cultural context. In addition, by considering the changing standard regarding 'taste', shown as shifts from the general to the particular, low-class to upscale and familiar to exotic, we are also able to examine the construction of cultural identity among Japanese.

The Yokohama Chinatown has been changing from a Chinese residential community to a Japanese style restaurant street, as many Japanese have observed. This is partly a reflection of how the local non-Japanese culture is suppressed, and at the same time, shows how consumerism has been cultivated to the exclusion of other occupations because it is what the Japanese-born Chinese expect. When I interviewed some second-generation (Japanese-born) Chinese who were running Chinese restaurants business there, I had the impression that they were more influenced by marketing values than by authenticity. For example, by examining how they conceptualize Chinese cuisine, I found that they put a strong emphasis on retaining the original taste of ingredients and how that taste is expressed. This mirrors the popular idea of *souzai* in Japanese cuisine, where the original taste of ingredients is not masked by other flavours, but is kept 'pure'. Therefore, by considering Chinese cuisine in Japan as a part of changing Japanese eating habits in the post-war world, we need to observe what is expected from the 'taste' of these cuisines. By investigating the changing foodways with its related values embedded in the society, I would like to emphasize that the choice of food not only clarify the process of one taste replacing another; but rather with the emergence of the new 'taste' from the more familiar kinds that have existed before. For example, Chinese food, or *chuka-ryori*, has been popular in Japan for a few decades, but there are still some Chinese regional cuisines with particular ingredients and spices that are considered exotic and special and are continuously being introduced into Japanese society. More theoretically speaking, the changing trends in Chinese cuisine in Japan can be seen as a long-term social process including importation, localization, and re-creation relating to the gain of status and identity for socio-political ends.

Studying Culture Through Food

Studying culture through food and its associated social forms is a delicate endeavour. Food, as it involves culinary traditions, dietary rules and trends in consumption, clearly fits into contemporary anthropological concerns. We are what we eat. Studies of food can help us to understand: first, the cultural meanings of various social relations involved in marriages, gifts, feasts and banquets; second, distinctions of caste, class, hierarchy and status; and third, metaphors through which the mechanism of self-construction with regard to ethnicity and social identity can be discerned (Sahlins 1976; Goody 1982; Bourdieu 1984; Mintz 1985). In Japan, this is not an exception either; as we know from many anthropological studies, food is (1) an exchange medium for social networking (Befu 1974; Edwards 1989); (2) an indicator of roles played by individuals (Moeran 1986; Allison 1991); and (3) a mean for the understanding of identity and self-construction in contemporary society (Noguchi 1994; Ohnuki-Tierney 1990, 1993). None the less, by looking at some 'foreign' food in Japan as a reflection of the society, Tobin (1992:27) mentions that

> foods once marked as foreign are being domesticated by young Japanese: perhaps by the turn of the century spaghetti and hamburgers will have lost all traces of their foreign origins. Signs of the domestication of the hamburger can be seen in its inclusion (without bun) in the okosama teishoku (the special children's lunch) served in department store restaurants and in the success of McDonald's Japan, whose Biggu Makku and Makku-furai (French fries) have become so thoroughly a part of Japanese life that Japanese tourists in Waikiki and Paris wait in line to order them when they are feeling homesick and want to eat something familiar.

In this short paragraph, Tobin significantly points out that the domestication of foreign food in Japan reflects not only the changing Japanese diet and eating habits, but also how foreign 'cultures' are adopted and localized for different ends. Likewise, the development of Chinese cuisine in Japan shows the complexity of 'taste', being expected and chosen in the last few decades after the Second World War.

My observation of Chinese food in Japan actually extends back to 1984 when I first went to Tokyo for a Japanese language course. At that time, I can remember that Cantonese food was not popular and that there were only a few Cantonese restaurants even in the Tokyo area. Apart from upscale Chinese restaurants, I went to some ordinary and inexpensive Chinese restaurants from time to time. There were two kinds of popular Chinese restaurant I used to go to: one served only fried rice, fried dumplings and noodles – the food was cheap and choices were limited; the other provided more kinds of Chinese food including typical Sichuan tofu, chili sauce shrimp, spring rolls, deep fried fish, stir fried pork with green pepper, sweet and sour pork, fried rice and noodles, etc. Both of these kinds of Chinese restaurant are still very common in Japan.

In *Cooking, Cuisine and Class*, Goody points out that by making use of the formation of haute or high cuisine, one can examine the social change and continuity embedded in food and cuisine. Goody (1982:105) emphasizes that high cuisine represents 'the higher in hierarchy, the wider the contacts, the broader the view of ingredients from outside', and he draws our attention to the transformation in terms of ingredients and technique within a global exchange context. Here, I would like to draw attention to Cantonese cuisine especially that distinguished as Hong Kong-style, in order to see how Japanese 'social taste' has been changing through the way food is chosen. By examining the case of Cantonese *dim sum*, we can see how a kind of popular style of breakfast in South China, eaten especially as brunch in Hong Kong, changed to become some upscale Chinese cuisine in Japan. There are several key elements involved in this so-called transformation.

First of all, *dim sum* contains some special ingredients (or combinations of meat and vegetables) which do not exist in ordinary *chuka-ryori*. Second, learning the techniques for making *dim sum* requires particular training, so most *dim sum* chefs were hired from Hong Kong to work in the Yokohama Chinatown. This probably gave the Cantonese food they served some kind of 'real and authentic' reputation, especially because Cantonese *dim sum* looks almost like the Japanese dessert (*wakashi*), which the Japanese appreciate for its craftsmanship. Third and most importantly, compared with the *chuka-ryori* that is served as the meal, Japanese eat *dim sum* as small dishes of snacks or appetisers before a regular meal, which normally includes staple food such as rice or noodles. Therefore, *dim sum*, represents Cantonese food as a supposedly high type of cuisine which was purposely introduced to give Japanese consumers extra and uncommon pleasure compared to the ordinary diet.

By investigating food as the medium for transmitting ideas and concepts, we can observe how its related selection and consumption mirrors the changing values and beliefs of a dynamic society. Therefore, the search for 'real and authentic' Chinese food and the re-creation of Yokohama Chinatown as the centre for the discovery voyage not only reflected the international relationship between Japan and China in the 1980s, as more attention was paid to Chinese culture and tradition, but also reflected the idea of the search for real and authentic forms of delicacy as an invented lifeways. In Japan, gourmet tours became very popular from the early 1980s, serving as an activity that anyone could participate in to search for *bishoku* or refined and distinctive food and *oishii-mono* or tasty food.

I use the word 'delicacy' instead of food or cuisine to shed light on not only the emergence of different kinds of Chinese cuisine, but also on the reasons why the Japanese are seeking different and unusual food. According to the definitions given by Webster's *Third New International Dictionary*, delicacy is defined as something is dainty or delicate and that gives extra and uncommon pleasure, and is something pleasing to eat that is accounted rare or luxurious. For example, fresh fruit in winter was once a delicacy available only to the very rich. By looking at Cantonese cuisine as an invented delicacy in the 1980s, we might ask what it means to Japanese consumers. Why is it popular in Yokohama Chinatown? Is it because of the Cantonese backgrounds of the neighbourhood? And, how is Cantonese cuisine distinct from other Chinese cuisine popularized in Japan over the last few decades, such as dumplings, fried rice and noodles? Referring to these questions, I will use Cantonese *dim sum* (in contrast to the popularized *chuka-ryori*) in Yokohama Chinatown to investigate how tastes and choices are forced on consumers though they do not realize how they are being manipulated.

Cantonese *dim sum* in Yokohama Chinatown

Let us take a look at the history of Yokohama Chinatown in relation to the reinvention of Cantonese *dim sum* for the interests of the Japanese consumer, *yum cha* (meaning to drink tea) is a typical Cantonese foodways with both distinctive food and a distinctive manner of being served and eaten. As I mentioned in the earlier section, Yokohama Chinatown began with Cantonese-speaking migrants who went to Japan directly from the southern part of mainland China. The history of migration can be traced back to the late nineteenth century. During the Meiji era the community was called Tojin-cho (literally, meaning Chinaman Town), and in the early part of the Showa era it was called Nankin-cho (literally, meaning Nanking Town, the same name as the one in Kobe city). Finally, it came to be called Chukagai (literally, meaning Chinatown) after the erection of the Zenrinmon (literally, meaning Neighbourly Gate) in 1955. In this Chinatown neighbourhood, there are streets with the names Hong Kong Street, Beijing Street, Chang-an Road, Kuangti Road, etc., representing a world that is obviously non-Japanese and Chinese in miniature. However, nowadays, Yokohama Chinatown exists more as a commercial neighbour-hood than as a local ethnic residential community; some Japanese have told me that they consider Yokohama Chinatown to be a 'restaurant street' like those commonly found in department stores. It bears little similarity to the type of Chinatown that can be found in North America, Australia or other Asian countries.

In order to understand how the change in Yokohama Chinatown took place, we need to look back to the post-war era. With Japan's defeat in the Second World War bringing dramatic changes to Japanese society, the insufficient food supply was seen as the most urgent issue facing Japanese society in the 1940s. During the 1940s, Yokohama Chinatown was known as a black market (in Japanese, *yami-ichi*) for food (especially, rice, flour, beef, etc.) since the Chinese were able to obtain those resources from the United States; this made Yokohama Chinatown important not only for the Chinese but also for the Japanese as a place where food was available. In the 1950s, Yokohama Chinatown began to be known as a place where ingredients could be purchased. The whole neighbourhood was considered a spatially separate business area, and was probably regarded as a centre for food resources different from other regions. In the 1960s when Japan was undergoing rapid economic development, it began to be a market centre rather than a black market, especially for retailing goods. Regarding the change in Yokohama Chinatown in the past few decades, I was told that Yokohama Chinatown previously had a bad or 'dark' image (in Japanese, *kurai-imeji*). This bad image probably helps us to understand what kind of neighbourhood it was. Until the early 1970s, it consisted of: (1) tiny, old, non-Japanese restaurants that had been there since the pre-war period; (2) foreigners, including sailors, traders and residents; and (3) drinking places such as bars and pubs.

Another factor that probably gave Yokohama Chinatown a bad image was the political conflict between the Taiwan and the mainland China. In 1952, the Chinese community of Yokohama split into two groups, reflecting the hostile relations between the pro-Taiwan and the pro-mainland China groups. And, before 1978, mainland China was ideologically different from Japan as well as all capitalist countries. From the early 1980s, warming international relations between Japan and mainland China and Japan's concern for internationalization led to a search for familiar but exotic specialities within the Japanese society. (I speculate that this might be one of the reasons that the image of Hong Kong, as an area with a neutral image for both groups, serves as the compromise between the two different political groups with common economic interests, and is able to link up their business partnerships.) This can be epitomized by the rediscovery of Chinatown as a nearly yet ethnically different spot for local consumers. In addition, by using the image of Hong Kong to promote Yokohama Chinatown as a tourist destination for local tourists, meant that the contentious relationship between the pro-mainland China group and pro-Taiwan group could be avoided.

Awareness of internationalization in Japanese society was aroused not as an isolated social phenomenon, but occurred at various levels such as lifestyle, leisure, foodways and experience with foreign cultures. Of course this awareness affected the construction of the ethnic Chinese neighbourhood – Yokohama Chinatown – inasmuch as it served as a place for foreign cultural experience mainly based on food and cuisine. As I have observed in different Chinese food advertisements, the meaning of Chinatown seems to contain a hybrid image in Japanese society. This hybrid image was explicitly shown through an advertising campaign for *dim sum* by Mister Donut, a franchised café that normally sells sweet cakes and doughnuts.

Here, I would like to bring in the development of the H restaurant which specialized in Hong Kong style Cantonese cuisine and is also considered one of the oldest existing Chinese restaurants in Japan. It was founded by an overseas Chinese living in Japan with his son succeeding him as owner. It was also the largest restaurant in Chinatown before the Second World War. But like any other town in Japan, Chinatown in Yokohama was devastated by the war. Before the H restaurant recovered to its pre-war scale, a close Chinese friend of the owner's family bought it and ran it under the same name. In 1975, the son of the new owner became the president of the newly established company structure. Renovations were undertaken and the H restaurant was promoted again for its traditional Cantonese cuisine in Yokohama Chinatown and also in Japan. From 1978, the H restaurant set up branches in various locations in Japan, and then, in 1988, its first international operation began with the establishment of a restaurant in Tsim Sha Tsui, Hong Kong. In Hong Kong, the H restaurant is famous for its décor and upscale image. By looking at how Cantonese *dim sum* became popular in the early 1980s, it is apparent that the H restaurant contributed a great deal to making it well known to the masses. In other words, the H restaurant not only contributed to remake or repackage Cantonese cuisine in Chinese food, but also changed the image of Yokohama Chinatown as a local ultimate destination for 'real and authentic' Chinese cuisine, and Cantonese *dim sum* was the key factor in the process.

As Ohnuki-Tierney (1997) mentions, the image of fast food – McDonald's – is actually a local construction of American culture. This construction is differentiated from conventional manners and etiquette in terms of eating habits as well as shared social values. Likewise, I would suggest that the reinvention of 'real and authentic' Cantonese *dim sum* in Yokohama Chinatown reflects the co-existing characteristics of inter-nationalized lifeways and localized foreign culture in contemporary Japanese society. *Dim sum*, a cuisine representative of Hong Kong, has served as the key element in the search for an exotic overseas (Hong Kong) cultural experience through food consumption. However, Cantonese *dim sum* is being localized in several ways, such as: (1) it is being served in the form of *teishoku* (meal set); (2) it is being chosen through menus with photos; (3) it is being changed as the concentration of ingredients familiar to the Japanese is increased, for example, more dumpling-type ingredients are used rather than chicken feet, intestine and pig blood, etc.; and (4) it is available whenever a restaurant is open, instead of being served only at certain times as in Hong Kong, where *dim sum* is available mainly for breakfast and lunch.

Apart from the emergence of an image of that correspond to Hong Kong as one of the most popular tourist destination among Japanese, I would also like to focus on the changing meanings of Chinese food in Japan as an index to show how food is valued. Considering the meanings of Chinese cuisine in Japan, it is also interesting to see how the image and meanings have changed in respective eras. For example, *ramen* (meaning noodles), fried rice, and dumplings are supposed to be the most typical elements of Chinese cuisine found in Japan, as they can be found almost everywhere. However, Cantonese *dim sum* probably shaped Yokohama Chinatown as the centre of Chinese cuisine; likewise, Hong Kong-style cuisine was invented as the high Chinese cuisine in Japanese society.

Why Chinese Cuisine is Hong-Kong-style

How did the emergence of different Chinese cuisines reflect post-war socio-cultural changes in Japanese society, especially as related to Hong

Kong-style cuisine and the idea of internationalization in Japan. With its defeat in the Second World War, Japan suffered from various economic and social disadvantages, with food shortages having the most serious consequences for the Japanese people. As Y, the inventor of instant noodles, mentions, when he looked at a large group of people lining up in front of a noodle shop on a freezing cold day, he came up with the idea of inventing some noodles that could be eaten elsewhere (Asahi Shimbun 1994).

The economic resurgence that Japan experienced following the period of post-war shortages is of important for this study. By examining the status of certain elements of Chinese cuisine we can better understand why Hong-Kong-style cuisine was sought after and reflected Japan's growing sense of place in the international arena. Since the early 1960s Chinese delicacies replaced more traditionally accepted forms of Chinese food, such as *chuka-ryori*, dumplings, fried rice and noodle dishes that were both popular and common as standard Chinese face for the Japanese masses. Chinese delicacies however, were scarce and considered to be of premium value.

In 1962, two years before the Tokyo Olympics were held, many high-class Chinese restaurants with a regional emphasis were opened in Tokyo, and many large-scale hotels were built with upscale Chinese restaurants. Chinese cuisine became the topic for television cooking programmes and cookbooks. With the emergence of a new middle class during the 1960s and the rapid increase in television sets among families during the Tokyo Olympics, Japanese lifestyles changed due to the influences of the mass media and improvements in living standards. Increasing social stability allowed people to eat out more often and to seek a new dining experience.

As I mentioned earlier, family restaurants and some kinds of mass-produced, inexpensive *chuka-ryori* restaurants (which combined different regional cuisines) became popular, and remain so even now. This kind of popular *chuka-ryori* can be found near most train stations, restaurant floors of department stores, *shoten kai* (shopping streets) and residential areas. Another kind of Chinese cuisine catering to Chinese delicacies appeared in the early 1960s, but only for small numbers of people. At that time, such restaurants were not centrally located, but were spread throughout metropolitan Tokyo. These restaurants emphasized China's regional cuisines such as Beijing, Shanghai, Sichuan and Canton. However, starting in the early 1980s, there was a shift in location from Tokyo to Yokohama Chinatown. One of the reasons for this shift was probably the urban redevelopment in Tokyo that made it difficult for restaurants to survive the high rent burden. Moreover, Yokohama Chinatown is a neighbourhood mostly formed by Cantonese speaking people and restaurateurs took advantage of the availability of good chefs from Hong Kong to work in their restaurants.

179

Another reason for the growing emphasis on Hong-Kong-style Chinese cuisine in Japan was the result of advertising and tourism. Hong Kong is advertised as a 'Heaven for Eating and Drinking', it has become one of the most popular tourist destination for Japanese, including company tours, packaged charter bus tours and independent tourists. And the desire to replicate the travel experience probably led the Japanese to search for Hong Kong-style delicacies at home. In addition, tourist experience demands a centre for the food discovery voyage through which Yokohama Chinatown is able to foster an exotic environment regarding travellers' expectations.

Apart from a shift in interests on the part of consumers, the reason why the neighbourhood adopted the image of Hong Kong for the economic benefit of both the consumers and business needs to be considered. Another key feature concerning the meaning of delicacy among the Japanese should not be overlooked, and that is what I call the 'informationalization' of food and delicacies. Moreover, influences from the mass media are significant and should not be overlooked. For example, in 1987, the motion picture called *Tampopo* (meaning Dandelion), directed by Juzo Itami, talked about different aspects of eating while the main story was about how the owner of a *ramen*/noodle shop learnt to prepare a bowl of delicious *ramen* with the help of a truck driver's eating experience. During the process of learning, the two characters also comically learned about how noodles should be cooked, ideas of originality, tradition and westernization in contemporary Japanese society.

Instead of showing how to cook food, competitions on how ingredients can best be cooked become one main way that food can become a delicacy. In other words, delicacy has become something that is not necessarily consumed by eating, but also can be consumed by watching and learning. So, it is not only the food as a product, but how ingredients are selected, prepared and cooked up, which produces the expected delicacy. In addition to the special documentaries, including the first Man-Han Imperial Banquet held in a Chinese restaurant in Yokohama Chinatown in 1977, television programmes such as gourmet tours led by movie stars, comics (*oshinbou* which is one of the popular comics about how to cook good food) and motion pictures which use the cooking process to reflect different kinds of social values, I would like to mention some television programmes of cooking contests. In the last decade, television programmes about cooking contests such as *ryori-no-teitsujin* (iron man of cooking) and children's cooking contests became very popular in Japan (some of these programmes were even translated and shown in other Asian countries). From these changes, we can see that food and cuisine is not only formulated according to recipes, but appears as a whole set of undefined rules which can be changed, manipulated and personally reinvented both by famous chefs working in mainstream restaurants and children who are not supposed to cook in their daily lives.

Conclusion: Delicacies are Good to Eat and Good to Know

Food and delicacies exist as information instead of as substantial and edible products among consumers. This can even be considered as an expression of individualism with an emphasis on food that is supposed to be enjoyed as knowledge (shared among people) instead of as taste. Regarding the idea that eating is a social event in that it brings people together, it is important for us to rethink how 'informationalized' food consumed through the media is strongly related to the individual consumption of 'taste' in the coming decade. For example, a person sitting in front of the television can probably enjoy the most exotic delicacies on his or her own in terms of information as well as knowledge of the daily social life experience.

We are what we eat or know how-to-eat; likewise, at the present, we expect to know more than we are able to eat since choices need to be made. As Mintz (1996:93) states: 'Many people who are not interested in food as food are quite interested in food as thought'. In Yokohama, there is a Ramen/Noodle Museum that uses *ramen* to display and represent the social change that Japan has experienced; the idea using food to represent such a concept acknowledges that food can be consumed as knowledge as well as nutrients. Furthermore, I would like to add that Chinese chefs from restaurants in Yokohama Chinatown are very popular and influential in various television programmes; their popularity is probably related to the images of Yokohama Chinatown, being the centre of delicate as well as high-class Chinese cuisine. Finally, through studying the emergence of Yokohama Chinatown as the centre for discovering the real and authentic in contemporary Japanese society, I conclude that food and cuisine are mostly reinvented to meet different social interests, and here, Cantonese food marks the turning point from delicacy as food to delicacy as information in the modern world.

References

Allison, Anne (1991) 'Japanese Mothers and Obentos: The Lunch-Box as Ideological State Apparatus', *Anthropological Quarterly*, 64:195–208.

Asahi Shimbun (1994) *Asahi One Theme Magazine: Chinese Overseas* (in Japanese). Tokyo: Asahi Shimbun.

Befu, Harumi (1974) 'An Ethnography of Dinner Entertainment in Japan', *Arctic Anthropology*, 11 (Supplement):196–203.

Bourdieu, Pierre (1984) *Distinction: A Social Critique of the Judgment of Taste* (translated by Richard Nice). London: Routledge & K. Paul.

Chen, Hsiang-shui (1992) *Chinatown No More: Taiwan Immigrants in Contemporary New York*. Ithaca and London: Cornell University Press.

Edwards, Walter (1989) *Modern Japan Through Its Weddings: Gender, Person and Society in Ritual Perspective*. Stanford: Stanford University Press.

Goody, Jack (1982) *Cooking, Cuisine and Class: A Study in Comparative Sociology*. Cambridge: Cambridge University Press.

Karatani, Kojin (1993) 'The Discursive Space of Modern Japan', in M. Miyoshi and H. D. Harootunian (eds) *Japan in the World*, pp. 288–316. London: Duke University Press.

Mintz, W. Sidney (1985) *Sweetness and Power: The Place of Sugar in Modern History*. New Viking: Viking.

— (1996) *Tasting Food, Tasting Freedom: Excursions into Eating, Culture, and the Past*. Boston: Beacon Press.

Moeran, Brian (1986) 'One Over the Seven: Sake Drinking in a Japanese Pottery Community', in Joy Hendry and Jonathan Webber (eds) *Interpreting Japanese Society: Anthropological Approaches*, pp. 226–242. Oxford: JASO.

Noguchi, Paul (1994) 'Savor Slowly: Ekiben – The Fast Food of the High-Speed Japan', *Ethnology*, 33 (4):317–340.

Ohnuki-Tierney, Emiko (1990) 'The Ambivalent Self of the Contemporary Japanese', *Cultural Anthropology*, 5 (2):197–216.

—— (1993) *Rice as Self: Japanese Identities through Time*. Princeton: Princeton University Press.

—— (1997) 'McDonald's in Japan: Changing Manners and Etiquette', in James L. Watson (ed.) *Golden Arches East: McDonald's in East Asia*, pp. 160–181. Stanford: Stanford University Press.

Sahlins, Marshall (1976) *Culture and Practical Reason*. Chicago: University of Chicago Press.

Tobin, J. Joseph (ed.) (1992) *Re-made in Japan: Everyday Life and Consumer Taste in a Changing Society*. New Haven: Yale University Press.

Tsu, Y. Timothy (1999) 'From Ethnic Ghetto to "Gourmet Republic": The Changing Image of Kobe's Chinatown in Modern Japan', *Japanese Studies*, 19(1):17–32.

Vogel, F. Ezra (1971) *Japan's New Middle Class*. Berkeley: University of California Press.

Watson, L. James (1975) *Emigration and the Chinese Lineage: The Mans in Hong Kong and London*. Berkeley: University of California Press.

—— (ed.) (1997) *Golden Arches East: McDonald's in East Asia*. Stanford: Stanford University Press.

Yokohama Archives of History (1994) *Yokohama chukagai* (Yokohama Chinatown). Yokohama: Yokohama Archives of History Publisher.

CHAPTER ELEVEN

Chinese Food in the Philippines

Indigenization and Transformation

Doreen G. Fernandez

The bedrock of the Philippine food landscape is indigenous food, drawn from land, sea and air, cooked in simple ways (roasted, steamed, and boiled). This includes such dishes as *sinigang*, fish, meat or fowl stewed with vegetables in a sour broth; *laing*, taro leaves in coconut milk; *pinais*, river shrimps steamed with young coconut in banana leaves; *pinakbet*, mixed vegetables steamed in a fish or shrimp sauce, and *kinilaw*, seafood dressed in vinegar. Foreign influences came to play upon this matrix which built up the totality now known as Philippine cuisine. The earliest input was Chinese, brought by merchants who, according to historians, have certainly been trading in the Philippines since the eleventh century, and quite probably as early as the ninth century (from the evidence of ceramic and other trade ware). Later came the Spanish-Mexican food traditions, then the American, brought in by two waves of colonization (1571–1898; 1899–1947). The Chinese influence on Philippine food is thus several centuries old, and as a result almost invisible. Most Filipinos do not realize that ingredients they buy in markets, and dishes they cook for everyday meals and for feasts, are Chinese in origin. They are so familiar now, so much part of the diet, that even though their names are not in any Philippine language, they are simply part of Philippine life.

Language Clues

By their names one may know them, these Chinese contributions to Philippine cuisine. Gloria Chan-Yap (1976), in a study of 'Hokkien Chinese Influence on Tagalog Cookery', lists 19 categories of Hokkien loanwords. These start with the names of cooking instruments, like *siyanse* (food turner), *bilao* (flat round food basket), *lansong* (bamboo steamer), *bithay* (bamboo sieve) and *pohiya* (ladle). Hokkien terms for raw food suggest that the foods may have been brought in by the Chinese, or their use as food popularized by them. Pork (especially wild boar) had long been part of the native diet, but Chinese names for pork cuts (*tito* for stomach, *kasim* for lean pork, *liyempo* for fatback), still used today, may mean that the Chinese taught Filipinos their ways of butchering and cooking. Names used today for beef cuts are predominantly Spanish (*lomo, cadera, punta y pecho*), although of Chinese origin are *goto* (tripe), and *kamto* (beef flank, also a dish in which it is stewed with radish). The black chicken (white skin, dark meat) favoured in Chinese cuisine is called by a Chinese term: *ulikba*, as are some fish and seafood native to the islands: *tuwabak, tuwakang, swahe, pehe*, and *hibe*.

Chan-Yap (1976:294) suggests that the Tagalogs may have acquired from the Hokkien speakers 'the habit of eating pork and beef cuts as well as certain kinds of fish and seafood ... they were not eating heretofore'. Chinese names are definitely for soybean products: *tokwa, tahuri, tawsi, toyo*; and for flour, rice or bean noodles: *miswa, miki, bihon, suwatanghon*. Neither soybeans nor noodles are native to the Philippines; they were introduced by the Chinese. Many of the merchants who came to the Philippines, and eventually married and settled here were Hokkien, and so these loanwords appear throughout the cuisine; in addition to the above, they describe the names of processes and especially of dishes. In restaurants, cafeterias, food counters, and even in the street carts of food vendors, one can find *siopao* (filled buns), *siomai* (dumplings), *mami* (noodles with broth and chicken or beef), *pansit* (fried noodles), and snacks such as *buchi, ampaw, bitsu-bitsu*. On trips to China, I have found street food and breakfast dishes instantly recognizable because of their existence within the Philippine experience.

Indigenization

All these foods eventually came to be adapted to Filipino tastes and ways, and thus indigenized and eventually Filipinized. Nowhere in the Philippines will one find dishes done exactly the way they are in China, or tasting exactly the same, because of the indigenizing process. *Pansit* makes an excellent case study. The development scenario may be imagined: a Hokkien merchant, to whom the word (*pian + e + sit*) means 'something that is conveniently cooked', comes to the Philippines and stays awhile, perhaps to wait for the payment in kind (forest and sea products like rattan, beeswax and *beche-de-mer*) for his pottery and silks. Missing his homeland cooking, he ventures to make noodles, and cooks them with the local ingredients available. The noodles are thus changed by local conditions. If he married a Filipina, as many did, and taught her how to cook his food, the dishes made with local materials would be further changed by her Filipino taste buds, which had never tasted anything Chinese before.

In the Philippines today, indigenization has made *pansit* a name only for noodles and noodle dishes (not anything else conveniently cooked). It has taken a myriad guises and shapes, according to the local context. *Pansit* Malabon, native to the fishing town of Malabon, usually includes shrimps, oysters and squid. *Pansit* Marilao, from the town of Marilao in Bulacan within the Central Luzon rice-growing area, features rice crisps. *Pansit* Molo contains not noodles but filled *wontons* in a broth; it is named after a town in Iloilo in which many Chinese settled. *Pansit* Guisado (*guisado* being the Spanish word for sautéed) consists of noodles sautéed with tomatoes, onions, shrimp, vegetables and pork. *Pansit* Luglog (*luglog* being a Tagalog word for 'to shake') has noodles shaken in hot broth, and flavoured with a shrimp-based sauce. In *Pansit* Palabok (*palabok* denoting added flavour or adornment), flaked smoked fish, crumbled crackling, sliced *bilimbi*, etc., are sprinkled over the basic noodles. Most are served with *calamansi* (*Citrus madurensis* Lour; *Citrofortunella mitis* Blanco, the native lime) and *patis* (fish sauce), both of these fine-tuning the dish further to the Filipino taste.

Pansit is now part of everyday meals, being 'conveniently cooked', but is also the traditional take-home food men bring home as a treat for their families. Also, served on large platters, and rendered luxurious by special ingredients, it is festive food. Everyone's mother, aunt, grandmother, sister or cook has her own *pansit* recipe – certainly Philippine in flavour, although Chinese in remote origin. This is indigenization, or cross-cultural transformation. *Pansit* is now definitely a Philippine dish.

Lumpia, the spring roll, is another example. All over Southeast Asia, the Chinese dish in which food (often a mix of vegetables) is wrapped in edible wrappers has become indigenized. In the Philippines it is often filled with a mixture of sautéed vegetables. Some Tagalogs add ground peanuts. Most serve it with a sweet-sour sauce laced with chopped garlic on the side. Silay City, Negros Occidental, in the Western Visayas, my hometown, is famous for *lumpiang ubod*: very fresh heart-of-palm sautéed with garlic, pork and shrimps, then wrapped in a paper-thin wrapper, a scallion stalk jauntily tucked in. The heart-of-palm must be so fresh that some *lumpia*-makers demand that the *ubod* come from a tree felled only that morning. My father used to plant small trees only for *ubod*, never meant to grow tall or bear coconuts. *Lumpia*, fried (when pork-filled it is called Lumpia Shanghai) or not (called 'fresh'), is now part of many daily meals, of restaurant menus, and of feasts; it is another indigenized Philippine dish.

Public Eating

When restaurants were first established in the Philippines in the nineteenth century, many were called – as they still are today – *panciterias*. The word is derived from *pansit*, but formulated the Spanish way (as in *zapaterias*, shoemakers' shops, and *carnicerias*, meat shops). These were Chinese restaurants, quite possibly the first eateries in the current restaurant mold. Native eating places found in markets, for example, were called *carinderias* because they served *kari*, or cooked food. They usually featured cooked food in trays on open counters, with perhaps a bench for customers, but without tables and chairs arranged in an indoor space and served by waiters.

The *panciterias*, which had tables, chairs and waiters, had menus in Spanish, obviously to make the Chinese dishes understandable to Spanish or Spanish-speaking customers. This started the phenomenon called *Comida China*, or Chinese food with Spanish names. An older generation (e.g. the grandparents of today's youth) still refer to them in those terms. Fried rice is *morisqueta tostada* (a reference to Moorish connections in Spanish culinary history); bird's nest soup, *sopa de nido* (nest), or *nido* for short; sharkfin, *aletas de tiburon*. *Pinsec frito* are fried *wontons*; *pinsec con caldo*, *wontons* in broth; *pescado en salsa agrio-dulce*, fish in sweet-sour sauce; *camaron rebozado*, batter-fried shrimps, and *torta de cangrejo*, crab omelette (similar to crab *foo yung*). *Arroz caldo*, literally rice soup, is the Chinese breakfast *congee* or porridge. In the Philippines it is usually cooked with chicken or with tripe, and Filipinized by flavouring with *patis* (fish sauce), *calamansi* (native lime), chopped green onions and crisp-fried chopped garlic. It is now considered comfort food, down-home food by many Filipinos. When served in flight on Philippine Airlines, for example, it is a favoured choice of Filipino passengers, as well as of the pilots and the crew. All these names came to be institutionalized as nomenclature for Chinese food served from the Spanish times onward in the country's homes and public eating places. All the tastes, without a doubt, were tempered by the culture, not only with the addition of *patis* and *calamansi* (which are generally still served on tables in Chinese restaurants along with soy sauce and hot sauce), but through ingredients and spices.

In later years, semantic shifts brought in English words and Tagalog words. *Amargoso* (bitter melon) *con carne* might become *Ampalaya con carne*, or *Ampalaya* with Beef. Liver with vegetables, which we found in a small restaurant in Binan, Laguna, was called *Atay con Gulay*, the only Spanish word remaining being the connective '*con*'. In the changing panciteria menus (courtly and correct in large Manila restaurants; largely misspelled in provincial menus, having been passed from menu to menu or printer to printer with little idea of the original Spanish), moving from Spanish to Spanish-Tagalog, Spanish-English, and then English or Filipino, lies the story of the evolution of Filipino-Chinese restaurant food. They provide evidence of the way Chinese food slid into Filipino lives with the mediation of the Spanish language.

These Sino-Philippine restaurants still exist, now alongside large restaurants with cooks from Hong Kong, Taipei, and Beijing. In the latter the meals consist of 'imported' rather than indigenized Chinese food, as they are cooked with imported ingredients by foreign chefs for a clientele not exclusively Philippine, Spanish, or Chinese.

Chinese Food in Philippine Life

The Chinese influence on Philippine food, which started with the interaction of trade centuries ago, is now deeply imbedded in Philippine history, hearts, and tastes. No mother considers *camaron rebozado* or *lumpia frito* or *pansit* anything but Filipino when she prepares them at home. To her they are not Chinese; she generally does not realize their foreign origin. They are now native Philippine dishes – food from tradition, for the home, for children's and school parties, for feasts at many levels.

Few Chinese may realize what an impact their cuisine has had on the Philippines. Chinese food entered Philippine life at ground level, so to speak, among traders and workers and their families, in contrast to Spanish food, which, with its imported and expensive ingredients, became principally food for feasts and other special occasions. Chinese cuisine depends mainly on ingredients available on land and sea. It is so thoroughly integrated into the culture that it provides a definition, a case study of indigenization, of how the foreign is transformed by, subsumed into, and made part of the local culture. It is daily food. It is also food for eating out, especially when one treats a large family group, from babies to grandmothers. Certainly it is food for gifts, for treats. And it is celebratory food (noodles still symbolize long life), even for Christmas, or the feast of the town's patron saint. As part of public eating, it is found in small neighbourhood eateries, where traditionally *pansit* can be ordered to take home, wrapped in a cone of paper lined with banana leaf. It is also found in more expensive, upscale *panciterias*, with such names as Panciteria Antigua, Panciteria Moderna and Panciteria Wa Nam. Further; it is also now available in large, glossy Hong Kong style restaurants, catering for large wedding and other parties, for example, Garden Restaurant, Shang Palace, Mandarin Villa, Ocean Dragon Seafood Restaurant, West Lake Garden, Han Court, and the like. The transformation is caused not only by ingredients used, dipping or other sauces added, by the nationality and training of chefs, by the restaurant orientation, or by the clientele being served. It is caused by a deep cultural change in a particular context and time.

Chinese food in the Philippines is different from Chinese food in Hong Kong, just as Chinese food in America and in London are different from the homeland originals. Of course it has to be different, except in the establishments with imported ingredients and chefs. The difference in flavour, orientation, service and social role comes from the transformation wrought by the cross-cultural interaction that resulted in indigenization.

Appendix: Some Filipino Names for Chinese Food

Aletas de tiburon	shark fins (usually in soup)
Am	the water from boiled or steamed rice
Ampalaya con carne	bitter melon cooked with beef
Ampaw	puffed rice or corn, served pillow-shaped
Angkak	red-coloured rice grains used for colouring food
Arroz caldo	rice soup or gruel with chicken and ginger
Bam-I	Cebuano noodle dish
Batsoy	a dish of pork loin and variety meats, sometimes with noodles
Bihon	rice noodles
Bihon guisado	rice noodles sautéed with condiments
Biko	rice cake cooked by steaming
Bilu-bilo	small sticky steamed rice balls, often cooked in coconut milk
Bitsu-bitsu	a Chinese doughnut or cruller
Butchi	fried taro balls rolled in sesame seeds
Camaron rebozado	battered, fried shrimps
Camaron rebozado dorado con Jamon	battered, fried shrimps with ham
Goto	tripe; also a rice porridge with tripe
Gurgurya	a cruller of sugar, flour, egg, etc. fried crisp
Kamto	beef flank, also a dish of beef flank with radish
Kekiam, Quikiam	minced shrimp or pork rolls wrapped in leaf lard or other wrapper
Kinchamsay	dried banana blossoms
Kinchay	Chinese parsley
Kutchay	Chinese chives
Heko	the liquid from fermented fish sauce
Hibe	dried shrimps
Humba	pork stewed with soy sauce
Liempo	pork belly
Lomi	wide noodles in broth with shrimps, meats, vegetables, etc.
Lugaw	rice gruel, congee, porridge
Lumpia	spring rolls filled with vegetables, shrimps, pork, or combinations of these
Mami	noodles in broth, with chicken or beef
Miki	thick flour noodles
Miso	soy bean cake; boiled bean mash
Misua	thin flour noodles
Morisqueta tostada	fried rice
Nido	edible bird nests

Pansit, pancit	a generic term for noodles or noodle dishes
Pansit bihon	a dish of rice noodles
Pansit Canton	egg noodles
Pansit guisado	sautéed noodles
Pansit luglug	noodles shaken in hot broth
Pansit mami	noodles with soup
Pansit Marilao	noodles with rice crisps, from Marilao, Bulacan
Pansit Molo	pork-filled wonton soup, from Molo, Iloilo
Pao	steamed bread
Pata tiim, patatim	pork leg steamed in soy sauce and vegetables
Pato tiim, patotim	duck steamed in soy sauce and vegetables
Pesa	chicken or fish boiled with vegetables and served with a soybean mash
Pinsec	filled wontons
Pinsec con caldo	wonton soup
Pinsec frito	fried filled wontons
Pospas	rice gruel, often with chicken, often made with broken rice grains
Siomai	meat, vegetable or shrimp dumplings
Siopao	steamed filled bun
Sopa de Nido	bird's nest soup
Sotanghon	'crystal' or 'cellophane' noodles, made from mung beans
Suwam, sinuwam	cooked with broth from rice or porridge
Taho	soft soybean cakes in syrup
Tahuri	fermented cakes of salted soybean curd
Tokwa	soybean curd
Torta de cangrejo	crab omelette
Togue, toge	mung bean sprouts
Ukoy	fried grated-vegetable shrimp patties
Ulikba	black chicken
Wansoy	coriander leaf

Reference

Chan-Yap, Gloria (1976) 'Hokkien Chinese Influence on Tagalog Cookery', *Philippine Studies*, 24:288–302.

Index